This book is dedicated with affection and respect to my parents,
Wanda and Lewis Cornelius.

-- Thanks for watching my girls, Mom. You rock.

BLOOD WILL TELL:

A Medical Explanation of the Tyranny of Henry VIII

BLOOD WILL TELL:

A Medical Explanation of the Tyranny of Henry VIII

Kyra Cornelius Kramer

Original text copyright © 2012 by Kyra C. Kramer

First United States Edition

All rights reserved. No part of this book may be reproduced in any form or by any electronic or mechanical means, including information storage and retrieval systems, without permission in writing from the publisher, except by a reviewer who may quote brief passages in a review.

Ash Wood Press

Bloomington, Indiana

Acknowledgements

This book would not have been possible without the research that went into the article "A New Explanation of the Reproductive Woes and Midlife Decline of Henry VIII" (*The Historical Journal*, 53:4, (2010) pp.827-848), written by Dr. Catrina Banks Whitley and myself. Although I was the first to suggest that it was Henry, not his wives, who was the true source of his difficulty in fathering heirs, it was Dr. Whitley who figured out the solution to the puzzle by unearthing the obstetrical problems that arise from having a Kell positive progenitor, and the potential complication of McLeod syndrome. I am deeply indebted to her medical and bioarchaeological expertise.

I would also like to thank some very important people who helped me in the making of this book. First, there is my wonderful husband, Casey Kramer, who gave me love and support throughout the writing process. Also, many thanks to The Goddess of Editing and her son, The Young Lobster, both of whom worked heroically to free this work from typos, split infinitives, rogue punctuation, unfathomable sentences, and mushy metaphors. Any mistakes that remain are solely my fault. I am additionally grateful to Paul and Lisa Lewandowski, for help above and beyond the call of friendship. Finally, I would like to express my profound appreciation of all the exemplary historians who have made so much information about Henry VIII's remarkable life and reign available to scholars and the general public.

Table of Contents

Chapter One	King Henry VIII	11
Chapter Two	Katherine of Aragon	34
Chapter Three	Anne Boleyn	73
Chapter Four	The Bloodbath Begins	117
Chapter Five	Tudor Medicine	170
Chapter Six	Tyranny Unchecked	205
Chapter Seven	The Great Flanders Mare	228
Chapter Eight	Katheryn Howard	256
Chapter Nine	Kateryn Parr	285
Chapter Ten	The Blood Burns	316
Bibliography		323

Chapter One
King Henry VIII:
The Man, the Monarch, and the Myth

Henry VIII did *not* have syphilis.

  The belief that this incredibly famous English king had syphilis is one of the most enduring myths circulated about him. It was first postulated by a Victorian physician in 1888 as an explanation for Henry's checkered reproductive record and his nightmarish tyrannical behavior (Keynes, 2007:179). Since the King was renowned for indulging his lusts this hypothesis seemed to fit the facts like a glove, and was more or less accepted as an enjoyably scandalous certainty for the next few decades. Even after the theory was soundly and conclusively debunked in 1931 by Frederik Chamberlin, the premise that Henry was riddled with syphilis continued to be promulgated. Today, in spite of the fact that syphilis has been ruled out as the cause of Henry's troubles *for almost 100 years*, the idea that the

King had this particular sexually transmitted disease keeps resurfacing. Regardless of the fact that it is untrue, it continues to be taught in history classes, included in non-fiction works, and is now discussed ardently on the internet. It shows up in books that are in all other respects well researched, where it has been quoted from an otherwise reputable source. Scholars have insisted for decades that neither Henry, nor any of his wives, showed symptoms of syphilis, but the popular conviction that the King was syphilitic has nevertheless persisted unchecked. Reality has been no match for this everlasting scandal. Why?

      Although the myth that Henry had syphilis is still being mistakenly given as a "fact," the scientific evidence that Henry was *not* infected with syphilis is incontrovertible. For syphilis to have affected Henry's first wife's pregnancies, the King would already have had to be infected by 1509, at the latest. He died in 1547. This means he would have had syphilis for more than 30 years. Symptoms of the tertiary, or late stage, of syphilis present themselves between 15-30 years after contracting the disease (Gross, 2011). The signs of syphilis that has reached this point are hard to miss. Moreover, it is not as though the physicians of that time were unaware of syphilis. It has often been assumed that Columbus and his crew brought this venereal disease back from the New World, but a body has been exhumed from a graveyard in London by archaeologists which proves that the English were already suffering, and dying, of syphilis years before that famous voyage took place (Glass, 2001). Columbus was probably linked with syphilis simply because of an unfortunate coincidence: shortly after his ships returned from North America, a syphilis epidemic began to affect troops fighting in Italy and rapidly expanded outward into the populations of Germany, Switzerland, and France, eventually spreading all the way into England by 1496 (Lancaster, 1990:188). The most common treatment for syphilis in the Tudor period involved dosing patients with massive quantities of mercury "salts", yet there is no record of Henry ever having been prescribed mercury for any medicinal reason, nor of any of his wives, mistresses, or children having taken them (Keynes, 2007:180). In contrast, Henry's contemporary, King Francis I of France, who was diagnosed with syphilis (although modern medical experts suspect he may have had gonorrhea instead), is known to have been dosed with "Chinese wood" and mercury by his court physicians.

    Had it been suspected that Henry had syphilis, word of his condition would doubtlessly have circulated in European courts. The fact that he was the English monarch would not have stopped the doctors from reporting his disease, any more than it stopped royal physicians from making the King of France's condition common knowledge. Doctors would not have been the only ones able to see that Henry had syphilis. The symptomatic lesions common in syphilitic patients would have been difficult to conceal from the courtiers who attended him in his bath and even helped him with toilet hygiene. Royalty suffering from a sexually transmitted disease would have been too juicy a tidbit of malicious news to have been kept quiet. Additionally, passing on such gossip was an ambassador's supreme duty; if Henry had been syphilitic, all the crowned heads of Europe would have heard about it from their representatives at the English court.

    Furthermore, none of Henry's surviving offspring showed signs of congenital or tertiary syphilis, which, as has been noted in several scholarly works, is not exactly a subtle physical condition (Whitley and Kramer, 2010). Since three of his surviving children were the firstborn offspring of their respective mothers, it could be argued those infants survived because the women had not yet contracted syphilis from the King, but that could not account for the health of Henry's daughter, Mary, who was the result of his first wife's fifth (or possibly sixth) pregnancy. If her father had been syphilitic, then Mary would undoubtedly have been infected, especially if the disease was to blame for all of the miscarriages which ended the Queen's earlier pregnancies. Mary, who lived into middle age, never showed any of the characteristics of congenital syphilis.

Without a doubt, Henry did *not* have syphilis. So why does the belief that he was syphilitic persist? What is it about this particular king that makes people want to believe he had a sexually transmitted disease? Come to think of it, what is it about Henry VIII that captures the imagination and spurs investigation into every lurid detail of his life?

Henry, unlike most of England's other Kings, is still vividly remembered more than 500 years after he ascended the throne and he remains an abiding topic of interest, not only for scholars but also for the public at large. He is the focus of academic study and popular entertainment, including books, documentaries, dramas, and blockbuster films. In contrast, think of Edward III. Few people other than historians know much about him, even though Edward III was an extremely important monarch who reigned for fifty years during a particularly eventful time in English history. Why is Henry VIII engraved on people's minds when so many other rulers, even strong ones such as Edward III, have faded from the public imagination? Perhaps it is due to his infamous reputation as a wife-killing tyrant and his ruthless quest for a male heir. Certainly most people find his marital exploits to be a fascinating story, full of intrigue, lust, murder, and power. From an academic standpoint, Henry's legacy centers mostly around his break with the Catholic Church, which laid the foundations for the Church of England. Considering that Henry's split with Rome was so momentous, it is ironic that he is probably more well-known for his connubial exploits and his obsession with fathering a son than for helping to change the religious climate of Europe.

The most famous of Henry's romances was his pursuit of, and eventual marriage to, Anne Boleyn. His passionate attachment to Anne began while he was still married to his first Queen, usually referred to as Catherine of Aragon, but who signed her name "Katherina", which will be the spelling used in this book. The public, and even many historians, have therefore viewed Anne as a home-wrecker who induced Henry to cast aside his first wife. She is often depicted as a calculating Jezebel who led Henry by the nose and encouraged his cruelty toward rivals, politicians, priests, the Catholic Church, Katherina, and even his daughter, Mary. Anne is frequently depicted as a schemer who destroyed a family, and the traditional forms of English worship, in order to get a crown. However, the fact her husband executed her on what appear to be false charges has also rendered her sympathetic. Even if she had seduced the King, did she deserve her gruesome fate? Curiosity about Henry and his relationship with his most famous ladylove has spawned hundreds of books, both serious historical accounts and titillating historical fiction. It is arguably one of the most famous love-triangles in the English-speaking world, and serves to keep Henry's life story at the forefront of popular culture.

Another part of Henry's allure may lie in the numerous unanswered questions about his extraordinary life. One of the most significant mysteries is his difficulty in obtaining a male heir. His six marriages produced only three living children. In fairness, there were some extenuating circumstances in his reproductive history with his later Queens. Jane Seymour, his third wife, died before they could try for a second child. He never consummated his fourth marriage, and there is a strong possibility that he couldn't have sex with his sixth wife either. In spite of these explanations for the lack of offspring in his later marriages, it is notable that his reproductive attempts outside of wedlock were no more successful. Although Henry had few mistresses, compared to other kings of his era, there were still a number of young women he was sexually intimate with for an extended period of time, yet only one of his amours is definitely known to have given birth to a child he fathered. It is also suspicious that his first two Queens, Katherina of Aragon and Anne Boleyn, had such similar obstetric histories. Both women endured myriad stillbirths, miscarriages and neonatal deaths. Could this be attributed to living in an era without sufficient medical care, or to a physiological flaw in *both* of the women? It seems unlikely that the two women's experiences could mirror each other so closely simply due to chance. It seems more plausible that something about Henry VIII himself was actually the reason there were so few children in the royal nurseries. After all, he was the common factor in every single pregnancy.

      A further cause of the persistent interest in Henry VIII is his dynamic image. Most people have seen the famous painting of the bloated, middle-aged King, standing with his fists anchored pugnaciously to his hips, wearing sumptuous clothes covered in embroidery and jewels. The force of his personality can still be felt, even from a two-dimensional depiction in oil. He appears to stare out of the portrait with his cold disdain for the viewer, secure in the knowledge that he holds the power of life or death over everyone around him. His appearance thoroughly matches his reputation as a brutal thug who murdered women when he tired of them.

The celebrated portrayal of Henry as a philandering beast is the reason syphilis is so readily connected to his name. The acquisition of a sexually transmitted disease is, erroneously, culturally conceptualized as the end result of promiscuity, rather than of the bad luck of having one infected sex partner. There is a fixed social ideology about illnesses that are transmitted through sexual activity; there is an assumption that they are indicators of wanton lasciviousness on the part of the infected person, as opposed to being the unfortunate consequences of sex with a single infected partner. Sexually transmitted diseases are also socially imbued with a feeling of "punishment", a sort of retribution for an impure life, so the idea that the King could not easily have the son he wanted because he was infected with syphilis further reinforces this narrative. Henry is associated with a dissolute lifestyle, and was unable to beget a male heir until his third marriage, so *of course* he must have had syphilis. It provides a neat tie-in between the cultural trope about 'the kind of person' who gets sexually transmitted diseases and the King's characterization as a skirt-chasing monster. Nevertheless, beliefs about who *ought* to get sexually transmitted disease have no basis in reality, and the King did not have syphilis. Nor was he the immoral swine folklore has made him seem.

Henry is popularly remembered as a fat, covetous, and womanizing lout, but this image is less than half the story. The aged King, with his cruel disdain for others and his harsh authoritarianism, is very different from his younger self. When

Henry first ascended the throne he strove to bring harmony and chivalry to his court; he was not the contentious and brutal man he was to become. It was not until he was in his forties that the Henry of the popular myth emerges, the caricature of a corpulent, rancorous King with a disturbing habit of executing his subjects for little or no reason. By the time Henry was fifty, he had indeed turned into the savage behemoth of legend. The kind-hearted and loving monarch transformed into someone who could routinely behead friends, family, and wives without remorse. No one was safe; he was utterly merciless. When faced with the multiple atrocities he committed, it is hard for most people to imagine what a true Renaissance man Henry was when he was younger.

Why did Henry's personality alter so significantly after his fortieth birthday? What made him change from a reasonable and affable, albeit overly pampered and selfish, young monarch into a tyrannical madman? Furthermore, why did his health deteriorate so dramatically during the last fifteen or so years of his life? Was it a lack of proper nutrition and exercise, or some larger medical issue? Could either his personality change or his health problems be connected to his difficulties in fathering heirs?

Academics and non-academics alike have offered multiple theories to explain these mysteries. There are even questions and debates *about* the questions and debates. For example, there is a dispute about whether the first two children of his former mistress, Mary Boleyn, who was the older sister of his future wife, Anne Boleyn, were actually his progeny. If Mary Boleyn's children are really his, could he have had more illegitimate children that simply were not acknowledged at court? Did he actually have reproductive problems, or was he simply unfortunate enough to marry several women who all had compromised fertility? There is also serious disagreement about the nature of Henry's personality change. Some ask whether his personality really changed at all, and if it *did* change, when this change first took place (Starkey, 2008). Many historians argue that there was no sudden and abrupt change in the King's personality, maintaining that Henry simply grew older and more aware of his power, or that his failing health made him irritable, and that was the real cause of his tyranny (Scarisbrick, 1970; Smith, 1982). Alternatively, they argue that it was a change in circumstances and threats to his rule which pushed him into becoming a more ruthless monarch (Lipscomb, 2009). There is a further assertion that Henry had always been a narcissistic bully, but before his attempt to end his marriage to Katherina of Aragon no one had ever really challenged his will on anything important, and thus his true malevolence had lain dormant (Lindsey, 1995). Nevertheless, it is practically indisputable that his moodiness, paranoia, and erratic behavior became more extreme, and therefore more noticeable, after he turned forty.

  Many people, from many different fields of study, have offered explanations for the enigmas which surround Henry VIII. There is conjecture about the effects of his diet, possible diseases, and the potential rhesus incompatibility of his wives, to name but a few. Does a combination of several factors account for all of his problems? Or is there a simpler answer? Could there be a medical reason to account for the high rate of miscarriage and stillbirths experienced by Henry and his unfortunate wives, as well as for his emotional instability and physical decline after midlife? Interestingly enough, there is something that could provide an answer all these questions -- and it involves Henry's blood.

Henry VIII hoped to be the legendary center of a new Camelot, and desired "to create such a fine opinion about his valor among all men that they could understand that his ambition was not merely to equal but to excel the glorious deeds of his ancestors" (Erickson, 1980:73). Sadly, it seems that the blood type he inherited from some of those ancestors had predestined him for distinction, but not in the manner he hoped. It is very plausible that the King's blood type was Kell positive (Whitley and Kramer, 2010). A person whose blood is Kell positive has an additional antigen on the surface of their red blood cells. Often being Kell positive does not cause an individual any significant trouble. However, sometimes a Kell blood type can have serious consequences, just like the problems that plagued Henry.

The Kell blood type, which the King would have inherited from his mother, was probably the cause of the troubles that have made him so prominent in the public imagination. For one thing, having a Kell positive blood type would explain why he had such difficulty siring heirs. Henry is seldom identified as the possible reason for the obstetrical losses of his first two wives, primarily because of the socio-cultural conditioning that makes most people, even medical professionals, assume that obstetrical issues are a 'female problem'. Henry might have been identified as the source of the trouble if none of his wives had become pregnant, but so few people are cognizant of the fact that the father can still cause negative reproductive outcomes even *after* conception that no one connected Henry with the miscarriages, stillbirths and newborn infant deaths. The myth that factors related to the father cannot affect a pregnancy after conception is so ingrained that even when people did speculate that the problem may have been caused by Henry, they usually ascribed it to impotence or sterility. Considering the fact that the King's first two wives had at least eleven, and possibly thirteen or more, pregnancies, and the fact that he impregnated his third wife and one of his mistresses, it is obvious that *fertility* was not Henry's problem. Fetal and newborn mortality were the crux of his reproductive troubles, not an inability to get women pregnant.

The obstetrical losses suffered by Henry's first two Queens are similar to documented cases of Kell affected pregnancies (Whitley and Kramer, 2010), which only occur when the father of the fetus has a Kell positive blood type but the mother has the more common Kell negative blood type. When a Kell negative woman conceives a baby with a Kell positive man, she experiences Kell sensitization, wherein her body becomes "allergic" to any fetus that is Kell positive like the father. Although the first pregnancy is usually safe, since the mother's body needs at least one Kell positive pregnancy to become sensitised, any subsequent Kell positive fetus will almost always die. This means that a Kell negative woman whose partner is a Kell positive man has an increased risk of suffering from repeated late term miscarriages, stillbirths, and the death of her newborns shortly after they are delivered (Santiago, et al. 2008). This is exactly what happened to any woman who had more than one pregnancy with Henry VIII. If the King was Kell positive, there is nothing whatsoever that his Queens could have done to prevent the deaths of their babies, and they have therefore been mistakenly blamed for their tragic losses for centuries.

Since most people with the Kell positive blood type can pass either a Kell positive or a Kell negative gene on to their children, every pregnancy fathered by Henry had a chance of being Kell negative. A Kell negative fetus would not be attacked by the mother's antibodies and would have as much chance of survival as any other healthy baby born during this era. This explains why at least one of his children, Mary, survived even though she was not the first-born of Katherina of Aragon. If Mary, the fifth baby born to Henry's first Queen, did not get the Kell positive gene from her father then she would have been safe in the womb, unlike her Kell positive siblings. The pregnancies of Henry's second Queen, Anne Boleyn, were a textbook example of a healthy first child and subsequent late-term miscarriages; any of Anne's pregnancies conceived after the birth of her daughter, Elizabeth, had unsuccessful outcomes. Henry's third Queen, Jane Seymour, had only one child before her death, but a healthy firstborn is normal with a Kell positive father. The only mistress formally acknowledged to have given Henry a child was Bessie Blount, who produced a healthy firstborn son, but then had no more children by the King.

A miserable history of lost babies is not the only thing Kell positive blood could have given Henry. If the King was Kell positive, then it is also possible that he developed a rare disease called McLeod syndrome, which occurs when a person has the "McLeod phenotype" of the Kell blood group (Miranda, et al., 2007). If you've never heard of McLeod syndrome before, you are not alone. It isn't well known except to a few doctors who are specialists in this kind of blood-antigen linked illness. Usually the symptoms of McLeod syndrome begin around a patient's fortieth birthday, and increase with time. McLeod syndrome has both physical and psychological symptoms that would explain why Henry became physically weaker and more mentally unstable after he turned forty in 1531, and why his condition continued to deteriorate until his death in 1547. McLeod syndrome explains why such a dashing young King who wanted to be the flower of English chivalry in his youth made such bad political decisions and had so many of his wives, friends and family executed in his middle age.

There is extreme difficulty in proving, beyond doubt, that Henry suffered from McLeod syndrome. For one thing, historical records may not have noted many of the symptoms needed to diagnose his condition. Additionally, symptoms may have been recorded in a manner which makes them difficult to correlate to modern diagnostic criteria. As a result, it is difficult to confirm exactly how *many* of the physical symptoms consistent with McLeod syndrome the King actually displayed. Moreover, he had other aliments which also affected his health. This problem of "co-morbidity" makes it very difficult to be sure precisely which aspects of his ill-health were caused by McLeod syndrome.

Take, for example, the well-known fact that Henry found it increasingly difficult to walk as he grew older. He had the "worst legs in the world" and was often wheeled around in a "tram", or traveling chair (Erickson, 1980:360). This could have been a result of McLeod syndrome, since a patient with this illness will often experience muscle weakness and nerve deterioration, especially in his lower limbs (Wada et al., 2003). However, taking this as conclusive evidence on which to base a diagnosis of McLeod syndrome would be problematic because he had other health problems that could have affected his ability to walk. It has been convincingly argued that the King had osteomyelitis, a chronic bone infection that makes it very painful to walk (Keynes, 2005:180). Furthermore he was, without question, vastly overweight by the time he entered his fifties. His lack of mobility may have been as much a consequence of his excessive bulk, coupled with his agonizing leg ulcers, as it was a result of McLeod syndrome. For obvious reasons the passage of time makes it impossible to figure out *exactly* which malady was causing which problem for the King. To further complicate the issue, there is extreme inconsistency in the severity of symptoms associated with McLeod syndrome. It is normal for McLeod sufferers to exhibit symptoms to differing degrees, so that one patient may have noticeable facial tics while another patient displays no facial tics at all.

Obviously the physical problems the King suffered were varied and are hard to pin on just one cause, but Henry's mental and emotional symptoms provide stronger evidence for the McLeod theory. The psychological symptoms experienced by patients with McLeod syndrome include erosion of memory and executive functions, paranoia, depression, socially inappropriate conduct, irrational personality alterations, and even schizophrenia-like behaviors (Whitley and Kramer, 2010; Jung and Haker, 2004). In some severe cases the schizophrenia-like symptoms and personality changes are the key to diagnosing McLeod syndrome (Jung and Haker, 2004:723). There is certainly strong evidence to suggest that Henry underwent a significant personality change after his fortieth birthday, in a manner consistent with the mental problems that are often linked to McLeod syndrome.

As a young man, Henry was a handsome, genial, and rational ruler. The youthful King was described, in the private letters of more than one foreign ambassador or other court contemporary, as having incredible physical beauty. His hair was red, he had very fair skin, and his face was considered as lovely as that of "a pretty woman" (Scarisbrick, 1970:13). Even in 1531, when the King was middle-aged and had lost the golden glow of youth, the Venetian ambassador to England, Ludovico

Falieri, found reasons to heap praise on England's monarch, writing that:

> "In the 8th Henry such beauty of mind and body is combined as to surprise and astonish. Grand stature, suited to his exalted position, showing the superiority of mind and character; a face like an angel's, so fair is it; his head bald like Caesar's, and he wears a beard, which is not the English custom. He is accomplished in every manly exercise, sits his horse well, tilts with his lance, throws the quoit, shoots with his bow excellent well; he is a fine tennis player, and he practices all these gifts with the greatest industry. Such a prince could not fail to have cultivated also his character and his intellect. He has been a student since his childhood; he knows literature, philosophy, and theology; speaks and writes Spanish, French, and Italian, besides Latin and English. He is kind, gracious, courteous, liberal, especially to men of learning, whom he is always ready to help. He appears religious also, generally hears two masses a day, and on holy days High Mass besides. He is very charitable, giving away ten thousand gold ducats annually among orphans, widows and cripples." (Froude, 32-33:1891)

Henry was also uncommonly tall for his time, well over six feet, with the chiseled physique of a champion athlete. The fact he was an excellent dancer and a model of chivalry further added to his attractiveness. He was a master horseman, able to ride for more than thirty miles without needing a break. He also excelled at jousting, consistently outperforming any of his court contemporaries. Since jousting was a dangerous and demanding sport with the potential to cause severe injuries, or even death, the King's skill and athleticism was no small matter. He hunted almost every day, ignoring bad weather to pursue his prey for hours at a time. Henry also played an excellent game of tennis, a sport that was more like modern squash than tennis as we know it in modern times, which required a lot of physical exertion. This kind of active lifestyle meant that the King remained a gorgeous court luminary until he was in his forties, when he had to stop, or at least restrict the amount of his participation in, most forms of exercise because of his chronic pain.

In addition to his physical accomplishments, the King had a brilliant mind. Henry's intellect impressed many of the most famous thinkers of his day. Although Henry would one day set England down the path to a complete separation from the Church of Rome, he was a devout Catholic until his midlife, and he even wrote a book in 1521 defending Catholicism from the criticisms of Martin Luther, entitled *Assertio Septem Sacramentorum*, which when translated from Latin means "The Defense of the Seven Sacraments". Notwithstanding his devotion to his religion, when he was young the King was not the implacable zealot he became in his later life. Early in his reign Henry enjoyed theological debates and would listen to opinions which differed from his own with remarkable calm. Erasmus, the famed Dutch scholar and priest who was one of the most renowned humanists of the Renaissance, praised Henry highly. Erasmus called the young King a "universal genius", and wrote that Henry "never neglected his studies; and whenever he has leisure from his political occupations, he reads, or disputes -- of which he is very fond -- with remarkable courtesy and unruffled temper" (Pollard, 1919:123). The King was not just well-mannered and gracious in matters of religion: he was lauded for his easy-going and cheerful nature in general. He also had an almost insatiable curiosity and interest in mental pursuits. He was taught mathematics, engineering, and astronomy by the most learned men in his kingdom. He spoke several languages, and was as fluent in Latin and French as he was in his native tongue. Moreover, he respected the pursuit of knowledge, establishing the Royal College of Physicians in 1518 and endowing two Regius Professorships in medicine at Oxford and Cambridge in 1540 (Furdell, 2001:9).

      Adding to the bounty of accomplishments with which he was gifted, Henry was musically adept. He was an amazing musician who could play several instruments. Moreover, he could sing beautifully and certainly appreciated the vocal talents of others. The King employed almost sixty musicians for his entertainment and accepted only the very best singers in England for his Chapel Royal; the music of the Chapel was so good it was described as "more divine than human" by a visitor to his court (Roden et al., 2009:278). His interest in music was not just limited to playing and singing what others had written; he also composed his own melodies. The King's musical interests serve to illustrate his keen intellect, since modern research shows that the brains of people who are musically talented are highly developed, making musicians more broadminded and curious about learning new things (Travis et al., 2011).

      It is hard for the modern reader to understand just how spectacular Henry must have seemed to those around him. To get a comparison, you would need to envision a man so athletically superb that he could win Olympic medals in several sports, make him as beautiful as any male supermodel, have him be fluent in three languages, then give him the ability to compose critically-acclaimed classical music, and finally have him earn a Ph.D in both engineering and Latin. Now, think of him as heir to the English crown as well. Only then would you have a good idea of how impressive Henry appeared to his contemporaries.

In spite of all his talents, the King was not an intense killjoy devoted to practicing his many skills. Far from it. When he was younger the King also enjoyed more relaxed pursuits, such as card games and other kinds of friendly gambling. He obviously didn't value winning enough to cheat, because he frequently lost huge sums during games of cards or dice (Loades, 1992:96). He must have been, contrary to his popular image, a very good loser, since there was never any retaliation against those who won large amounts of money from him. This did not mean he gambled foolishly. He quickly figured out when he was being scammed at cards by a group of French con men, and had them dismissed from his court (Scarisbrick, 1968:19). Not only did the King love games of chance, he was not snobbish or elitist about his gaming partners; between 1527 and 1539 he often played with his sergeant of the cellar, Robert Hill, who was a upper-level member of the kitchen staff. Hill would have been in charge of keeping track of the beer, wine, and ale consumed by Henry's household, a position far removed from the court luminaries the King could summon for games if he wanted to (Sim, 1997:33). The easy-going, cheerful, and gregarious nature of the King is a far cry from the monstrous bully that most people believe him to have been.

Although he clearly had his virtues, Henry was not a saint. Even during his youth it can be argued he was egocentric, with a propensity to show off. These qualities should probably be expected in such a talented young man, considering that athletic and musical talent were no less appreciated in the Tudor period than they are today. When such abilities are combined in a man who had been taught to believe that he was God's chosen leader of the English people, "and by the very logic of his office could do no wrong" (Smith, 1982:25), he could hardly fail to develop a swollen ego. Henry was considered the embodiment of England, and was the most important man in his Kingdom. He was so relentlessly flattered and feted by those who wished to profit from his favors that it would have been nothing short of miraculous if he had not been conceited and spoiled. Certainly the young King was vain about his looks, as he had every reason to be.

Henry was also something of a slave to the concept of romance. He loved to woo and flatter the ladies of his court, but this does not mean he was a lecherous womanizer. He formed amours for various women, and often overestimated his appeal to all members of the fairer sex, but he was so devoted to the concept of chivalry that he was never a coarse libertine. He wrote poems and sent women presents and needed to believe that the heart was always present in the bedroom; he was neither a lecher nor a rapist.

One cannot help but wonder how this man, who gave every indication of being a magnanimous and progressive sovereign, could have become the hidebound and reactionary dictator of his later rule. How did a man so devoted to the chivalrous ideal go on to legally murder his wives? The change seems so preposterous that it almost *requires* a medical explanation for the difference. What else could have affected him so strongly, in such a short time?

Even those historians who do not believe Henry experienced a radical alteration in character cannot help but recognize that the King behaved very differently in his old age than he did in his youth. Lacey Baldwin Smith, a well-respected biographer of Henry VIII, observes that in his youth Henry was "a man of honour, a warrior knight and a noble gentleman" (1982: 25), but in his later years he "became the most dangerous kind of tyrant, secretive, neurotic and unpredictable" (1982: 268). Moreover, Smith noted that since the day of the King's death, "apologists and critics have been struggling to penetrate the ambivalence of Henry's personality. Two images keep merging and reappearing: the angelic-faced athlete who inherited a brimming treasury, a stable throne, and boundless good health, and the Henry of later years who ... [died] degenerate in body and soul" (2009:123). Another distinguished historian, David Starkey, acknowledges that "Henry's is a life which naturally falls in halves" (2008:7), meaning that the Henry who was crowned in 1509 "is not the same as the man who revises [the coronation oath] . . twenty-odd years later" (2008:7). Other scholars are more willing to concede that Henry's personality did change abruptly. Recently, historian Susannah Lipscomb argued that a distinct difference in Henry's personality emerged in 1536, and that many of "the flaws in his character were fashioned or catalyzed by the events of this one year" (Lipscomb, 2009:205). There is also speculation that Henry sustained brain damage when he fell from his horse while jousting, in 1536, explaining a rapid and radical switch in his behavior (Lipscomb, 2009:205). A brain injury in 1536 is not, however, a satisfactory answer for the King's personality change, since he showed signs of the transformation several years earlier (Whitley and Kramer, 2010:839). What is certain is that Henry's moodiness, paranoia, and erratic behavior progressively became worse, and he became "markedly more distrustful and despotic" (Lipscomb, 2009:184) during the last 15 years of his life .

The theory that Henry had a Kell positive blood type and McLeod syndrome is the result of extrapolating from historical clues. As any historian will attest, piecing together the facts from the bits of information which survived for centuries is very difficult. Often information is gleaned from letters written about court gossip and relaying only second-hand knowledge. Additionally, the writers of those letters were not impartial. The court teemed with intrigue and factional jockeying for power. Those who were in the favor of certain ministers, or wives, of the King could view the same event very differently. For example, those who favored unchanged Catholicism, and Henry's first Queen, were naturally hostile toward Anne Boleyn and wrote scathing reports of both her and the King. Those who favored religious reform and were sympathetic towards Henry's need for a male heir wrote much kinder assessments of Anne.

A great deal of what we know about Henry's court and scandals during the time of his relationship with Anne comes from the letters of Eustace Chapuys, one of Queen Katherina's most ardent supporters and the ambassador of her nephew, Charles V of Spain. They are well written, descriptive, and detailed. However, are they as accurate as they are plentiful? It was in Chapuys' interest to portray Katherina as favorably as possible, and to describe Anne as a wanton, vicious, dangerous harpy. He clearly wanted Charles V to invade England and remove Henry, who had hurt Katherina and was openly rebelling against Papal authority, from his throne, thus allowing Katherina's only daughter, Mary, to rule in Henry's place. Chapuys was far from unbiased, and he was skilled in political maneuvering. Lord Paget described Chapuys as "without respect of honesty or truth … He is a great practicer, with which honest term we cover tale-telling, lying, dissimulating, and flattering"

(Froude, 112:1891). This is probably unfair, but it does show that not everyone agreed with Chapuys' version of events. Yet historians frequently use his letters to ascertain the "truth" of Henry's situation and actions. Often this is from necessity. There is only scanty evidence left after the passage of 500 years, and Chapuys is frequently the closest scholars can come to an eyewitness account of life at Henry's court.

Considering the challenges that face historians in their attempts to ascertain the truth, imagine, if you will, how difficult it has been to make a medical diagnosis just by using information gleaned from those same slanted historical records. How can there ever be certainty about whether or not Henry was in the Kell positive blood group and suffered from McLeod syndrome? Fortunately, there are genetic markers for the suspected conditions, and new techniques for extracting DNA from very old remains. Thus, if Henry's body were exhumed for analysis, a DNA test could prove, beyond doubt, if the King had Kell positive blood and McLeod syndrome. However, until such analysis is allowed, historical clues will have to suffice.

The idea that Henry had McLeod syndrome is an important one. If the King's brain functions were compromised because of McLeod syndrome, his successively more paranoid and violent behavior would have been a result of his illness, rather than because he was a psychopathic murderer. One of the biggest tragedies about Henry VIII is that few people remember the fair and caring monarch he was when he first ascended the throne; most simply remember the vile despot he became. It is a shame that Henry is remembered not for the lives he spared before he was thirty-nine, but rather for the lives he took after he reached his forties. If the King had McLeod syndrome then he was as much a victim of his own illness as the people that his condition compelled him to execute. Whatever he became, the young idealist who took the throne in the spring of 1509, who was so warmly praised by Erasmus as a "lover of justice and goodness" (Erickson, 1980:62), deserves to be remembered just as much as the bloodthirsty tyrant he was when he died more than four decades later. It would be appalling were Henry to remain condemned for behavior he could not control.

Chapter Two
Katherina of Aragon: Daughter of Spain, Princess of Wales, and Queen of England

Some of Henry's wives have become as famous as the King himself. It therefore seems fitting that his wives and the record of their pregnancies should figure so prominently in the story of his health. His first Queen, Katherina of Aragon, is the unfortunate woman who encountered the most extreme obstetrical complications, probably as a result of having married a Kell positive husband. Although she was not one of the Queens who lost her head to Henry's displeasure, in many ways Katherina's life with the King was even more tragic than the fate Anne Boleyn or Katheryn Howard suffered. For every good thing that happened to Katherina, there were an excess of contrasting tragedies. She married Henry in his prime when he was a handsome and dashing young monarch who loved her and rescued her from an untenable political limbo. However, this romantic rescue had disastrous consequences for Katherina. If Henry was Kell positive, then his love was the reason that she had to endure the agonizing heartbreak of multiple fetal losses, the birth of stillborn infants, and the deaths of almost all of her newborn babies. Furthermore, the loss of so many of her children is also the primary reason her beloved husband eventually attempted to annul their marriage, claiming that they were never legally wed in the first place.

Katherina was born in mid December of 1485, the youngest living child of Isabella of Castile and Ferdinand of Aragon. Her parents were very capable military leaders who shared power equally, which was highly enlightened for their time. Sadly, their enlightenment did not extend into other areas. Isabella and Ferdinand helped facilitate the Spanish Inquisition, which was one of history's greatest examples of inhumane oppression, but for many people religious intolerance and persecution were, unfortunately, part and parcel of being devoted to a theological ideology during that era (Perez, 2006:30). Katherina's mother, and her formative role model, was smart, strong, and tough, as well as being a fanatical Catholic. Isabella was extremely strong-willed, ruling Castile in her own right. She was also the bane of anyone who met her armies on a battlefield. There is a persistent myth that Katherina was born in the midst of a combat zone, but it is inaccurate. However, Isabella did remain on a heavy military campaign while pregnant with Katherina, withdrawing to prepare for birth only after a major victory (Starkey, 2003:11). While she had many admirable qualities, Isabella was also stubbornly dogmatic and unwilling to compromise, or even be lenient, about matters of the Catholic faith. Like her mother, Katherina was intelligent, stalwart, and would later prove herself to be equally adept at leadership. She would also prove to be her mother's equal in her devotion to Catholicism and her determination to fight for what she felt was hers and hers alone.

Katherina was engaged to Arthur, the oldest son of Henry VII and the elder brother of Henry VIII, when she was still a toddler. At the time, England was an unsophisticated, rather unimportant country that had been immersed in a civil war for years, and Henry VII was an upstart with a dubious right to the throne (Lindsey, 1995:13). He had only become King after he had won the Wars of the Roses, which had been fought between two separate branches of the Plantagenet royal family. On one side was the House of Lancaster, whose emblem was a red rose, and on the other side was the House of York, symbolized by a white rose. In spite of the fact that Henry VII had a very shaky claim to the throne, he was declared King after he defeated his Yorkist rival, Richard III, on Bosworth Field in 1485 (Starkey, 2008:8). Richard III is most famous for having allegedly murdered his young nephews, who are often called the Princes in the Tower, because they had a more legitimate claim to the throne than he did. Historians are still debating the matter, but evidence appears to identify Richard III as the culprit in their murders (Ross, 1984:97-100). Henry VII, after killing Richard III and becoming King of England, wisely married Elizabeth of York, the eldest sister of the Princes in the Tower. She was the putative heir to the House of York, and her marriage to Henry VII thus united the warring factions. To signal that the civil war had finally been brought to a conclusion by this merger of the Houses of York and Lancaster, Henry VII combined the red and the white rose to create a new symbol which is now called the Tudor Rose. The reign of the Tudors had begun and would last for 117 years.

There had been one small impediment to the marriage of Henry VII to Elizabeth of York. They were distant cousins, and their "shared blood" meant their union could be prevented on the grounds of consanguinity. Therefore, they had to get a Papal dispensation, in which the Pope "dispensed" with the Church objections to their familial relationship, so that they could wed (Chrimes, 1999:330). European royalty, in general, had to obtain Papal dispensations to allow their marriages, since the interbreeding among the monarchies was extreme. How extreme? Well, Katherina of Aragon was the descendant of one of Edward III's children, just as were her future grooms, Arthur and Henry. They were, all three, the great-great-grandchildren of John of Gaunt, who was Edward III's third surviving son. Arthur and Henry were also descendants of Edward III's second surviving son, Lionel of Antwerp, through their mother. With these kinds of tangled family lineages, you can see why Papal dispensations were necessary ... and frequent.

Henry VII and Elizabeth of York's marriage was very successful, especially by royal standards. There seems to have been genuine affection between the two. They were also lucky in their reproductive success. Henry and Elizabeth had four children who survived childhood. Their firstborn son, Arthur, was heir to the throne, while his sisters Margaret and Mary had the potential to make marital connections to other European royal houses, which would increase England's political importance. The King and Queen's youngest son, Henry, who would leave such a lasting legacy as King, was initially thought to have a future in the church, perhaps to make sure he had no children who would one day challenge their cousins for the crown. After all, England had endured its fill of civil war, and Henry VII was understandably cautious and worried about the future.

Nevertheless, fate had a different destiny in mind for Arthur's younger brother.

As adults both daughters became Queen consorts. Margaret Tudor was married to James IV, the King of Scotland, and gave birth to a son and heir. In keeping with the tradition of royal intermarriage, two of Margaret's grandchildren, Mary I of Scotland and Henry Stuart, were wed in the summer of 1565. Their marriage was short and unhappy, but it did produce Margaret's great-grandson, James VI of Scotland, who eventually became James I of England when Margaret's niece, Queen Elizabeth I, died and left him her throne.

Mary Tudor was married, briefly, to Louis XII, the King of France, but they had no children, probably because of Louis' advanced age. She then boldly wed Charles Brandon, the 1st Duke of Suffolk, without asking permission from her family. After having sacrificed herself for her country by becoming the bride of a man old enough to be her grandfather, she felt entitled to marry for love after she was widowed. She and Brandon had two daughters who lived to adulthood, but all of their surviving grandchildren were victims of the political machinations of their cousins, and died young. The most famous of Mary and Brandon's grandchildren was Lady Jane Grey, who was Queen of England for only nine days and was subsequently beheaded on the orders of Henry VIII's eldest daughter, Queen Mary I of England.

Henry VII and Elizabeth of York naturally wanted the best for their children, and finding Arthur a suitable bride was of utmost importance. Therefore, they were extremely happy that they had managed to arrange, with careful and persistent diplomacy, Katherina of Aragon's betrothal to their eldest son. Arthur's engagement to a Spanish princess was a major achievement for the English Crown, not just for her connection with a powerful European nation, but also because Katherina's mother, Isabella, was more legitimately connected to the throne of England than was Henry VII (Lindsey, 1995:13-14). Isabella was a descendant of one of the children born to John of Gaunt by his wife, Constance of Castile, whereas Henry VII was descended from the children of John of Gaunt and his mistress Kathryn Swynford, whose children were only legitimized after John of Gaunt was able to marry their mother. There were reasons other than Katherina's more legitimate blood ties to the English throne that made her a marital coup for the son of Henry VII. She also came with a hefty dowry, and Henry VII was reputed to be exceedingly fond of money. Moreover, an alliance with such powerful Spanish monarchs gained England greater influence. Henry VII had proven that he could wage an effective military campaign when he won the War of the Roses: he demonstrated his diplomatic leadership capabilities by obtaining such a high-level bride for his heir. In short, Katherina was quite a prize for the son of a parvenu King and was valued accordingly.

However, Arthur could not claim his bride until his father had satisfied Ferdinand and Isabella with a sacrifice of royal blood: they would not let Katherina come to England until Henry VII had executed Edward Plantagenet, the 17th Earl of Warwick. Warwick was the grandson of Richard Plantagenet, 3rd Duke of York, and thus the nephew of Kings Edward VI and Richard III. As a more direct descendant of Edward III and briefly Richard III's heir to the throne, Warwick was, in truth, the most legitimate contender for the English crown. However, for reasons that are not entirely clear, Warwick was not considered a good candidate for the throne. Perhaps he was "simple-minded" or otherwise unable to rule (Kendall, 1956:349). Regardless of the reason, he was unlikely to challenge the Tudors' right to the throne. Nonetheless, the very existence of Warwick made England's new royal family nervous. After the Spanish ambassador communicated some concerns about the "doubtful royal blood" still threatening Henry's crown, and imparted news of Ferdinand and Isabella's reluctance to send their daughter to England when there might someday be contention about Arthur's right to rule, the King had Warwick "framed" and executed on November 28, 1499 (Loades, 1999:91). Henry VII had probably been seeking an excuse to kill Edward Plantagenet, and the Spanish anxiety was a further motivation to have him beheaded. As politically pragmatic as the execution/murder was, it meant that Katherina and Arthur's union started under a cloud, and Katherina herself was later to claim that some of the tragedies that would befall her were "a judgment of God" because her first marriage was "made in blood" (Sullivan, 1838:165).

Katherina came to England in 1501, when she was not quite sixteen. She was a pretty girl, with a pleasing face and long reddish-gold hair that she had inherited from her English ancestors (Starkey, 2003:57). The people of England were enchanted with her and decorated London to welcome their future Queen in a grand style. Katherina further endeared herself to both the court and the populace by trying very hard to be friendly and to embrace the customs of her adopted country. She was charming to Arthur and even managed to deal well with her future father-in-law. This couldn't have been easy for a young girl who was surely suffering from homesickness, was adjusting to a different climate, and who couldn't speak much English (Starkey, 2003:65). Katherina was obviously possessed of more than usual fortitude, since she didn't let Henry VII shake her composure and she did her best to make Arthur, who was almost a year younger than she was, comfortable in his role as her husband.

Her future husband must have been pleased with her, because once he met her he sent letters to Spain assuring Isabella and Ferdinand that he "had never felt such joy in his life as when he beheld the sweet face of his bride. No woman in the world could be more agreeable to him" (Starkey, 2003:64). Arthur also assured his in-laws that he would do his best to be a good husband to their daughter.

Arthur's letter not only demonstrated a firm grasp of etiquette but also gives a good indication of contemporary beliefs and hopes about politically expedient unions. Most marriages in the 15th and 16th century were "arranged", in that the families of the prospective brides and grooms had a large say in whether or not a wedding would take place. However, this did not mean the happiness of the parties involved was not considered, or that their consent was not required. To the contrary, an ideal marriage was one arranged by the families to be economically and socially advantageous, yet which still enabled the wedded pair to form a sincere attachment to one another. Love was considered a crucial ingredient for a good marriage, and was eagerly hoped for (Cressy, 1997:260-262). Families were advised to take the wishes of the prospective bride and groom into account, since "where the fancie is not pleased, all the perfections of the world cannot force love, and where the fancie delighteth, many defects are perfected or tolerated" in the marriage partner (Whetstone, 1582 in Sims, 1996:7). It is certainly true, especially among the upper classes, that the family would arrange a marriage even if neither party had met, but even then it was sincerely hoped, by everyone involved, that the couple would grow to love one another, or at least have an amiable and successful relationship (Cressy, 1997:261). Often, however, the potential couple was more familiar with each other and had a chance to determine whether cordial feelings had the potential to develop, before the marriage was arranged. If a marriage had to go ahead without the couple getting a chance to get to know one another, as was the case for Arthur and Katherina's union, the new bride and groom often did their best to fall in love with each other. This 'fake it until you make it' approach was surprisingly successful, at least to the point where the newlyweds could have a happy and beneficial partnership. If young people became smitten with someone prior to any contracted betrothal, then their parents or guardians would usually try to arrange a match between them, provided that there was no important reason to prevent the union (Sims, 1996:6-8).

    Nevertheless, in spite of parental concerns for a child's happiness, if a person fell in love with someone who was considered unsuitable, their parents and other family members would discourage the match with all their considerable social and cultural power. To openly defy your family carried such a heavy stigma that it is hard for the modern reader to really understand just how *bad* it was to be a disobedient child, at any age, during this time. Thus, the family of an individual had a great deal of influence over the choice of a marriage partner, even if the person was of age and financially independent (Sims, 1996:4-6). Moreover, it was considered that passionate love alone was a bad reason for marriage, since a "hot love soon cooled" (Sims, 1996:6). Families may have considered stopping an imprudent union the best possible thing they could do to ensure the thwarted individual's future happiness.

It is frequently believed by many people in the West that an arranged marriage is always a loveless marriage. That is incorrect. Studies of Indian couples have found that people in arranged marriages are as happy, in general, as those who are in marriages which were made for romantic reasons (Eysenck, 2000:548). Certainly there are unhappy arranged marriages, but Western divorce rates demonstrate beyond a doubt that people do not always have a successful and happy union even when it was made without any familial input. Parents, throughout history and in every culture, have tended to love their children and want the best for them. Therefore, few people are going to knowingly arrange for their children to wed someone who would make them miserable. In the Tudor era there were certainly parents who were cruel and made horrible marriages for their children simply for their own greedy advantage, but these parents are the exception, not the rule.

In this context, it is easy to see that Arthur and Katherina would have been strongly motivated to try very hard to form an attachment to one another. Not only had they been trained since childhood to accept the political consequences of their royal status; they knew it would make their families very happy if they fell in love.

The age of the newly married pair would have been of concern to their royal parents. While marriages arranged from the cradle were normal for the very wealthy and the children in those matches were frequently wed in their very early teens, this was not at all common for society in general. The average age of marriage for a woman in the Tudor era was 25 or 26 years old, and men were typically 27 or 28 years old when they wed (Cressy, 1997:285). Therefore, Arthur and Katherina would have been considered very young to embark on the marital journey, and their parents would have watched them carefully and been prepared to help and offer advice at every step. Older councilors chosen by their parents surrounded Arthur and Katherina, and the newlyweds would have been expected to listen carefully to their recommendations, no matter how *intimate* the topic. Ferdinand and Isabella were so concerned about the youth of their daughter's groom that they wrote to Katherina's duenna, Dona Elvira, and told her that they would "rather be pleased than dissatisfied" if the couple postponed any attempts to find connubial bliss in the marriage bed (Gelardi, 2008:74).

Henry VII and Elizabeth of York may have had other reasons for worrying about the union. Arthur is usually described by historians as being in delicate health, so they may have been concerned that an early marriage would endanger his well-being. One of the few scholars to disagree with the consensus that the Prince of Wales was chronically ill is David Starkey, who argues that Arthur's indisposition is a myth, pointing out that there is "eye-witness evidence to the contrary" from contemporary sources (2003:27). Circumstances, however, would seem to favor the majority opinion about Arthur's constitution, since he died when he was only 15 years old. Whether or not the groom was sickly, and regardless of the fact that he and the bride were hardly more than children, Arthur married Katherina on November 14, 1501.

Whether their marriage was subsequently consummated would become a matter of huge debate and one that is still unresolved. Katherina's young husband certainly shared her bed several times. Arthur's body servant, William Thomas, testified that he would help the Prince get ready for bed, then "conducted him clad in his night gown unto the Princess's bedchamber door often and sundry times … and that at the morning he received him at the said door ... and waited upon him to his own privy chamber (Starkey, 2003:76). Furthermore, Arthur bragged that he had accomplished his marital duties, insisting that he had been "in the midst of Spain" (Fraser, 1992:162). However, the young groom may have been boasting from bravado, since when Arthur died a few months later on April 2, 1502, his bride declared that she was still a virgin. She would maintain her assertion was true for the rest of her life.

    Disagreement about whether the bride told the truth about the marital consummation continues in historical circles. Those that believe Katherina did not lie about her virginity point out that she was a staunch Catholic who stood by her story even to the Papal Legate, Cardinal Campeggio. Campeggio recorded that Katherina had sworn to him that she had become a widow while she was "intacta et incorrupta", which translates as untouched and pure (Okerlund, 2009:169). Furthermore, during the debates surrounding the annulment of her marriage to Henry VIII she put it to Henry's conscience if she had been a virgin or not and he did not refute her. If he had been able to work up even a shred of doubt it is almost certain he would have used it, since her marriage to Arthur was his excuse for nullifying their long union. Those who believe that Katherina was lying base their arguments largely on the papal dispensation for her betrothal to Henry VIII, which said the marriage had "perhaps" been consummated, and testimony against her given in a court that Henry had summoned specifically to help him find reasons to dissolve his marriage (Starkey, 2003:86-87). While it is true that Katherina had strong motivation to lie, since she was fighting for her marriage and the undisputed right of her daughter to remain heir to the throne, the evidence seems to side with the historians who support her version of events. Nevertheless, the truth of her marital relations will remain unknown for perpetuity, since there is no way for any concrete evidence to be presented.

After the death of her young husband there was some immediate diplomatic scrambling to figure out what to do with the newly widowed Katherina. Henry VII did not want to give up her dowry or her connections, so, having recently become a widower, he even talked about marrying her himself. It's disturbing to the modern reader to think about a man his age wedding a teenage bride, but that happened with distressing regularity to girls her age during this era. Nonetheless, people of that time were horrified at the thought of a man marrying his widowed daughter-in-law. Since she became, legally and morally his 'daughter' upon her marriage to Arthur, it would have been disgustingly incestuous for Henry VII to take her as a wife. Fortunately, Katherina's strong-willed and powerful mother was not about to let such an atrocity happen. Isabella wrote to the Spanish ambassador that it would be an "evil thing ... the mere mention of which offends our ears" (Jansen, 2002:114), making it clear she would never allow such a union for her daughter. However, even though Isabella wanted to find her daughter a suitable marriage, she was also trying to keep her expenditures to a minimum, so she began negotiating Katherina's marriage to the new Prince of Wales, the future Henry VIII, in spite of the close kinship between a man's widow and his brother. Isabella and Ferdinand had already sent a large amount of money and gold plate that they felt should count toward the full dowry for the new marriage. Henry VII, who was somewhat of a penny-pincher, did his utmost to raise the amount of Katherina's dowry to its absolute limit. Negotiations were further slowed by the fact that Prince Henry had once been Katherina's brother-in-law, so a dispensation from the Pope was required to allow them to marry.

Pope Julius II granted a dispensation for Katherina's marriage to Henry only after much hesitation and even Henry VII had some doubts as to whether or not the dispensation was enough to allow the marriage (Jensen, 2002:114). Henry VII apparently soothed his conscience by considering the wealth of Katherina's dowry and her political connections. On June 23, 1503 the Spanish royals and Henry VII finally came to an agreement regarding the terms and conditions of a marriage between Katherina and Prince Henry (Whitelock, 2010:10).

   In spite of the marital treaty, Katherina's situation became more precarious when her mother died in November of 1504. Isabella had been the monarch of Castile in her own right; her death meant that various factions, and her widower, Ferdinand, became engrossed in a struggle to rule her kingdom in her place. Ferdinand was much too busy trying to take possession of Castile to pay much attention to his daughter's problems. Likewise, Henry VII was much too busy trying to secure the entirety of her dowry from Ferdinand to give much thought to his once and future daughter-in-law's comfort or happiness. Moreover, while he still wanted the remainder of her dowry from Spain, Henry VII was also reluctant to let her marry the Prince of Wales, since Katherina was less valuable now that her powerful mother was deceased. Ferdinand, who clearly recognized that Henry VII was as crafty as himself, refused to send more dowry until Katherina was married to the Prince. Both men took their frustration with the intractability of the other monarch out on Katherina, who was left in relative penury.

   While her father and Henry VII were squabbling over her dowry, Katherina had to fend for herself. She was forced to pawn her jewels and household goods in order to pay her servants their wages, and to buy food and clothes (Lindsey, 1995:23). Her father named her ambassador to the English court, which was a shrewd move that allowed her to stay there without forfeiting her dowry. He also sent her some money, but it was never enough and she wrote to Ferdinand that her servants were ready to start begging in the streets and she was "all but naked" from lack of clothing (Okerlund, 2009:126). In response, her father mercilessly replied that she should remember her dignity, and even chastised her for having sold some of her gold plates to pay for her expenses (Lindsey, 1995:24). For years, Katherina was left to scrape by, but the death of Henry VII changed everything for the struggling Princess.

Henry VII died in April 1509. Henry VIII, who was still two months shy of eighteen years old, was now King of England. Katherina had been in England for almost eight years and had been an impoverished and miserable widow for most of that time. She was twenty-three years old, which was roughly five and a half years older than the groom. Although the age disparity was not such that it would prevent the marriage, her age was definitely not a point in her favor. Furthermore, she was comparatively poor, with little hope that her father would ever provide more dowry. She had no political power without her mother, and her father's disinterest was clear. Only a few weeks prior to the death of Henry VII, Katherina had written her father anguished pleas to be allowed to come home and spend her "few remaining days in serving God" (Starkey, 2003:105). The young widow had given up all hope of another English wedding. Her household was literally packing in preparation to return to Spain because everyone thought the newly crowned King would seek a different bride, one with more wealth or more powerful connections. There was certainly nothing that could force him to honor the marriage treaty, and only Katherina's personal charms to entice him to do so. To everyone's surprise, Henry VIII rode to Katherina's rescue, a true knight in shining armor, glorious in his athleticism and beauty, and declared his father had wanted him to marry Katherina and that was exactly what he planned to do. The new King claimed his father had, on his death bed, changed his mind about the marriage, and had approved it (Lindsey, 1995:24). Though rather unlikely, it made it very difficult for anyone to frame a persuasive argument against the union, and smoothed the way to a quick wedding ceremony. It is hard to imagine the relief and gratitude that Katherina must have felt when she heard the news. Her gratitude and love for her gallant hero would be enduring. Even though Henry turned into a monster who imprisoned her and tortured her psychologically, she still died declaring her love for him (Whitelock, 2009:72). No matter what happened between them, it seems as though she carried an image of that valorous rescuer in her heart forever.

When Henry VIII wed Katherina on June 11, 1509, it was probably a love match between the bride and groom, rather than a mere political alliance. Without doubt, Katherina was utterly dedicated to Henry, whom she loved with an unceasing passion. He could not have asked for a more doting and loving Queen. She made his shirts with her own hands, embroidering the white linen carefully with intricate designs in black thread. Even today, people who study the history of this style of embroidery, called blackwork, which utilizes the contrast of black thread on a white background, credit Queen Katherina for introducing it to England and note that she was so associated with that type of needlework that it was known as "Spanish work" in her honor (Gostelow, 1998). For Henry's part, he apparently loved his pretty and amenable wife. He dubbed himself Sir Loyal Heart, and neglected his political duties in order to enjoy her company instead (Starkey, 2003:122-3).

Everyone hoped that the newlyweds would have their first child, preferably a son and heir, as soon as humanly possible. Things seemed promising when Katherina became pregnant quickly, but the joy was short lived. Lamentably, she gave birth prematurely to a stillborn girl on January 31, 1510. Her loss was kept as secret as possible. Only the King, a couple of her waiting women, and her confessor were informed about the loss. This was probably done to protect Katherina, since in that time period people would openly speculate that women who miscarried had offended God or practiced witchcraft. To make matters worse for poor Katherina, after she delivered her stillborn daughter, her uterus swelled so much that her physician thought there might be another, still living, baby inside (Starkey, 2008:331). In spite of her doctor's hopes, the Queen was no longer pregnant and eventually her periods started again. All hope that she was pregnant should have been abandoned then, but her persistent swelling continued to persuade her physician that she might actually be pregnant with a second baby, in spite of the return of her menstrual cycle. Katherina, who probably wanted to believe her physician, even went into confinement to prepare for the birth of her phantom baby.

Confinement is an odd concept to modern readers. During confinement, the mother-to-be would go into a room that had been almost entirely closed off, in an attempt to keep out drafts or anything else that they thought might hurt the mother or her newborn (Cressy, 1997:53). Usually, the expectant mother was attended only by women from that point forward. The baby was typically delivered by a midwife, rather than a male member of the medical profession. Other female family members and friends, called "gossips", came to assist the midwife and the laboring mother (Cressy, 1997:57-58). Taking this enclosed environment into account, and the attendance of only the women she trusted the most and who were closest to her, it is easy to see how the events of Katherina's labor could be kept relatively secret.

    The midwife and the gossips would have helped the Queen get out of bed to give birth, or at least rise up into a sitting position in the bed, because lying on one's back is an incredibly bad way to have a baby (Thompson, 1999:55). The idea of lying prone to give birth, which is called the dorsal lithotomy position, has no modern medical basis. Many scholars believe this position for childbirth was popularized by King Louis XIV, who ruled France from 1643 until his death in 1715. Legend has it that King Louis liked to see his mistresses give birth, and the emergence of the baby is better viewed if the mother is lying on her back (Dundes, 1987). However, the dorsal lithotomy position was recommended by Aristotle, even though other Greek physicians from antiquity rejected it, and it was Francois Mauriceau, a French obstetrician in the latter half of the 17th century, who plagiarized Aristotle and probably brought the prone birthing position into vogue (Dunn, 1991). Since the prone birthing position had yet to come into fashion, Queen Katherina, like other women from her time, would have most likely given birth on a birthing chair or stool, or at least sitting as upright as possible in the bed. The birthing stool was usually placed in front of the fireplace for warmth, and straw was placed under the stool by the gossips in order to absorb the copious amount of liquids that come into the world with the new baby. For all practical purposes, childbirth was childbirth, regardless of how high the rank of the woman doing the pushing, or how fancy a cradle the baby would use.

While Katherina was in confinement the swelling in her uterus finally went down and everyone had to admit there was no second baby. Katherina did not receive much sympathy or understanding about her ordeal. She actually had to write her father a letter begging him not to be angry with her because she had given birth to a stillborn girl. At least one historian has declared that Katherina was clearly someone who played fast and loose with the truth, simply because she equivocated in her letter to her father, telling him that she had borne her lifeless daughter "some days before", but did not clarify that the days numbered over three months (Starkey, 2003:119). To impugn her reputation for honesty because of that is perhaps too harsh. People, as a whole, will hedge facts a little to spare themselves or others undue pain, and Katherina had certainly suffered her fair share. Moreover, she was *technically* telling the truth. She had given birth "some days before", and she wasn't under any obligation to give an exact count of those days. All that Katherina did was to remain politically vague and try to prevent some discord or chastisement. The unfortunate Queen was already dealing with enough trouble in her own court, considering that some courtiers were already beginning to whisper that maybe she would never have a baby, and certainly would not have wanted to deal with an emotional scourging from her rather negligent father.

Speculation about her fertility from the courtiers based on her single miscarriage was grossly unfair. During her time any pregnancy "had no better than a 50% chance of going to term" (Cressy, 1996:47). A pregnancy was always considered a fragile and tricky thing. Women were cautioned to avoid loud nosies, funerals, anything that would cause mourning or anxiety, hard physical work, and medical practices such as bloodletting, in order to protect the fetus from any "shocks to the mind or body [which] might dislodge a child from the womb" (Cressy, 1996:46). Midwives and 'wise women' had myriad concoctions that were thought to help prevent miscarriage. For example, sage was considered "the holy herb" because women with child, if they are likely to "come before their time and are troubled with abortions, do eat thereof to their great good; for it closeth the matrix, and maketh them fruitful, it retaineth the child, and give it life" (Cressy, 1996:47). In light of the fact there was widespread knowledge that pregnancy was an extremely iffy business, Katherina's loss would have been a very normal occurrence, and no real cause for alarm about her potential childbearing. Even women who were prolific had probably suffered at least one miscarriage or stillbirth. Negative reproductive outcomes were undoubtedly heartbreaking, but too common during this era to be considered abnormal.

Adding to Katherina's nightmarish experience was the fact that Henry had begun his first affair. The obvious affection between them had lulled her into thinking that Henry would remain faithful for the entirety of their marriage. This was probably unreasonable on her part, since they lived in a time period when it was accepted, even *expected*, for a wealthy and powerful man to keep a mistress or two. Moreover, it was believed that when a man's wife was sexually unavailable for any reason, he not only had the right to seek physical satisfaction elsewhere, but it was actually necessary that he do so to preserve his health. Pregnant women were advised to avoid sexual intercourse for the first four months of their gestation, as well as during the sixth month and the eighth month, "for fear of shaking the child and bringing down her courses", so Henry was unable to have sex with his wife during those times (Cressy, 1997:46). Since men were thought to be in physical danger if they let their "fluids" build up and get out of balance, sex was therefore a medical necessity for them, and the young King was probably encouraged by the prevailing social attitudes to find a mistress (Lyons, 2006:152).

Henry was still in his teens and doubtlessly had a strong sex drive. Temptation would have surrounded him. He was fabulously wealthy, incredibly handsome, and far from "unavailable" just because he was married. Moreover, if a woman was chosen to be his extra-marital companion, her family would reap immense financial, social, and political benefits, and these perks induced many of his courtiers to actively encourage his interest in their kinswomen. Often ambitious men did not hesitate to act as pimps for their pretty wives, daughters, sisters, nieces ... or nephews, if the monarch was inclined that way. Henry could not have lacked for willing partners. Yet, in his defense, it should be noted that compared to other European royalty, or even the lesser nobles in his own court, Henry was an unusually faithful husband. In spite of living in an atmosphere that sanctioned and assisted his adultery, he very seldom strayed from the marital bed. He had, when judged by the standards of his time, a rather prudish view of intimate relationships (Smith, 1982:72). Even when he eventually left Katherina for the young and alluring Anne Boleyn, he waited *seven years* to consummate his relationship with his new love. During that time he was essentially celibate, since he did not, to the best of anyone's knowledge, take a mistress while he was waiting to marry Anne. His enduring reputation as a profligate lothario is undeserved.

In spite of Katherina's familiarity with the social norms regarding male fidelity in royal courts, she still became exceedingly upset when she heard of Henry's romance. Although Katherina quickly learned to gracefully ignore her husband's amours, as was expected of her, the first affair clearly shocked and hurt her deeply. Faced with such upheavals in her life, she stayed in her chambers until the end of May. At least one prominent historian has written that it was odd that she withdrew from court life for a while, and essentially hid in her private rooms for several weeks (Starkey, 2003:118-119). However, this would seem to be a very natural response, since the loss of her child and her husband's infidelity would have doubtlessly depressed her, and pretending to be cheerful at court would have been too difficult for her.

    Katherina may not have been leaving her chambers, but Henry was definitely calling upon her in private. Proof of the royal visits comes from the fact that the Queen became pregnant again sometime in late April or early May. This is entirely consistent with the fact that it was commonly recommended that during the seventh and ninth month of pregnancy a woman should have as much sex as possible with the father of her baby. It was thought that the father could 'fashion' his child and "set his influence on it" by engaging in sexual activity with the mother at this time (Cressy, 1996:46). If both Henry and Katherina believed, based on the doctor's speculations, that there might be a remaining fetus in her womb, they would have thought it both prudent and pleasurable to engage in frequent sexual intercourse.

    On New Year's Day of 1511, Katherina gave birth to the son everyone was waiting for. The newborn Prince of Wales was named Henry after his father. He appeared to be a normal and healthy baby, prompting widespread and prolonged celebration. It is probable that this little boy was one of Katherina's Kell negative infants, and was thus able to thrive during gestation. Henry and Katherina were thrilled with their new son. Henry VIII went on a pilgrimage to a shrine dedicated to the Virgin Mary in order to give thanks for the birth of his heir, and the proud parents hosted a tournament at Westminster in mid-February to celebrate the arrival of the Prince, whom they hoped would be the first of many (Erickson, 1980:67). Regrettably, their adored son died on February 22. No one knows why for sure. Unfortunately, there was a seemingly endless number of reasons a baby could die in infancy during the Tudor period, so there is no way of knowing what killed the small heir. In spite of their power and wealth, all that the royal couple could do for their son was grieve his loss.

      In September of the same year it was rumored that the queen might be pregnant again, but suddenly it was no longer mentioned (Weir, 1991:111). It may have been just wishful thinking on the Queen's part, or Katherina may have had an early miscarriage. Until relatively recently, women had a very difficult time knowing if they were actually pregnant. They couldn't be really sure until they were about half-way through the pregnancy. Simply missing a menstrual period would not have been seen as anything other than a hopeful sign that she might have, maybe, possibly conceived. Adding to the confusion was the fact that women did not consider themselves to be truly pregnant until the fetus "quickened", or reached the point at which the mother could first feel movement inside her (Cressy, 1997:45). Quickening was crucial, because most people believed that the fetus did not receive a soul until the time when it could be felt moving (Hull, 1996:105). This understanding of ensoulment didn't change until the nineteenth century, when Pope Pius IX decided that souls entered the embryo at conception (Simon,

1998:2). Without a soul the fetus was not really a 'person' to the people of the Tudor time period. There was even doubt whether a fetus could be considered 'alive' prior to the quickening. As a result of these beliefs, pregnancies were often well into the second trimester before they would be announced. Regardless of uncertainty about conception and gestational age, a miscarriage often caused immense grief for the parents, especially once the pregnancy had quickened. The emotional pain people felt about the loss of a pregnancy or stillborn baby was not less painful simply because it happened more frequently then than it does today.

    Henry did impregnate Katherina again for certain in 1513, not long before he left to fight a war in France. Henry's father-in-law, Ferdinand, was his confederate in this war effort, and the alliance between England and Spain pleased Katherina immensely. Scotland was allied with France, and Henry left his wife to act as regent and defend the kingdom from their northern neighbors while he was away. She did a very good job at it. The stalwart Queen didn't let the fact she was carrying a baby slow her down. During her regency the English army defeated and killed the King of Scotland, James IV, during the Battle of Flodden on September 9, 1513. After the death of James IV the exultant Queen sent her husband a piece of the dead Scots King's coat-armor as a trophy. This seems a bit ghoulish, since James IV was, as mentioned before, Margaret Tudor's husband and thus Henry and Katherina's brother-in-law. However, it was just part of ruling a country in those days: as a royal you were occasionally called upon to fight, and kill, your relations. Margaret's seventeen-month-old son, James V, became King of Scotland in his father's place, which created roughly 15 years of inter-familial battles over his regency. James V eventually wrested royal power from his overbearing regent, and went on to lead troops against the forces of his uncle, Henry VIII, just as his father had done before him.

After the English victory at the Battle of Flodden, Katherina went on a pilgrimage to give thanks for her advancing, and seemingly healthy, pregnancy. Everything finally appeared to be going the Queen's way. However, her own father proved to be a more dangerous enemy than Scotland, in that he ruined the Queen's happiness with much greater success than James IV ever could. Ferdinand double-crossed his English ally by stealthily making a separate peace with the French, sending Henry into a rage. Since he couldn't get to Ferdinand, Henry unleashed his frustration on Katherina (Starkey, 2003:154). As a good daughter, the Queen had always encouraged Henry to ally himself with her father. Ferdinand repaid Katherina by betraying her husband and leaving Katherina to pay the consequences for his underhanded behavior. Then disaster struck: she lost her baby in October (Fraser, 1994:69). The baby was a much-desired boy, and it is uncertain whether she miscarried or was far enough along in her pregnancy that it could be described as a stillbirth. This event would have been emotionally painful enough, but problems between her husband and her father made it that much worse. The falling out between Henry and Ferdinand over the Spanish King's deceptions caused Katherina such distress that it was assumed she had lost the baby as a result of "grief, as it is said, for the misunderstanding between her father and her husband" (Starkey, 2003:154). Since this was considered to be a reasonable explanation for fetal death or a stillbirth in this time period, Katherina was spared most speculation that she had offended God or done something else to bring about this latest catastrophe.

The King's anger toward his wife and her father was the likely reason word started to spread that Henry was going to repudiate Katherina, ostensibly because they had no living children, and that he would marry a French noblewoman as soon as his marriage was annulled. It turned out to be simply a rumor, and Katherina was safe, at least for the moment (Starkey, 2003:153-154). Nevertheless, she was publicly and loudly rebuked by Henry for Ferdinand's perfidy; unable to reach the real culprit, the King vented his anger and frustration on Katherina. Henry's treatment of his wife was more egregious considering that she supported him fully in his ire against her father. Katherina was loyal to both her husband and her adopted homeland, so much so that Ferdinand's ambassador to Henry's court complained that Katherina had "become English, and forgot her duty to her father" (Starkey, 2003:154). The Castilian representative bemoaned the fact that the Queen wasn't assisting him more in his diplomacy with the King, and was not acting like a good daughter of Spain. Taking into consideration her adoration of her husband, and the constant betrayals of Ferdinand, who had never had the slightest consideration for his daughter's situation, it would hardly be surprising if the Queen chose to become English in her heart.

Henry may have been angry with his pretty and patient wife, but he and Katherina were still getting along well enough that she became pregnant yet again sometime in late spring or early summer of 1514. Sadly, a few months later, in February of 1515, the Queen gave birth to a son who "lived not long after" (Fraser, 1994:69). That's a total of four, maybe even five, pregnancies in just six years, with only one baby born healthy enough to live even for a month. It is beyond contestation that Katherina was fertile; she conceived with astounding frequency.

In contrast to other women of her era, who had an average of six or seven pregnancies over the course of their life spans, the Queen was doing more than her share of breeding (Cressy, 1996:30). There is a consistently repeated myth that women lived in a constant state of pregnancy during the early modern time period, but in fact a woman who bore a child almost every year was an exception, not the rule.

Furthermore, the lack of surviving offspring was hardly a rare problem, and Henry and Katherina were far from alone in their predicament. For the upper class men of Henry's generation, being childless or having no male heir was a frequent dilemma. Fully 19% of first marriages among the nobility in this era did not produce living children, and 29% had no male heirs (Lindsey, 1995:64). Multiple marriages weren't a guarantee of fruitfulness either, since 48% of second marriages were childless, and 58% produced no male heir (Lindsey, 1995:64). It was not unexpected that titles and wealth would pass to other heirs, such as nephews, nieces, and cousins. Henry may have urgently desired a son, but like all men of that time he should have been mentally prepared to pass the crown to one of his sisters' children, rather than plotting to replace his wife.

Katherina was now "middle-aged" by the reckoning of her time period, but certainly still young enough to have more children. However, having lost her youth, she had also begun to lose her good looks. She had started to "run to fat", and her face was becoming "round and blotched and bloated" (Starkey, 2006:37). This seems natural enough in light of the fact that she had undergone repeated and yearly obstetrical tribulations, had the added emotional burden of being blamed for not producing a living heir to the throne, had successfully acted as regent for her husband during a war, and had suffered a total breach with her father in favor of her husband, who incidentally was angry with her for her father's behavior. It would be very difficult to retain 'girlish' good-looks under such stress. This is not to say she had completely lost her charms, however, since one contemporary recorded that while the Queen "was not handsome" she was "certainly not ugly" either (Fraser, 1994:75-76). Moreover she was intelligent, a good wife, and was adored by her English subjects. An ambassador from Venice reported that while Katherina was "of low stature and rather stout", she had the virtues of being "very good and very religious", spoke "Spanish, French, Flemish, and English", and was "more beloved by the Islanders than any queen that has ever reigned" (Froude, 1891:32).

    Some historical writings emphasize the fact that she wasn't as pretty as she approached mid-life as she had been as a girl, particularly as a result of her weight gain. When Katherina's plumper body is discussed, Henry's desire to end his marriage is usually portrayed more sympathetically, on the assumption that a fat, middle-aged body could never be pleasing to a man. This is more a reflection of the modern bias against the fat female body than a true representation of Katherina's attractiveness. Clearly some of the writings about the Queen have been steeped in the modern socio-cultural belief that if an individual female is fat she must therefore be considered ugly, and her body is consequently interpreted "as reflecting moral or personal inadequacy, or lack of will", which in turns turn renders fat women 'bad' and repellent (Bordo, 1993:192). It is very problematic to ascribe this bias to Henry, who was the product of very different cultural norms. Since fashion in the Tudor time period "favored slimness", some historians have argued that this was Henry's own preference (Starkey, 2003:161). Notwithstanding the fashion for a trim waist, Henry was probably unaffected by the 'excessive' adipose tissue of his sexual partners. Although his second wife, Anne Boleyn, was very slender, his fifth wife, Katheryn Howard, with whom he was utterly infatuated and enthralled sexually, was plump with the "fetching beginnings of a double-chin" (Starkey, 2003:651). Clearly the King was attracted to many different body types. Katherina's weight gain may not have been an issue for Henry the way it can be for people reared in a modern fat-intolerant cultural climate. Regardless of the change in her physical appearance, the King still found her comely enough that she became pregnant again a few months after the loss of yet another son.

    Finally, Katherina's reproductive luck took a turn for the better and on February 18, 1516, she gave birth to a healthy daughter, who was named Mary. The King and the members of his court had kept secret from her the information that her father had died less than a month earlier, due to the fact that they were afraid that any emotional upset could cause her to lose the baby (Lindsey, 1995:39). They must have felt they were wise to have kept the secret, since the baby lived. In truth, Mary was most likely the lucky recipient of a Kell negative gene from her sire, making her Kell negative as well, and therefore preventing Katherina's antibodies from killing her in the womb. Katherina and Henry's only surviving child would eventually rule England, and would become known as "Bloody Mary", because of the number of Protestants she executed during her ultimately futile attempt to restore Catholicism to England.

    Although everyone was glad that there was now at least one child to be the heir to the throne, people were outspoken about how much better it would have been if the baby had been male. As misogynistic as this clearly is, the courtiers did have a reason to be concerned, since at that time England had never, in its recorded history as a kingdom, been successfully ruled by a Queen. The most recent civil war was still fresh in people's minds. A male heir seemed to be the best hope for political and social stability. Henry tried to soothe his court and defend his Queen by pointing out they were both young and, with God's help, they would also have sons to accompany their daughter (Starkey, 2003:158).

    Katherina was possibly pregnant again in August 1517, but it was never officially announced. It may have only been a rumor, or it may have been a factual pregnancy with another disastrous and heart-wrenching end; it is very difficult to say for sure (Scarisbrick, 1970:150). The Queen was known, without doubt, to be pregnant only one more time, in 1518. Courtiers, ambassadors, and even the Pope all expressed the wish she would have a boy (Fraser, 1994:81). The royal Secretary wrote that he prayed "heartily" for a prince, who would be the "universal comfort of the realm" (Starkey, 2003:158). One can only imagine how fervently Katherina must have been praying too. Undoubtedly she wanted another living child, considering her staggering losses, but more importantly she wanted to give the King a son. Not only would this please her beloved husband, but it would also mean that she would no longer be a 'failure' who had neglected to give England a male heir. Lamentably, she gave birth that November to a baby who died shortly after the delivery. Katherina was probably bitterly disappointed that the infant was a girl, but it is unlikely this lessened her distress at the loss of yet another of her babies.

    The King remained sexually involved with his wife for several more years, but there were no further pregnancies. The Queen probably believed that she was the cause of her reproductive misfortunes, and blamed herself just as much as everyone else did. Bear in mind that this was a time when the official 'medical wisdom' was that women were in truth only deformed men who were too 'cold' to extrude their penis, and therefore their penis was inside out and upside down inside their bodies, which created a womb (Lyons 2006:152-153). Men then deposited seeds, via sperm, to be mixed with the female seeds (which were naturally less potent than male seeds) that a woman carried around in her body (Thompson, 1999:68-69). After the seed was planted, it was up to the woman to be a good 'field' and grow the baby until it was big enough to be born. Of course, many people, including physicians, also thought menstrual blood killed plants and could cause dogs to go mad (Pinto-Correia, 1998:255). Moreover, it was believed that menstruation stopped when a woman was pregnant because the uterine blood turned into breast milk to feed the new baby (Thompson, 1999:64, 70). It really wasn't a great time for medical wisdom. Notwithstanding how ridiculous these theories seem when looked at with modern knowledge and from a modern perspective, Katherina would have had no reason to dispute accepted medical doctrines. She probably looked for things she had done to harm the fetuses, or alternatively, things she might have done to displease God and bring his wrath down on her.

To make things even worse for Katherina, Henry had started a clandestine relationship with a woman named Bessie Blount. That the King had any paramour was probably disquieting from the Queen's perspective, but a long-term affair meant that Henry felt an emotional, not just a physical, attraction for his mistress. Considering how much Katherina loved Henry, and there is ample proof that she loved him fiercely, the knowledge that he was involved with another woman must have cut deep. Then fate dealt Katherina the cruelest blow of all. On June 15, 1519, Bessie Blount gave Henry what his Queen had tried to give him so many times in the past -- a healthy baby boy. With a disturbing lack of sensitivity for the Queen's feelings, Henry VIII named the boy Henry Fitzroy and publicly acknowledged him as a royal offspring. The fact that Henry christened his illegitimate son with the same first name as the infant prince that he and Katherina had lost in 1511 is, to be frank, proof of an appalling lack of consideration for his wife. Katherina stoically bore up under her husband's callous disregard for her emotions. She probably even understood that he was motivated by the need to defend his pride. Doubtlessly, the King's ego needed to show the world that the lack of a legitimate prince wasn't 'his' fault, and that he was clearly capable of fathering healthy sons, and he was unconcerned what this display cost his wife.

    Some historians, such as Lacey Baldwin Smith, also thought the birth of Henry Fitzroy proved that any obstetrical problems were on Katherina's side of the equation. Smith, who is an otherwise peerless historian, wrote that the King "proved where the fault of sterility lay by siring a son" (Smith, 1982:128). However, it is a misstatement to identify Katherina as infertile, since the definition of infertility, according to *Merriam-Webster's Medical Desk Dictionary*, is a couple who is "incapable of or unsuccessful in achieving pregnancy over a considerable period of time (as a year) in spite of determined attempts by heterosexual intercourse without contraception." Katherina was pregnant on least six, maybe even eight, occasions between 1509 to 1518. Half a dozen or more pregnancies in as many years make the idea of her infertility ludicrous. It is clear that the Queen was fecund. Additionally, it is plain that Henry had no physiological, or psychological, problem preventing him from performing intercourse.

Henry Fitzroy's birth does not in any way contradict the theory that Henry VIII was Kell positive. Fitzroy was Bessie Blount's first known pregnancy and her only child by the King, so her body would not have been sensitized to the Kell antigen yet, and the fetus would have been safe from her antibodies. Some historians have speculated that Henry only had one child with Bessie because he was sexually unaroused by a woman who had borne his child (Starkey, 2003:274). That seems unlikely, since he had gotten Katherina pregnant annually, and she had definitely given birth to his children. However, she was also his Queen, and thus it was his duty to try to impregnate her in order to secure heirs, so perhaps he really did reject his mistress because she had become the mother of his son. Nevertheless, it is at least possible that he didn't have multiple children with his mistress because he *couldn't*. Any of Bessie's pregnancies in which she carried a Kell positive fetus would not have produced a viable baby, just like many of the losses experienced by Henry's wife. This must remain speculation, since there is no record of Bessie having ever been pregnant with any more of the King's children. However, she did have subsequent children with her husband, Gilbert Talboys (Fraser, 1994:83).

The King's once loyal heart had begun drifting away from his wife in the early 1520s. While he had been a remarkably faithful husband for the time and place, he now began to keep company with other women more frequently and more openly. It is believed that he started having an affair with Mary Boleyn, Anne Boleyn's elder sister, in 1522.

Although most scholars now believe that the affair took place, in the past there has been a great deal of historical debate as to whether or not Henry and Mary Boleyn were ever lovers. Historians who did not believe that the King had ever counted Mary among his mistresses advanced various pieces of evidence, usually extrapolations from what was *unsaid* during the time of Henry's attempted divorce form Katherina. For example, Cardinal Reginald Pole, one of Katherina's staunchest allies and a fierce opponent of both the divorce and the Reformation, did not refer to the putative relationship between Mary Boleyn and the King even as late as 1535 (Froude, 56:1891). This seems odd, considering that in the context of that era any past sexual relationship with Mary would have rendered Henry's marriage to Anne void without a Papal dispensation, even if his divorce from Katherina was unimpeded, since intercourse was enough to create consanguinity. If Cardinal Pole gave credence to the rumors of a relationship between Henry and Mary, why wouldn't he have reminded his allies of this? After all, rumors about Henry's sexual relationship with one or more of Anne's relatives had been floating around the court since at least 1529, when the Spanish ambassador, Chapuys, wrote to the Emperor in December of that year to tell him "People say that it is the King's evil destiny that impels him; for had he, as he asserts, only attended to the voice of conscience, there would have been still greater affinity to contend with in this intended marriage than in that of the Queen his wife" (Froude, 130:1891). If Chapuys was aware of the scuttlebutt, then it is almost certain he would have told Katherina what he knew, or would at least have told her allies. If the Pope and the pro-Katherina faction were reasonably certain that Henry had been Mary's lover, why wouldn't they have used this information? Katherina was no fool, yet she never mentioned this potentially explosive information, or gave any hint of it, in any of her myriad letters to her confederates (Froude, 59:1891).

What about the rumors that Anne's mother had also been one of Henry's lovers? It is highly unlikely to have occurred, yet innuendo about it began to spread at roughly the same time as whispers about Henry and Mary began. One piece of evidence affirming the affair between Mary and the King comes from Sir George Throckmorton. Throckmorton claimed that he had confronted Henry about the fact that the King "had meddled with both the mother and the sister" (Bernard, 2007:211). Throckmorton then said that Henry, startled, had replied, "never with the mother", leaving the King's quick-witted Lord Privy Seal to declare, "nor never with the sister either" (Bernard, 2007:211). When Throckmorton was asked why he had spread this account of the King's words, he confessed that "he spake it only out of vainglory, to show he was one that durst speak for the Commonwealth" (Froude, 59:1891). In short, this evidence for the idea that Mary was involved with Henry relies on the words of someone who admitted bragging about what he supposedly said to the King in order to impress his friends (Bernard, 2007:212).

The strongest support for the contention that Mary Boleyn was one of Henry's paramours is the fact that in 1527, after he had formed a serious intention of marrying Anne, Henry asked for a dispensation from the Pope allowing him to marry any woman he chose, "even if she were related to him within the prohibited degrees of affinity" (Friedmann, 1884:57). Most scholars believe that this stipulation in the request is proof that Henry had indulged in an affair with Mary Boleyn, and was eager to cover all his bases.

Mary Boleyn had married William Carey, a courtier who served as a Gentleman of the Privy Chamber, in February of 1520. William Carey was willing to overlook his wife's past as the mistress of the French King, since a connection with her meant that he was now a kinsman of the powerful Howard family. If she indeed had an affair with Henry in 1522, then he was willing to turn a blind eye to her present as well. In exchange for his wife's "services" to the English crown, Carey was rewarded with promotions and estates. History records Mary as a "great prostitute", since she was supposedly the mistress of the King of France as well as of the King of England (Erickson, 1980:188). Oddly, history fails to record her family and her husband as "great pimps", since they all benefited monetarily by trading Mary's sexual favors for fiduciary gain. Mary Boleyn had two children while married to William Carey, a daughter, Katherine Carey, who was probably born in 1524, and a little boy, Henry Carey, who was born in either 1525 or 1526. There is still intense debate among historians over whether or not they were the King's children (Cruz and Suzuki, 2009:132).

Considering that Henry's affair with Mary appears to have been short-lived, the children, especially the boy, would have been conceived long after their mother was no longer having intercourse with the King. Moreover, Henry's desire for sons was such that if he had been even reasonably sure the boy was his, one would think he would have been eager to acknowledge paternity. However, it must be admitted that there was a strong motivating factor for Henry to remain silent about the matter, even if he knew for sure he had another son. By 1525 the King was starting to become infatuated with Mary's sister Anne (Starkey, 2003:282). Even if the boy was his son, the King would not have wanted to claim him because of the huge scandal involved if a man was romantically involved with sisters. That kind of behavior was considered disgustingly incestuous in the Tudor world, and would have cast a shadow on his relationship with Anne.

Although it is very unlikely that both of Mary Boleyn Carey's children were fathered by Henry, even if they were this would not refute the theory that the King was Kell positive. As a firstborn baby, the little girl probably would not have been affected because her mother had not yet become sensitized to the Kell antigen. The little boy could also have survived even if he were the King's, provided that he had not inherited the Kell gene from his father. However, since there is no incontrovertible evidence that Mary Boleyn Carey's offspring were the King's progeny, the children cannot be included in an examination of Henry's reproductive record.

Mary's affair with the King was brief, but it is likely that Henry began to notice Anne during his relationship with her sister. Some historians have argued otherwise, but it appears that Henry had his chancellor, Cardinal Wolsey, forcibly end the engagement of Anne Boleyn and Henry Percy, the oldest son of the Earl of Northumberland, in 1524 or 1525 (Starkey, 2003:274-278). Apparently the King was already thinking about pursuing Anne and didn't want anyone to have her before he made his choice. The Earl of Northumberland was a powerful figure, and the heir to such an important title was not as likely to play a compliant cuckold as the far less important William Carey had done. If Anne married Percy, the King might have never gotten to enjoy her charms, and Henry was not about to risk this eventuality. Thus, he had Cardinal Wolsey exert his considerable influence to badger Percy into breaking off the engagement.

The fact that Henry torpedoed Anne and Percy's relationship does not paint him in a good light, since only a "grossly self-absorbed person" (Lindsey, 1995:53-54) would tear a loving couple apart just because he *might* want to indulge in an affair with the woman sometime in the future . However, this kind of selfishness was something Henry was capable of, even when he was in perfect physical and mental condition. Even before Henry became a monster in 1535, he was still spoiled beyond belief and perfectly capable of acting in just such a cruelly egotistical manner. He seemed to sincerely believe that if he wanted something, then, as the King, he should have it. Moreover, as King, he was pretty certain that God wanted him to have it too. From a psychological perspective, Henry was perfectly capable of ending Anne's engagement to keep her free for his possible advances.

Although he wasn't certain about his feeling for Anne Boleyn yet, Henry knew for sure that he did not want was his wife anymore. He had stopped having sex with Katherina entirely by 1524 (Ives, 2004:90). The Queen, although only in her late thirties, had ceased to menstruate, and Henry no longer loved her enough to share her bed without the motivation of creating a royal pregnancy (Lindsey, 1995:60). The causes of naturally occurring "premature menopause" remain largely mysterious, with most cases being attributed to either underlying genetic factors, or an autoimmune disorder, wherein a woman's own antibodies start attacking her ovarian endocrine tissues (Beckmann et al., 2009: 333-334). The reason for the Queen's unusually early cessation of menses is unknown, but the result is incontrovertible: Katherina could give Henry no more children. The hoped-for son and heir would never be produced while he remained married to his first wife.

In response, the Queen poured more of her time into her religion and her daughter. Even though she and Henry were no longer living as man and wife, the Queen continued to love him and was completely devoted to him and his needs. Therefore, she was absolutely crushed when he started trying to annul their marriage in 1527 on the grounds that marrying your brother's widow is forbidden in Leviticus. Katherina knew her husband well enough to know it was Henry's way of trying to justify, especially to himself, his desire to get rid of her and try for a son with some new, younger Queen. Moreover, she quickly figured out he wanted to replace her with a particular woman, the lovely and dynamic Anne Boleyn. Katherina was not about to let Henry displace her and push Mary out of the succession. Henry had no idea of the fight his usually docile Queen was going to give him. After all, she had always put his wishes ahead of her needs in the past. He was unaware that in this matter she was going to put herself and her daughter ahead of his desires. As far as Katherina was concerned, the annulment was only going to happen over her cold, dead body. You could almost feel sorry for Henry, if he wasn't being such a putz.

Henry's battle to annul his marriage to Katherina became known as the King's Great Matter. It turned out to be a Great Matter for many people, not just the royal couple.

Chapter Three
Anne Boleyn:
Hunted, Hated, Headstrong, and Headless

    The romance between Henry and his second wife, Anne Boleyn, has reached legendary status. Typically, Anne has been reviled as a wanton seductress, and Henry has been portrayed as a dupe who eventually became wise to his lover's malignant nature and found an excuse to have her executed. Sometimes the accusations against Anne, including the allegation that she had incestuous sex with her brother, are promulgated as literal truths, but they are as unsubstantiated today as they were in the past. Only rarely is she portrayed more realistically as a hounded woman who simply made the best of the hand she was dealt.
    When looked at from the point of view of the theory that Henry had a Kell positive blood type and McLeod Syndrome, the most interesting part of their love affair is the contrast between its beginning and its end. Henry adored Anne and pursued her

relentlessly for the better part of a decade before he was able to claim her as his wife. While there were the occasional storms between them after they were married, prior to that fateful May of 1536 there were no serious hints of the terrible way in which their relationship would end. In fact, as late as April of that same year the King was still lavishing presents on his wife and badgering other European courts to recognize her as his legitimate Queen. Henry's seeming devotion to Anne until just three weeks before her beheading makes the judicial murder of his wife even more shocking than it would otherwise have been. Why did Henry suddenly turn on Anne? What could have prompted such an extreme reaction? Is it possible that McLeod syndrome played a part in Anne's death?

    Although no one is completely certain when Henry first became infatuated with Anne, it may have been as early as 1524. At the time the King was in his early thirties, and he was still healthy, both physically and mentally. When Henry had Anne beheaded on May 19, 1536, he was almost forty-five and had recently earned a reputation as a murderous tyrant. If Henry had developed McLeod syndrome, which would have begun to affect him around the age of forty, then the King's relationship with Anne can be used as a yardstick to measure his deteriorating mental stability. When his behavior toward her during their courtship is contrasted with his actions in the latter half of their relationship, a distinct shift in his personality becomes evident.

    Anne Boleyn was the "It" girl of the Tudor court. What she lacked in idealized beauty she more than made up for with sex appeal (Ives, 2004:43-45). She has often been described as having deliberately ensnared the men of Henry's court with flirtatious games designed to keep them interested in her, but this seems to be an unjust accusation. Certainly she was innately charismatic, which is often viewed as 'sexiness' when expressed by women, and had learned flirtation as an art form during her time in France. However, this does not mean she was a malicious temptress. Often, the only currency and power that most women could truly call their own (prior to the women's liberation movement, which would come into existence centuries too late for Anne) was the ability to attract and influence powerful men. Her reputation as a Tudor Jezebel is also decidedly unwarranted since there is no evidence she ever had premarital or extramarital sex. Her chastity did not mean she was a stone-hearted temptress, who teased men with her allure but left them frustrated in order to keep them snared. Rather, it more likely indicates that while she knew that women at court needed to be considered attractive and witty, she also knew that her reputation, and thus her marital prospects and her life, would be ruined if she had sex with any of her many suitors prior to marriage. Although many of the court noblewomen took lovers after they were wed and faced few social consequences, an unmarried woman was expected to remain chaste if she wanted to make a good match (Rickman, 2008:203). Marriage was the best, and often only way, for a woman to obtain security, wealth, or power. Anne flirted because she needed to, in order to be successful. Moreover, a woman's ability to charm powerful men could also prove extremely useful to her family in the economic and social intrigues of the Tudor court. To be less than a coquette would have been politically naive for Anne, and potentially damaging for her family. Is it really fair to accuse her of being a strumpet simply because she obeyed the socio-cultural mores of her time? Is it fair to despise her simply because she was the best in the game?

Never doubt it, Anne was a very successful flirt. Apparently her "excellent gesture and behavior did excel all other" women in the court (Lindsey, 1995:53). Her sex appeal and courtly manners would have paid off handsomely, providing her with a marriage to the heir of one of the most powerful men in England, the Earl of Northumberland's eldest son, Henry Percy, who also happened to be the man she loved. Sadly, the King ruined that future for her, ordering his Lord Chancellor, Cardinal Wolsey, to browbeat Percy into renouncing the betrothal. Percy did not give Anne up lightly. He held out for as long as he could and to a remarkable degree, so much so that Cardinal Wolsey even summoned Percy's father to help pressure the young man into ending his romance.

Percy would have been under tremendous pressure to obey his father's commands. It is almost impossible to overstate the cultural pressure which existed to respect one's elders, particularly one's parents, and to submit to authority figures. Absolute obedience to one's parents and social superiors was drummed into people from their earliest youth. For Percy to have defied his father and married Anne anyway would not have been seen as 'romantic'; it would have been seen as an ignominious betrayal of common decency, marking the young man as a scoundrel, and the young couple would have suffered grievously for it. Thus, it was inevitable that Percy would give in to his father's demands and marry the woman chosen for him by his family. Henry's interference was underhanded, selfish, and even cruel, considering that Anne and Percy appeared to have been genuinely in love with one another (Starkey, 2003:275-277). However, Anne never knew Henry was the true author of her misery. Instead she blamed Wolsey. She formed a deep hatred for the Lord Chancellor, and swore that "if it ever lay in her power, she would work the cardinal as much [similar] displeasure" (Ives, 2004:64). In short, Anne promised to ruin Wolsey's life if she ever got the chance. Fate would deliver her that chance in the not too distant future, and she would make good on her threats. Anne was clearly a woman who made an implacable enemy.

Anne was obviously neither meek nor a saint, but she is still undeserving of her reputation as a scheming seductress. Rather than having been an unscrupulous siren, Anne was the victim of the King's libido. Henry destroyed her marriage prospects in order to try winning her favors for himself, and never stopped pressuring her to return his regard. Notwithstanding her innocence, for the last five centuries Anne has been predominately configured in the popular imagination as a duplicitous home-wrecker, who only refused Henry's sexual advances so that he would leave his loving wife and let Anne have the crown instead. This is grossly unfair.

Considering the fact that Anne tried every means possible to show the King that she was uninterested in him without actually telling him *to his face* that she did not want him, it seems unlikely that she clung to her chastity merely as a way to entice him (Lindsey, 1995:57-59). To have rejected Henry outright, or with a lack of proper diplomacy, would have been political suicide for her and her whole family. Anne certainly appears to have tried every method she could devise in order to discourage Henry. She even went so far as to leave the court for over a year, and would not come back, even with her mother there to act as chaperone (Ives, 2004:80). Wouldn't she have remained at court if she had been deliberately stringing Henry along?

The King wrote to her, in a woebegone yet incredulous tone, that he had "been told that the opinion in which I left you is totally changed, and that you would not come to court either with your mother, if you could, or in any other manner; which report, if true, I cannot sufficiently marvel at, because I am sure that I have since never done anything to offend you, and it seems a very poor return for the great love which I bear you to keep me at a distance both from the speech and the person of the woman that I esteem most in the world: and if you love me with as much affection as I hope you do, I am sure that the distance of our two persons would be a little irksome to you, though this does not belong so much to the mistress as to the servant" (Phillips, 2009:13). This is unmistakably *not* the writing of a man who has received strong encouragement from his would-be inamorata.

	However, one must wonder at the fact Henry found her opinion "totally changed". Plainly she had given him hope that she would come back to court, and his confidence that she loved him with "as much affection" shows that she was pleasant enough to him to give him a firm belief that she was being successfully wooed. Was this a sign she was stringing him along, involving herself in a deep game to entice him away from his wife and into her arms by playing hard to get? Or is it just that she was forced, by etiquette and prudence, to be be very nice to him, and his ego gave him the arrogance to assume this meant she returned his attraction? Considering her disappearance from court when his suit grew too hot, it looks as though she was only being nice to "the King", not the lover.

	It seems perfectly possible that Henry was having a very hard time taking her polite "no" for an answer. In one letter, Henry wrote that "On turning over in my mind the contents of your last letters, I have put myself into great agony, not knowing how to interpret them, whether to my disadvantage, as you show in some places, or to my advantage, as I understand them in some others, beseeching you earnestly to let me know expressly your whole mind as to the love between us two. It is absolutely necessary for me to obtain this answer, having been for above a year stricken with the dart of love, and not yet sure whether I shall fail of finding a place in your heart and affection, which last point has prevented me for some time past from calling you my mistress" (Phillips, 2009:1-3). Take note of the fact that Anne took care to "show" the King that she was uninterested, but that he felt he could "understand" her affections in other places. This probably means that the rejection was overt, but the diplomatic hedging she was forced to use was freely interpreted by the King as a sign she really did, after all, return his love (Lindsey, 1995:56-57)

    Henry offered Anne everything he could to tempt her, assuring her that if she would just "give up yourself body and heart to me … I promise you that not only the name shall be given you, but also that I will take you for my only mistress, casting off all others besides you out of my thoughts and affections, and serve you only" (Phillips, 2009:3). Anne was apparently uninterested in being his mistress. Although Anne's response is not known for certain, because her letter was not preserved, judging by Henry's reply she must have written to him that she was the King's loyal servant only. The King wrote to her, rather plaintively, that although "it is not fitting for a gentleman to take his lady in the place of a servant, yet, complying with your desire, I willingly grant it you, if thereby you can find yourself less uncomfortable in the place chosen by yourself, than you have been in that which I gave you" (Phillips, 2009: 4).

In at least one missive Henry complained about the fact that Anne had never replied to one of his earlier letters. The King grumbled to Anne that "it has not pleased you to remember the promise you made me when I was last with you that it, to hear good news from you, and to have an answer to my last letter; yet it seems to me that it belongs to a true servant (seeing that otherwise he can know nothing) to inquire the health of his mistress, and to acquit myself of the duty of a true servant, I send you this letter, beseeching you to apprise me of your welfare, which I pray to God may continue as long as I desire mine own" (Phillips, 2009:5). It seems clear that Anne was trying to extricate herself from the difficult situation Henry had placed her in -- that of having to discourage the attentions of a man who could control her entire family's fortunes -- by avoiding his pursuit. How can this shunning of the King's affections be seen as a come-hither ploy by a hardened vamp? Isn't it manifestly an attempt to escape an unwanted and overly-persistent suitor?

Her lack of response seems to be an extremely clear signal that she was uninterested in his romantic propositions. However, the King's ego was obviously too aggrandized for him to understand her rejection. He was used to being the object of love, adoration, and pointed flirtation. The idea that a woman would be uninterested in him, in spite of his wealth, talents, good-looks, and power, was apparently beyond his comprehension. Why, then, is Anne wrongly portrayed in history as a predatory harlot? It is possible that many are prejudiced against Anne because she did the unthinkable: she did not use her sexuality to please a powerful man but, instead, used it for her own purposes. The argument that she must have been plotting to entice Henry in order to gain the crown ignores too many facts clearly written in Henry's own hand.

Anne Boleyn was clearly not an enchantress casting an evil spell on Henry to make him forget his loyal wife and neglect his daughter; she was a woman trying to elude an over-eager suitor. In spite of all of her efforts to evade him, Henry would not be deterred. Even though she spent more than a year trying to gently let him down, he persisted (Lindsey, 1995:58). Rather than accepting that Anne did not want him, the King wrote to her that if he just knew for certain that she didn't want him then he could "do no other than mourn my ill-fortune, and by degrees abate my great folly" (Phillips, 2009:14-15). However, the King could not *really* believe Anne was immune to his magnetism, so instead of putting his folly from him, Henry transformed it into a more honorable offer: marriage. It would be Anne, not a foreign noblewoman, who would replace Katherina and give Henry his chance for more children. In the face of such determined pursuit, what was left for her to do but to try to achieve at least some of her own goals in exchange for her capitulation?

Thomas Wyatt, another of Anne's many admirers, wrote a very famous poem that most historians agree must be about her:

> Whoso list to hunt, I know where is an hind,
> But as for me, alas, I may no more.
> The vain travail hath wearied me so sore,
> I am of them that farthest cometh behind.
> Yet may I by no means my wearied mind
> Draw from the deer, but as she fleeth afore
> Fainting I follow. I leave off therefore,
> Sithens in a net I seek to hold the wind.
> Who list her hunt, I put him out of doubt,
> As well as I may spend his time in vain.

> And graven with diamonds in letters plain
> There is written, her fair neck round about:
> *Noli me tangere*, for Caesar's I am,
> And wild for to hold, though I seem tame.

The message of the sonnet is that Wyatt had unsuccessfully pursued Anne, and now she was exclusively Henry's prey (Lindsey, 1995:59). The part that should draw attention is that Anne is allegorized as a deer, something that was hunted down only by the gentry, and it is made explicit that she is trying to get away. Nevertheless, the King was the one hunter she could never fully escape. At some point, it is clear, Anne must have realized she wasn't ever going to be free of Henry's attentions. She probably began to hear rumors that Henry was planning to annul his marriage to Katherina and was looking for a new wife. She had to have realized that no one would contract a marriage with her as long as Henry was showing an interest in her. She must have decided that, if escape from Henry was impossible, then she should at least try to salvage something from the situation by insisting on marriage. Shortly thereafter she sent him a gift, probably for New Year's Day, as was customary. It was a diamond pendant of a ship being "tossed about", with the small figure of a woman on board, which Henry took to mean that Anne was asking him to protect her from the stormy seas of life (Lindsey, 1995:60).

Henry wrote her an impassioned letter thanking her for the gift, and her willingness to become his beloved: "The demonstrations of your affection are such, the beautiful mottoes of the letter so cordially expressed, that they oblige me for ever to honour, love, and serve you sincerely, beseeching you to continue in the same firm and constant purpose, assuring you that, on my part, I will surpass it rather than make it reciprocal, if loyalty of heart and a desire to please you can accomplish this" (Phillips, 2009:11). Obviously, he took her gift as a confirmation that she wanted him to keep her safe, and that her heart was now his (Ives, 2004:87). However, historian Karen Lindsey (1995:60) speculated in her book, *Divorced, Beheaded, Survived*, that Anne was secretly implying that she was going to attempt to steer her own course. If so, then Henry should have been much less effusive in his thanks for her gift.

Although she accepted the fact she was the object of the King's desires, some suspect that Anne never fully returned Henry's affections. If his letters lamenting her absence are anything to go by, she certainly didn't seem to want to be with him as often as he wanted to be with her. Henry wrote to Anne to assure her that, " by absence your affection to us may not be lessened: for it were a great pity to increase our pain, of which absence produces enough and more than I could ever have thought could be felt … on my part the pain of absence is already too great for me" (Phillips, 2009:7). Clearly the King was deeply enamoured of Anne, and he just as clearly assumed that she felt the same intense emotions for him. Was this a delusion created by Henry's egotism which could not fathom someone he loved not loving him in return? Or had she come to return his sentiments?

Some historians argue that she did love the King, pointing out the fact that she kept his letters (Ives, 2004:86). Yet it should be considered that retaining a flattering piece of correspondence sent to you by the King is not the same as sentimentally keeping a love letter from the man you adore. Moreover, Anne refused to consummate her relationship with Henry for almost a decade. She seems to have been sincerely religious, so feeling a deep moral responsibility to remain a virgin until marriage might have helped her firm her resolve, but if she had really loved Henry and desired him, she would have been more likely to consent to a sexual relationship, considering the length of time they were together. This is especially true considering that in this time period to be pre-contracted to marry, and then to consummate the relationship, was almost as good as a wedding, since she would have become Henry's common-law wife. Sexual relations between two unmarried people who were precontracted to each other would not have been frowned on by the moral authorities of the era. Disputes about the legitimacy of any children born to such a union could be resolved later, as they had been for the children of John of Gaunt and Kathrine Swynford. John of Gaunt, who was the third surviving son of Edward III, and his then-mistress Swynford had three sons, John, Henry, and Thomas, who were given the surname Beaufort, as well as a daughter, Joan. When John of Gaunt married Swynford, their children were declared legitimate by an Act of Parliament during the reign of Richard II (Bevan, 1994:4). Thus, there was a clear precedent to follow if Anne and Henry had become lovers and had children. Of course, some people maintain that she and Henry were engaging in an illicit sexual liaison, as well as an emotional affair, for many years before their wedding. Nevertheless, it is completely plausible that they did not begin the physical aspect of their romance until they were actually married by a priest.

      It should be noted that even if Anne had loved Henry with the same incendiary passion he felt for her, the King had done several things that might have cooled her ardor. When one of Anne's maids contracted the 'sweating sickness' in the summer of 1528, the King ordered Anne to stay at Hever Castle, in case she had already caught the disease, while he *fled to the countryside with Katherina* (Lindsey, 1995:73). The sweating sickness was an extremely virulent disease that frequently resulted in death, sometimes within hours of the patient first showing symptoms. Not only did he abandon the woman he supposedly loved to a frighteningly communicable and fatal disease, he took with him the spouse from whom he was supposedly separated, thus indicating his respect and deference for Katherina's position as wife, Queen, and mother to Mary and any additional future heirs. This was unlikely to have inspired Anne to great heights of love.

  Henry did, however, write Anne a letter to assure her that although he was leaving her behind while he absconded with his wife to a safer place, she shouldn't worry too much. The King wrote that the "uneasiness my doubts about your health gave me, disturbed and alarmed me exceedingly, and I should not have had any quiet without hearing certain tidings" (Phillips, 2009:25). It is obvious from the letter that Henry is very concerned for Anne's safety, but he was still able to abandon her in order to keep himself from being exposed to the sweating sickness. Although it could be argued that Henry needed to take this prudent course with his own health, due to his position as the King of England, there was no reason why Katherina needed to accompany him on his retreat. The Queen could have been ordered to another castle or manor with little comment. Moreover, the King could have sent Anne away to a safer place, as well, even if the risk that Anne was already infected meant that he could not have taken her with him.

  It gives insight into the nature of Henry's ego, which appears to have been so enabled by those around him that he was unaware of its unnatural size, that he cautioned Anne not to worry too much about him. He had left her behind to take her chances with the contagion, yet felt the need to comfort her by sending her another letter assuring her of his well-being. Henry did not seem to understand his desertion might have been perceived negatively by Anne, and he assumed that she was consumed with fear for *his* health, probably even more than her own.

When Anne, not surprisingly, did come down with the dreaded disease, the King claimed to have the utmost concern for her condition, even wishing he could bear part of her illness (Phillips, 2009:22). He even sent one of his personal physicians to care for her. While it is nice that he would have given up *half* of his heath to make Anne well, for all his sweet words Henry still fled, leaving her behind to be exposed to the deadly disease, and stayed far away from his afflicted love until the illness had run its course and she could return to court. Unfortunately, there is no record of what Anne thought about the contrast between his words and his actions.

There was also Henry's attitude toward his former mistress, Mary Boleyn Carey, which would have doubtlessly encouraged Anne to remain chaste. Watching how contemptuously the king treated her sister must have strengthened any feelings Anne had about the inadvisability of sex before marriage. The same summer that Anne fell ill from the sweating sickness, William Carey also caught the disease. Unlike Anne, William died as a result. His death left Mary in penury with two small children. Anne wrote to Henry and pleaded with him to do something to help her sister. Henry promised Mary one hundred pounds a year, and also wrote to Thomas Boleyn, Anne and Mary's father, to insist that Mary receive some financial assistance from her family. While this was certainly appreciated by the widow Carey, Henry also used the letter as an opportunity to denigrate Mary for her sinful past, as if he hadn't recently been a willing part of that same past (Lindsey, 1995:73). The hypocrisy and judgmental attitude Henry displayed surely reinforced Anne's determination not to surrender her body until she was safe within the bonds of holy wedlock.

Henry wasn't wholly driven by gross selfishness and hypocrisy, however. His behavior during his courtship of Anne Boleyn demonstrates some of the complexity of his character. He tried very hard to make everyone happy, even while he was determined to make *himself* happy at all costs. The opposition to his nullity suit caused him extreme vexation, but he still did his best to avoid causing Katherina undue pain, even as he was trying to get rid of her. He kept her at court and they continued their appearances as man and wife (Lindsey, 1995:70-86). The King clearly hated to hurt the woman who had been his wife for so many years, but he was simply too spoiled to deny himself anything he really wanted, and he wanted Anne very badly indeed. Furthermore, it was in the best interest of the country, and therefore his duty, to secure male heirs if at all possible. It did not seem to occur to him that lavishing affection on Anne Boleyn at the same court where his wife lived must have hurt the Queen deeply. For the King, it was enough that he showed Katherina the outward symbols of respect.

The King's scruples about his first marriage were not entirely a fiction he created as an excuse to rid himself of Katherina and replace her with another of his choosing. The succession was even more important than Henry's obsession with Anne. England had never been successfully led by a Queen, and the one prior attempt had thrown the country into a vicious civil war. Henry, like many of his ministers, was afraid to leave his throne to a daughter. It is true that Henry could have wed Mary to one of his maternal cousins, such as Henry Courtney or one of Margaret Pole's sons, and thereby ensured that he was succeeded by a male heir who was closely related to him by marriage, as well as more distantly related by blood. But perhaps his potential son-in-law would have been *too* close to the crown for comfort? A Yorkist heir might have cast doubt on the validity of Henry VII's claim to the throne, and caused people to question whether his victory as Bosworth had truly made him a king. Perhaps God was displeased with the false kingship claims of the Tudors, and had thus denied Henry VIII sons? To show the divine right of the Tudor line, Henry needed a direct male heir from his body to reign after him. The succession was so important that the King and his ministers even considered "marrying the Princess Mary to the King's natural son [the Duke of Richmond] if it could be done by dispensation" (Froude,79-80:1891) from the Pope.

    Although people tend to remember his Great Matter as a manifestation of his desire for Anne, it would seem that Henry genuinely convinced himself that his marriage to Katherina had been a false one, cursed by God (Scarisbrick, 1970:152). The King really did try to be a good man, but his conscience was too easily soothed; as long as he could persuade himself that he was in the right, no matter how much hypocritical speciousness was involved, he was content. He was so sure of his inherent rightness that he expected Katherina, and even the Pope, to agree that the annulment was needful. The King probably believed that once he explained his 'logic', Katherina would be willing to quietly agree to the annulment, after grieving for a suitable amount of time, of course.

It is also apparent that Henry desperately wanted to avoid being the 'villain' of the annulment. For example, in November of 1528 he gave a speech to his courtiers and the London elite to explain his decision to annul his marriage to Katherina, and he praised her to the skies, declaring that "if the marriage might be good, I would surely chose her above all women" (Ives, 2004:97). He expected public sympathy to be on his side, as the man who was clearly trying to do the right thing, not for the selfish reason of his urgent desire for another woman, but simply to alleviate the "sores" and "pangs" of his worried conscience (Scarisbrick, 1970:217). However, the public was singularly unimpressed with his pleadings. The people of London apparently did not see a troubled and pitiable King; instead they behaved as though they saw a man who wanted to throw off an old wife in order to wed a younger lover. Henry did not take this rejection well. The popular "support for [Queen Katherina] and the poor reception by the notables of his speech" (Ives, 2004:98) sent him fleeing to Anne for comfort.

Henry, secure in the belief that he was entitled to everything he desired, and having had everything his own way for most of his life, was unprepared to be thwarted. Therefore, his courtship of Anne Boleyn and his Great Matter must have been shockingly frustrating to him. Not only was Anne making him wait for the wedding before she would consummate their affair, his Great Matter was also dragging on in a way he had not expected. Henry seemed frankly shocked when Katherina flatly refused to believe any of his theological sophistry. Instead, the Queen used every means at her disposal, including her extremely powerful nephew, to block the nullity suit (Starkey, 2003:204).

Katherina's weapons were not insubstantial ones. Her nephew was a very powerful man, being simultaneously the Holy

Roman Emperor Charles V and Charles I of Spain. Charles V didn't see Henry's attempts to dispose of Katherina in a good light, but he also used the excuse of defending his kinswoman to impede Henry in Europe's political arena. Perhaps if Katherina had been married to a lesser noble, or one with less military power, Charles might not have cared as much about the sanctity and validity of her marriage. His real motivations aside, the threat of intervention by Charles provided Katherina with a means to defend herself, which she used to good effect (Lindsey, 1995:76-78). Furthermore, the Queen was very smart and strong willed, which helped her outmanoeuvre Henry's attempts at annulment.

Even without believing himself to be absolutely in the right, Henry had good reason to think that his nullity suit would be resolved fairly quickly. Papal annulments, at least for the wealthy and the nobility, were not that hard to get. Henry's sister Margaret received an annulment from her husband, the Earl of Angus, in December of 1527, for a variety of implausible reasons. She even dredged up rumors that her first husband might be alive, despite the fact he was conclusively dead (Lindsey, 1995:71-72). The relative ease with which Margaret obtained an annulment enraged Henry. Henry could not see that, unlike himself, Margaret had grounds to nullify her marriage. The Earl had been precontracted to marry another woman. This was a commonly accepted reason to void a marriage. The power of the Papacy was not an issue. Of course, the real reason Margaret wanted to end her marriage was that her husband had kidnapped her son, James V, in order to usurp her power as Regent and rule Scotland in her place. Looked at in context, her nullity suit makes sense both legally, in that a precontract was a legitimate excuse to grant her request, and politically, because her soon-to-be-ex was her enemy. Not only did Henry not view this as reasonable, he was incensed by the fact that Margaret was in a romantic relationship with a man whom she planned to wed as soon as her marriage to the Earl of Angus was no longer an issue. Henry wrote to Margaret, exhorting her to respect the "divine ordinance of inseparable matrimony" and warning her about the "danger of damnation" to which she was subjecting herself (Pollard, 1919:209-210). He further castigated Margaret over her negligent parenting, since her daughter from her union with the Earl would become illegitimate once the marriage was voided (Lindsey, 1995:71). Henry was blind to the fact that this was *exactly* what he was trying to do to his daughter Mary, but with much less reason. Henry was unable to perceive his own hypocrisy. His inflexible sense of moral superiority only allowed him to understand other people's frailties, but never his own.

  To make matters more complicated, Henry was his own worst enemy in the Great Matter. Katherina was certainly a significant obstacle in the way of Henry's successful annulment of his marriage, but he was inadvertently hampering his own success by stubbornly insisting that his first marriage had been wrongfully sanctioned by the Pope. Not only was he arguing that he was right, he was insisting that the Vatican admit the Pope had been *wrong* to allow him to marry Katherina in the first place (Scarisbrick, 1970:152). The King thought the Papacy would willingly throw the jurisdiction of the Pope into question, while the Reformation raged around it, just so Henry could marry the woman he loved. Absurdly, this unreasonable request was not even necessary, since the King's Great Matter could have been resolved by other means than the Papal dissolution of his first union. The Pope was open to alternative solutions, and even toyed with the idea of permitting royal bigamy, or legitimizing the offspring of any royal adultery (Smith, 1982:125). Henry closed all other avenues to marry Anne by steadfastly demanding that his first marriage be recognized as a sinful abomination by the Church (Smith, 1982:126).

Another choice that Henry eschewed was to simply have Katherina clandestinely murdered (Smith, 1982:126). This was never truly an option, since he was not yet a monster who killed his wives. It has been argued that the Queen was too beloved of the English people for Henry to risk assassinating her, but it is unlikely that her popularity would have stopped the King had he been determined to get rid of her. After all, the support of the King's subjects did not save any of the martyrs Henry would execute in the very near future. Concerned as ever about the "discharge of our conscience", he fervently needed to believe himself in the right, as a representative of God upon earth (Smith, 2009:128). Murdering Katherina would have tarnished his sterling reputation. The King wanted nothing less than an admission from everyone, including the Pope, Katherina, and all Katherina's defenders that he was correctly and legitimately following God's will as made manifest in the text from Leviticus: "And if a man shall take his brother's wife, it is an unclean thing: he hath uncovered his brother's nakedness; they shall be childless."

This belief in his own correctness leads one to wonder if he wasn't just egotistical, but had actually become a narcissist. Narcissistic personality disorder (NPD) is a serious mental illness. It produces a galaxy of symptoms, all guaranteed to make narcissists unpleasant to be close to. Those with NPD have ridiculous feelings of self-importance and expect to be treated favorably under all circumstances, they are obsessed with fantasies about their own abilities and/or ideal love, they require constant attention and admiration, they will take advantage of others in order to promote their own needs, react to any criticism of this behavior with rage or wild self-pity, and their selfishness makes them devoid of empathy, therefore they do not feel remorse about hurting or using others for their own gain (First and Tasman, 2009:504). Narcissists can hide their real nature under a veneer of charm for *years*. No one is sure what causes this personality disorder, but theories tend to center around the idea that narcissists are people who are either abused (especially mother-son incest), or people who have just been cosetted and enabled to the point where they start to believe the attention is their due, or people who had very emotionally distant and critical parents as children (Gabbard, 2005:52-504; de Vires, 2009:177). Henry had a very indulgent and loving mother, and a very harsh and demanding father, so he may have already been predisposed toward this mental illness by the time he became King. Narcissism usually shows up by the time a person is a young adult and it is nearly impossible to cure, since almost all narcissists refuse to admit they have anything wrong with them. It is possible that Henry became a narcissist simply as a result of the constant assertions from those around him that he was completely magnificent. Given his beauty, brains and talent, he had some reason to believe their flattery. He was probably still a normal, albeit self-centered, young man when he took the throne, but years of kingship and an adoring wife who felt it was her duty to make him happy, may have pushed his conceit into narcissism.

    Whatever truly spurred Henry on in his difficult quest for an annulment on his terms, the Great Matter was quickly becoming a matter of international intrigue, and Anne Boleyn was reaping an unfair share of the blame. Diego Mendoza, a diplomat serving Charles V, wrote to the Emperor on August 15, 1527 to tell him that people had begun to say that Henry planned to marry a daughter of Master Boleyn, who had at one time been an English ambassador to Charles' court (Froude, 1891:48). Once Anne's name became common knowledge, Katherina and her faction knew who to hate. Katherina still loved Henry and wanted to seize on anything other than the cessation of his affection for her as the cause of his desire for an annulment. Anne, whom she could despise with ease, was cast as the temptress and witch who had lured Henry away from his good wife with her evil and wanton charms. Those who supported Katherina could not vent their ire directly at the King, because that would have been political, social, and economic suicide, so they turned their anger on an easier target, his presumed mistress.

    Nor were all those whom Henry considered his allies in the pursuit of his annulment as interested in procuring him a nullification of his first marriage as he assumed they were. At first Cardinal Wolsey was an enthusiastic proponent of the annulment, hoping to marry Henry to a foreign noblewoman in order to cement political ties and secure a large dowry. However, when it became clear that Anne would be the new Queen, the Lord Chancellor became steadily less helpful, and after a time he began to surreptitiously aid Queen Katherina's cause.

    Charles V was well aware that Cardinal Wolsey had a great deal of influence over the King and very little love for Anne Boleyn. In September of 1527 the Emperor wrote to Mendoza with instructions on "befriending" Wolsey, telling his ambassador to "make him the following offers ... payment of all arrears on his several pensions, amounting to 9000 ducats annually ... Six thousand additional annually until such a time as a bishoprick or other ecclesiastical endowment of the same revenue becomes vacant in our kingdom ... The Duke (of Bourbon), who is to have Milan, to give him (Wolsey) a Marquisate in that Duchy, with an annual rent of 12,000 ducats, or 15,000 if the smaller sum be not enough; the said Marquisate to be held by the Cardinal during his life, and to pass after him to any heir whom he shall appoint" (Froude, 1891:45). Clearly Henry's Lord Chancellor had good reasons to be less than wholehearted in his attempts to get his King the annulment from Queen Katherina.

    Theoretically it did not matter who did, or did not, support Henry's decision to marry Anne. The only thing Henry needed was the cooperation of the Pope, Clement VII. If Clement granted the annulment, there was nothing Katherina or Charles V could do to prevent Henry from fathering legitimate children on a new wife, even if she was a commoner like Anne Boleyn. Far from being staunchly against the annulment, Clement was sympathetic to Henry's request. Nonetheless, Clement was not in a position, Pope or not, to help the King. The Papacy had aligned itself with France and several powerful Italian city-states against Charles V, but unfortunately for the Pope the Emperor's army had defeated all opposition in its march through Italy, eventually sacking the city of Rome and the Curia itself. The Pope had been held as the Emperor's prisoner in Castel Sant'Angelo for six months. Humiliated and defeated, Clement had disguised himself in order to escape to Orvieto, where he attempted to perform his duties as head of the Catholic Church. He was hampered in this, however, by his great (and justifiable) fear of Charles V.

    Henry sent his secretary, Dr. Knight, to try and get an audience with Clement in Orvieto. Knight was unable to see the Pope in person, but he did get a letter to him. Knight reported to Henry in December of 1527 that the Pope had promised to "send him all the King's requests in as ample a form as they were desired" (Froude, 1891:51), confidently assuring Henry that he would have everything he needed for the divorce soon. Moreover, Sir Gregori Casalis, one of Henry's agents in Rome, wrote in the spring of 1528 that the Pope was, "not unwilling to please the King and Wolsey, but fears the Spaniards more than he ever did. The Friar-General has forbidden him in the Emperor's name to grant the King's request. He fears for his life from the Imperialists if the Emperor knows of it. Before he would grant the brief he said, weeping, that it would be his utter ruin. The Venetians and the Florentines desired his destruction. His sole hope of life was from the Emperor. He asked me to swear whether the King would desert him or not. Satisfied on this point, he granted the brief, saying that he placed himself in the King's arms, as he would be drawn into perpetual war with the Emperor. Wolsey might dispose of him and the papacy as if he were the Pope himself" (Froude, 1891:68).

    The Pope finally returned to the traumatized city of Rome in October 1528. He was now in a position where he was going to have to resolve the issue of Henry's marriage one way or another, and soon. Clement preferred to stall, hoping to avoid the wrath of Charles V without losing his friendship with the King of England. The Pope was a man who was dearly in need of powerful friends, being beset by enemies on all sides. Wolsey tried desperately to warn Clement that if he did not grant Henry his divorce, then the King would reject Rome's authority. The Pope was not impressed with Wolsey's admonishment, and apparently thought that Wolsey was just worried about his own power and his position with Henry (Froude, 80-81:1891). The Defender of the Faith wouldn't really turn apostate! The idea was ridiculous. Clement would have been wise to heed Wolsey's advice. Wolsey's greater knowledge of Henry's nature had forewarned him that the King was not a man who would submit himself to any authority that was not directing him to do exactly what he had wanted to do in the first place.

Clement tried to buy more time by sending Cardinal Lorenzo Campeggio to England to see what could be done about the King's Great Matter. First Campeggio tried to argue with Henry, but that failed. The Cardinal wrote to a friend that even if God Himself sent an angel to tell Henry that his marriage to Katherina was valid, the King wouldn't believe it (Starkey, 2003:222). Obviously, Henry wasn't going to be amenable to sweet reason, so the Cardinal's best hope of achieving a resolution to the Great Matter was to talk Katherina into tolerating a solution which would be acceptable to Henry. So when Campeggio met with the Queen, he tried to highlight the advantages for everyone if she would decide to join a nunnery (Starkey, 2003:223). This, with the benefit of hindsight, would have been Katherina's wisest course of action. She would have kept her status and wealth by taking the veil and becoming an abbess, as other royal women had done before her. An abbess was the highest position of authority a woman could attain in the Catholic faith, and some of the wealthiest and best-connected abbesses had power which rivaled that of a Bishop. Furthermore, she would have been rewarded and praised for smoothing things out between Henry and the Pope. Best of all, Mary could have been declared still legitimate and kept in the line of succession, since she was conceived in good faith between people who believed they were married at the time. However, it was a risk the Queen could not take.

There is no way Katherina could have known that the reproductive problems she had suffered were most likely caused by Henry, and would therefore also affect Anne. From the Queen's perspective, there was every reason to fear multiple sons from a second union, sons who would have driven her daughter far down the line of succession. There were also intensely personal reasons why Katherina rejected the nunnery. She was deeply and sincerely devoted to Catholicism, and to become a nun without feeling that it was a call from God would have been sacrilegious (Lindsey, 1995:74). Moreover, marriage was a sacrament, and to allow Henry to break their union without just cause or without a formal Papal ruling to dissolve their marital bonds would also have been sacrilegious. Nuns are considered Brides of Christ, and the Queen would be committing a kind of spiritual bigamy if she became a nun while still considering herself the wife of a living man. Katherina would never voluntarily commit sacrilege, so taking the veil was never truly an option for her. Furthermore, it is probable that she did not join a nunnery because she loved Henry with a devotion that was second only to her worship of God, and therefore she didn't want him to marry another woman.

    The Queen was not above yanking the chains of those who were trying to bully her. She held out false hope to Campeggio, telling him that she would *think about* joining a nunnery, but then added the codicil that the King would have to take a similar vow of celibacy, rendering her decision moot as far as Henry's personal goals were concerned (Lindsey, 1995:74). Katherina was no one's fool, and was not about to be duped by the Cardinal's supposed concern for her predicament; she knew she was in the right but that the Pope would prefer not to have to do the right thing at the expense of Henry's good will.

    Katherina had set her course and now she would follow it, regardless of obstacles or hardships. Not only was she not going to let Anne Boleyn usurp her role as Henry's wife without a fight, she had convinced herself that to let her husband wrongly put her aside would burden him with a grave sin. She was able to justify her obstinate adherence to her principles at any price as a duty to Henry, because it would save his soul. Finally, she obviously did not expect that Henry would resort to such draconian measures against her, and she certainly did not believe he would turn against the daughter he loved. Neither she, nor anyone else in England, knew that Henry, who had previously been so loving and gentle in spite of the fact that he was doggedly determined to get his own way, would become a fiend not long after his fortieth birthday.

      Katherina fought the annulment, tooth and nail. She used friends to get messages out to her nephew, Charles V (Starkey, 2003:230-231). She waged a public relations battle, and got popular opinion on her side, which kept Henry on the ropes, and thus on the defensive. The Queen used every legal and theological argument she could to eviscerate Henry's flimsy case against her. She had many, many loyal friends at court who reported Henry's every plan to her so she could plot a counterattack (Starkey, 2003:214). In public she was holding herself together so well that Henry became petulant. The King sent her a message speculating that she must not love him, because she showed "no pensiveness in her countenance, nor in her apparel nor behavior" (Lindsey, 1995:76). Her regal dignity chafed Henry's ego, since he assumed she would be devastated by the withdrawal of his love. In fact, she was heartsick because of his betrayal, but had too much pride and self control to make herself the object of mockery or pity by showing her emotional devastation in public.

The Queen demonstrated her determination and wits at the 'trial' Henry convened so that Campeggio, as the Papal Legate, could rule on the legitimacy of the King's marriage to Katherina. Henry was tired of waiting for the Pope's decision and was trying to force the issue by holding a trial in England. The legal proceedings began in June of 1529, a week before Henry's thirty-eighth birthday. When the Queen was summoned to testify, she quickly proved herself to be a formidable opponent. Katherina first protested that the trial wasn't lawful, arguing that only the Pope could decide the matter. She then asked Henry why it took so many years for him to develop scruples about their marriage. Her question backed the King into a corner, and he defended himself by saying, in open court, that he had waited because he loved her so much and wanted their marriage to be declared valid "more than anything else" (Starkey, 2003:241). After the Queen wrested this statement from the King, she demonstrated outstanding theatricality by coming over to Henry and kneeling at his feet. From this abject position, she pleaded with him in heavily accented English. Then, while he tried repeatedly to get her to rise, she begged him to tell her why he was doing such a terrible thing to her. Thus, she wounded him where he was most vulnerable -- his proud belief that he embodied the code of chivalry. What knight errant of old would do this to his Lady? Having discomfited the King thoroughly, Katherina swore that she had been, "a true maid, without the touch of a man" when she married him, and demanded of Henry "whether this be true or no, I put it to your conscience" (Lindsey, 1995:79). Henry's response was silence, which, frankly, was as a good as a verbal admission that she had been a virgin on their wedding night. This was devastating enough, but Katherina wasn't done yet. She asked him why, if he was concerned with her honor and the preservation of their marriage, he did not approve of her appeal to the Pope? Henry, wanting to look better in the eyes of the audience, foolishly agreed with her. She could now go over Henry's head and appeal to Rome, and she could communicate freely with her allies there (Starkey, 2003:242). Katherina, having obtained every concession she needed, then walked out of the court *before he could say or do anything to compromise her victory*.

    Campeggio used Henry's agreement with Katherina to redirect the verdict back to Rome, which he and the Pope had planned to do all along (Starkey, 2003:244). The King had been utterly checkmated by his Queen and her faction. Henry then sent a letter to the Pope which was full of disappointment, but which left an opening for a complete reconciliation with Rome, if the Pope would simply behave the way he had assured Henry's representatives he would. The King wrote,

> "[w]e could have wished, not less for your sake than for our own, that all things had been so expedited as corresponded to our expectation, not rashly conceived, but according to your promises. As it is, we have to regard with grief and wonder the incredible confusion which has arisen. If a Pope can relax Divine laws at his pleasure, surely he has as much power over human laws. We have been so often deceived by your Holiness's promises that no dependence can be placed on them. Our dignity has not been consulted in the treatment which we have met with. If your Holiness will keep the cause now advoked to Rome and your own hands, until it can be decided by impartial judges, and in an indifferent place, in a manner satisfactory to our scruples, we will forget

what is past, and repay kindness by kindness." (Froude, 124:1891).

Again, it should be remembered that what Henry was asking for was not something that was rare for the Pope to grant. Nor was the idea that the Pope needed the goodwill of secular rulers a new one. After all, Rome itself had been sacked and a Pope had been held hostage until he had been intimidated into meeting the Emperor's political demands. In 1529 Micer Mai, the Imperial agent to the Vatican, cautioned the Curia that it had better show respect for the Emperor. If any Cardinal spoke slightingly of Charles V, then that prelate would be "beheaded or burnt alive within his own apartment", and he further warned that the members of the Curia should not "speak evil of princes, or make themselves judges in the affairs of kingdoms" (Froude, 90:1891). The Emperor was willing to force the Holy See to do his bidding, yet Charles V was considered a very devoted Catholic. Is it any wonder Henry began to chafe under Papal authority?

Astoundingly, the King then continued to try and live with both Katherina and Anne at the same time. While he spent most of his leisure hours with Anne, he made court appearances, and even enjoyed the occasional family meal, with Katherina. He appears to have been trying desperately to have both his beloved, Anne, without really losing the ersatz mothering of his wife, Katherina, the woman who had been taking care of him so long.

Even though he was beginning to show a lack of empathy for others, his narcissism (even if he did not have narcissistic personality disorder, his egotism is clear enough that it seems justifiable to call it narcissism) had not yet become so bad that he was cruel. He still wanted everyone, including Katherina, to support his agenda, but he also wanted them to be happy. Therefore, he tried to woo Anne, fight the Vatican, keep Katherina happy, and maintain the facade that he was only getting an annulment because he absolutely *had* to do it, all at the same time. It must have been mentally and emotionally exhausting. Henry had both Katherina and Anne installed at court, and while Katherina was still officially the Queen, Anne was being treated as the de facto wife of the King (Ives, 2004:128). This caused extreme confusion among his courtiers. By 1530 his subjects, and even the populace of other European nations, were openly mocking Henry's situation. He was so publicly smitten with Anne that he had become a laughingstock, the caricature of a moonstruck swain (Ives, 2004:127). It weakened him politically as well, and his international opponents, including the notoriously womanizing King of France, did little to hide the fact they were bemused by Henry's behavior. Anne handled the confusion with great aplomb and used her influence to encourage the King to read the Evangelical and/or Protestant works that she favored. Katherina refused to acknowledge Anne's presence at court. She seemed certain that if she were patient, Henry would tire of Anne and return his affections to his true Queen, who had not ceased to love him. Katherina excused Henry's desire to nullify their marriage, and soothed her own wounded heart, by blaming his desertion of his true wife on the evil machinations of Anne and Wolsey.

    Katherina and Anne were, oddly enough, birds of a feather. Both were deeply religious, smart, strong-willed, and frequently outwitted Henry. The King was often caught between them, and it never went well for him. One such famous incident happened on St. Andrew's Day, November 30, 1529, not too long after Katherina had maneuvered Henry into allowing an appeal to Rome. Henry went to have dinner with his wife, who was still recognized formally as the Queen. During the course of the meal she accused him, correctly if not wisely, of neglecting her and treating her badly. The King then tried to argue that his behavior was understandable, since everyone in the court agreed with him that their marriage would be found to be unlawful. Katherina lined up his arguments, broadsided them, and sank them with all hands on board, leaving him dumbfounded and fuming. She finished her mental annihilation of his assertion that they were not married by telling him that "for each doctor or lawyer who might decide in your favor and against me, I shall find a thousand to declare that the marriage is good and indissoluble" (Starkey, 2003:393).

    For twenty years his gentle wife had seemed to defer to his wisdom; her intellectual victories over him must have astonished and dismayed the King. Nevertheless, Henry did make a rash threat that he would later prove good, saying that he would "denounce the Pope" and "marry whom he pleased" (Starkey, 2003:393). This was a momentous occasion, since it showed that Henry was beginning to regard the Pope's authority as less than divinely mandated, and heralded the eventual break from Rome. The King then fled to Anne, his dignity in tatters, hoping for comfort. But the Lady Anne, who was witty when she was in a good mood, but could verbally eviscerate those who angered her, wasn't inclined to sympathize. Instead of comforting him, she told him that he was foolish to argue with Katherina, because the Queen *always* won. She then went on to vent her annoyance with the whole situation by telling him that he would probably one day return to Katherina, abandoning Anne after having destroyed her chances of marrying anyone else. She pointed out that she could have had several children by now if she had been left alone to wed a lesser nobleman. Anne, having whipped herself up into a righteous froth of indignation, cried "alas!" and bid "farewell to my time and youth spent to no purpose at all" (Starkey, 2003:393).

    It cannot have been easy for Henry to have lived in close proximity to two such indomitable women, but he had only himself to blame. The King wanted Anne, but he also wanted the comfort of the woman who had taken such good care of him for so many years. As late as June of 1530, the Queen was still sewing Henry's shirts. Naturally, when Anne found out that Henry, who was promising that he would be able to marry her soon, was still having Katherina make his shirts, she was enraged, since she knew that his behavior only strengthened the Queen's position as his lawful wife (Fraser, 1994:172). It was little wonder that Katherina thought Henry would eventually come back to her: he was still acting, in many ways, as if they were still a happily married couple. Anne was very public with her displeasure, and Henry placated her by reallocating his linens to her, so that she could sew his shirts, rather than allowing Katherina to continue to do so (Starkey, 2003:434). Having won her point, and having cut one of the ties that connected Henry to the Queen, Anne soon after hired a seamstress to actually do the work involved.

    We think that Anne's ability to manipulate Henry accounts for why so many historians have charged that she enticed the King for her own purposes. Her deeply held religious convictions are often downplayed or overlooked, since religious motivations are incompatible with the idea of Anne as a scheming temptress. It is possible that Anne convinced herself that Henry's desire for her was part of God's plan, and demonstrated divine support for Evangelicalism and the Reformation. After all, as the object of Henry's passion she was able to introduce him to radical and forbidden works that criticized the Papacy. For example, she showed him a pamphlet by the exiled reformer Simon Fish, called *The Supplication of Beggars*, which was a blatant attack on the clerics of the Catholic Church (Scarisbrick, 1970:247). One of the ideas in the pamphlet was that the Church, because it took tithes and other monies from the populace, interfered with Henry's taxation and drained his treasury, while giving nothing back to the Crown and inciting rebellion against the King (Wilson, 2003:258). In sum, the clergy were leeches who were disloyal to their sovereign. This idea intrigued Henry. As a result, the King pardoned Simon Fish and had him brought him back to England (Ives, 2004:134). Anne might have wondered: if she was able to help the reform movement that much simply by being Henry's ladylove, how much more could she do to further the cause as a Queen? This is not to imply that Anne was a model of Christian virtue. She certainly had her faults. She was hot-tempered and could be both rude and vindictive, especially where she felt she had been personally wronged.

Without doubt she bore a grudge against Cardinal Wolsey, and she did her best to destroy him. Wolsey called Anne "the midnight crow" and was convinced that it was her influence that had him removed from favor (Ives, 2004:128). However, his fall from grace was not entirely her doing. The King was open to Anne's suggestions that Wolsey was secretly hindering the attempts to nullify Henry's marriage to Katherina because, for the first time, Wolsey had failed to achieve the desired results. Henry seems to have been convinced early on that Wolsey was trying to prevent the successful completion of the nullity suit, and he willfully ignored the realities of Wolsey's situation: it was hardly Wolsey's fault that the Pope could not risk alienating Charles V in order to give Henry his annulment (Holmes, 1993:190-192).

In spite of Henry's ire, the Cardinal's fall was not a sudden plunge toward the chopping block; it was more of a descending slither, full of sudden starts and stops. Henry dithered about dismissing Wolsey, in spite of Anne's open animosity toward the Cardinal. The King had grown used to having the support of his Lord Chancellor, and was fond of Wolsey's toadying. The Cardinal had long known that the best thing he could do with Henry was to "heap praise on his opinions" (Ives, 2004:126), and this constant reinforcement of his own ideas was pleasing to the King. Nevertheless, Wolsey was falling from favor and Anne, with her faction, encouraged his downward trajectory to the best of their abilities. Late in September of 1529 the King appeared to decide, with Anne's encouragement, that Wolsey was the enemy of the annulment, and Henry commanded Wolsey to hand over the Great Seal (Scarisbrick, 1970:234). However, Henry had trusted and depended on his former Chancellor for a long time and was hesitant to give him up completely. After Wolsey had departed in humiliation, the King sent a messenger after the Cardinal with a ring and the King's promise that Henry had not really abandoned him (Scarisbrick, 1970:235). Overjoyed, Wolsey waited for Henry to bring him back to court. He waited in vain. In October, the Cardinal was found guilty of *praemunire*, or supporting Papal authority instead of the King, which would cost Wolsey his head (Ives, 2004:118,125). Yet, once again, Henry changed his mind and pardoned the Cardinal. Keeping matters ambiguous, the King continued to send him occasional gifts, leaving Wolsey hoping for a return to royal favor (Scarisbrick, 1970:235). Wolsey did everything he could to please the King, including bribing all those who might help him with lavish gifts of money, although this made no impression on the hard-hearted Lady Anne (Starkey, 2003:425-426). The "midnight crow", ever mindful of the hurt he had done her, would not relent. Henry, however, proved more easily swayed by pretty presents. Cardinal Wolsey, in a wise yet assuredly painful move, signed over the title of his splendid manor, York Place, to the King in February of 1530. This pleased the King so greatly that he granted his former Chancellor a full pardon, and restored him to his former position as the Archbishop of York (Starkey, 2003:426). This must have infuriated Anne.

    Wolsey, motivated by his hatred of Henry's new love, then acted foolishly and offered his clandestine support to Katherina in order to frustrate Henry's plan to gain an annulment. Apparently the Cardinal's pride meant more to him than his life, since he then committed treason by "advising foreign powers on the best tactics to use against his sovereign", and attempted to "foment unrest in England", all in order to "coerce Henry into leaving Anne" (Starkey, 2003:428). Anne became aware of the Cardinal's activities, and with the dangerous determination that made her Wolsey's nemesis, she threatened to leave the King if he did not arrest his pernicious former Chancellor (Starkey, 2003:429-430). Henry had Wolsey arrested for treason on November 4, 1530. It will never be known if the King would have relented once more, because Wolsey died a natural death on the trip back to London, on November 29, 1530 (Starkey, 2003:432). The Cardinal would suffer one more posthumous insult: Henry changed the name of York Place to Whitehall and gave it over to Anne's use (Lindsey, 1995:81). Did

Anne feel a sense of satisfaction when she was at Whitehall, thinking of how unhappy Wolsey would be to know his worst enemy was enjoying the home he worked so hard on? Did she feel this would "work as much displeasure" for the Cardinal as she felt after Henry Percy was torn away from her?

  The Cardinal's arrest was a scandal, and the tales doubtlessly grew in the telling. Shortly before Wolsey's death, Chapuys wrote to Charles V to tell him an item of gossip he had gleaned from Wolsey's personal physician. According to Chapuys, the doctor had admitted to him that Wolsey had urged the Pope to excommunicate the King unless he sent Anne away, and that the Cardinal hoped to "raise the country and obtain the management" by these intrigues (Froude, 1891:140). It is completely understandable that the Cardinal would want to rid himself of Anne Boleyn, but it seems doubtful he was planning to take over England by force. However, Chapuys was desperate to coax Charles V into an invasion of England, in the hopes of placing Princess Mary on the throne, and any rumour of a plot to overthrow Henry was something to be shared and perhaps exaggerated.

  Nevertheless, a Spanish invasion of England was not such a far-fetched possibility that it could be ignored. Two years earlier, in November of 1528, an English agent had written to Wolsey in order to warn him that the Spanish Chancellor had bragged that "if we wished we could expel [Henry] from his own Kingdom in three months. What force had the King? his own subjects would expel him" (Froude, 1891:82). In spite of Chapuy's claims and the Spanish Chancellor's boasts, the people of England were not so eager to get rid of their King. When the words of the Spanish Chancellor were reported in London they were received poorly, and turned popular opinion against the

Emperor. A letter from one English nobleman to another stated that Charles V "lost the hearts of one hundred thousand Englishmen" that day (Froude, 1891:83).

The threat of a foreign invasion was not the only problem facing Henry. Unhappily for His Majesty, the Queen and Anne began turning the court into a social battleground, which Henry enjoyed much less than he enjoyed real warfare. Before the Christmas of 1530 neither Katherina nor Anne had ever really fought openly with each other, but that would change during the Yuletide. It started with a fracas between Henry and Katherina. The Queen, after all the years of ignoring Anne, finally snapped and accused Henry of wanting a divorce not for moral reasons, but so that he could marry his strumpet (Starkey, 2003:434). The King was finally able to reply to one of her attacks with confidence; he *was not* cavorting with some cheap tart! He was in love with a virtuous woman and he would marry her whether the Pope liked it or not.

It is very likely that Henry believed that if he was not physically committing adultery with Anne, then he was blameless; the idea of an "emotional affair" was not something people thought of in those days. It is even possible that he was now as emotionally invested in Anne's chastity as Anne was herself. Anne's virginity was his proof that his desire for an annulment from Katherina was wholly motivated by a sincere wish to do God's will in accordance with the text of Leviticus, rather than by prurient carnal urges. Since Henry's interest in Anne predated his nullity suit, he was plainly being disingenuous, but it's possible he was trying to deceive himself as much as other people. Henry wanted his motives to be pure, as befitted a King. Much of Henry's robust ego seems to have rested on his belief in himself as an arbiter of moral rectitude.

The King was not allowed to savor his victory over the Queen long, because he then became embroiled in a battle with Anne as well. Historians are unsure what provoked their argument. Possibly the fight began when Henry foolishly told her what the Queen had said. Instead of reacting with gratitude for Henry's defense of her chastity, it is likely she vented her frustration that his actions, and inaction, had forced her into such an insupportable situation in the first place. Considering Anne's temper and nature, she was undoubtedly embittered by constant slurs on her morals, and was vexed with Henry as the source of her problems. It must have irritated her that she now had a reputation throughout Europe as a home-wrecking slut, especially since she had done everything in her power to avoid the King's interest for over a year and was (in all likelihood) still a virgin. Being thought of as a harlot must have rankled greatly.

Certainly friends of Katherina and Mary were scathing in their opinion of Anne's character. Chapuys called her "the concubine" in his letters, which is hardly complimentary and strongly implies that he thought the King and Anne had a sexual relationship (Lindsey, 1995:82). In light of the fact that an ambassador's stock-in-trade was court gossip, he was unlikely to have been alone in his assumption. By 1533 Chapuys had begun to refer to her as "*la putaine*", or "the whore", in his letters (Starkey, 2003:359). The King's subjects were also calling Anne a "naughty paikie", which was a very coarse and vulgar word for a prostitute, a word that made "whore" seem tame in comparison (Fraser, 1994:171). For a woman of Anne's piety and pride it must have been intolerable. Goaded beyond endurance by the insults to her honor, she lashed out at Henry, and unquestionably started to hate Katherina, since the Queen was prolonging Anne's misery by obstinately refusing to allow the annulment.

Whatever the reason for Anne's wrath that January of 1531, it must have been nearly transcendent. Henry actually went to Anne's relatives, pleading with them to intercede for him and encourage Anne to forgive him (Erickson, 1980:231). This shocked everyone at his court and throughout Europe. To love and appease a woman, rather than dominating her, was considered unmanly behavior for a commoner, let alone for a King (Erickson, 1980:231). Henry was unable to subjugate Anne, and it was a scandal. This was also another strike against Anne in the popular mind. She was independent, she had her own opinions, and she wasn't docile. What's more, Anne fought with men, including her male relatives and even with the King himself. She was, in short, not a 'good' woman in the context of the Tudor world. She repeatedly violated socio-cultural norms of feminine behavior. The Queen, in contrast, was seen as a model of womanly virtue. She may have been as headstrong and smart as Anne, but she was more subtle and knew how to lead while pretending to follow. Public sympathy was firmly on Katherina's side, and was vehement in its condemnation of Anne.

Anne had previously ignored the presence of Katherina at court, just as she had been ignored in turn, but this changed after Anne's momentous quarrel and reconciliation with Henry. The Queen was now on the receiving end of Anne's temper and harsh words. Anne said to one of the Queen's Ladies-in-Waiting that she wished "all Spaniards were at the bottom of the sea" (Ives, 2004:138). Katherina, in spite of her many years in England, was still considered a "daughter of Spain", so the insult was unmistakable. Moreover, Anne declared that she would rather see Katherina "hanged than have to confess that she was her Queen and mistress" (Ives, 2004:138). This was blatant treason against the Queen, but Anne, safe in Henry's affections, clearly did not care.

Why did Anne turn so viciously against Katherina? Perhaps Anne had simply reached the point where she had lost all sympathy for the Queen, and had transformed any guilt or pity she had once felt into rage and scorn. Katherina was refusing to annul her marriage when everyone in Europe knew that Henry was desperate to leave her, thus she had forced Anne into the disreputable position of an apparent trollop for more than three years. This was bad enough, from Anne's point of view, but the Queen was also clinging to a form of Catholicism that Anne was moving away from, which made Katherina an inherent enemy of those, like Anne, who favored the Reformation (Lindsey, 1995:75). Furthermore, it is possible that Anne's own lukewarm feelings for Henry made her underestimate the strength of Katherina's love for the King, which encouraged her to assume that the Queen had avaricious motivations for blocking the annulment. Finally, it might have been easier for Anne to despise the woman that she and Henry were treating so badly, because hate is usually a much easier emotion to feel than guilt, from a psychological perspective.

Henry, prior to his fortieth birthday, clearly felt differently than Anne, and still treated his wife with at least some semblance of respect. As angry as he would become toward Katherina at times, he was convinced she loved him and seemed to feel remorse for causing her pain. Additionally, they both loved their daughter Mary, which maintained an emotional bond between them. However, even as he maintained myriad connections with Katherina, it appears that he was exhilarated by Anne's fierce temper, and was also desperate to sever his matrimonial ties. It is likely that he misunderstood Anne's rage at the whole situation, believing her anger to be a mark of her great love of him and her desire to marry him as soon as possible. Thus, Anne had implicit permission to be openly uncivil to the Queen's supporters and disdainful of Katherina, even though Henry continued to enforce Katherina's status with his courtiers. Additionally, it is probable that the more people who told him he couldn't have Anne as his wife, the more the public supported Katherina, and the more difficult it was for him to annul the marriage, the more he wanted to marry Anne Boleyn. His romance with Anne, since it was forbidden, retained all of its earliest excitement, and it probably seemed to him that it would be a testament to his chivalry if he could destroy all the obstacles between himself and his True Love. Likewise, it would be proof of his Kingship, and his absolute authority in his domain. This challenge would have appealed to both the King's romantic notions and, in theory, his narcissism, if he were indeed afflicted with that psychological ailment.

    The years between 1529 and 1531 were not only difficult for Henry because of the increasing tension between Anne and Katherina, but also because of burdens of state. With Wolsey gone, Henry needed a new Chancellor. He turned to his friend, the renowned humanist scholar Thomas More, to fill the vacant position. Henry's relationship with More was long-standing. More had tutored Henry when the King was a boy, and had helped form a large part of Henry's religious, moral, and philosophical beliefs. Henry respected and loved the man who had taught him so much, and could think of no one who could better fill the position of Chancellor. With little taste for power, More tried strenuously to decline the position (Scarisbrick, 1970:236). For one thing, he did not want anything to do with Henry's attempt to put aside the Queen. He believed the King's marriage was valid. Additionally, as a loyal and devoted Catholic, More did not want to see the Pope's authority destroyed. Nevertheless, as Anne Boleyn had discovered before him, More was to find that once Henry was determined to achieve something, he was impossible to resist.

The King was well aware that More could not, with good conscience, agree that Katherina was not Henry's lawfully wedded wife. This saddened Henry but he had not, as yet, become a hardened villain, so he promised More that he would never "molest his conscience" by making More fight on behalf of the annulment (Bernard, 2007:131). In turn, More gave the King his silence, promising that he would not publicly oppose Henry's nullity suit, even if he could not support it. More kept his word, even up to the moment of his death.

Unfortunately, Henry's fortieth birthday was rapidly approaching, and soon afterwards the King would cease to honor his promises, much to the detriment of not only More, but many others. Prior to his forties, he had been, in general, a reasonably commendable man. In his youth, he attempted to live up to the ideals of a just ruler and loving husband. As he grew older, he grew more narcissistic and hypocritical, so that when he experienced a mid-life crisis he acted like a disgraceful cad to both his loving wife and his reluctant amour, but his behavior was nothing that would have earned him the label of "tyrant". Some would argue that he treated Wolsey almost as unethically as he treated Katherina, rewarding Wolsey's years of devotion with callous ingratitude. Unlike Katherina, however, the Cardinal was far from an innocent victim. Wolsey had used his service to Henry as an excuse to amass considerable wealth for himself through very shady means, and eventually tried to betray his monarch for his own gain. Wolsey's duplicity serves as a strong argument against any accusation that Henry acted with malice and ungratefulness toward his former Chancellor. If Henry had never suffered a radical alteration in his personality, or if he had died suddenly in 1531, he would have been remembered by posterity only as a passable monarch with an extreme mid-life crisis.

Pondering what-might-have-been is an interesting mental exercise, but the reality is that the King turned forty on June 28, 1531. His behavior and mental stability began to deteriorate shortly thereafter, securing him a place in the popular imagination as a brutal despot, and radically altering the course of English history.

Chapter Four
The Bloodbath Begins: Martyrs, Conspiracies, and Jane Seymour

If Henry had McLeod syndrome, then it would explain why the King slowly grew more dangerous and erratic after he turned forty. In the early stages of Henry's personality shift his cruelty was still aimed almost solely at his first wife. Shortly after his birthday, in the summer of 1531, the King banished Katherina of Aragon, Princess of Spain, Queen of England, loyal wife and mother, from court and sent her to live at the More, which was one of Wolsey's former estates. Adding insult to her injury, Anne Boleyn, the daughter of a minor noble, was given ascendancy in her place (Lindsey, 1995:86). Katherina's daughter Mary was also sent away, to Richmond, and the Queen would never see either her beloved husband or her adored child again (Porter, 2007:76). Perhaps even Henry did not yet know that he was separating mother and daughter forever; he may have assumed Katherina would eventually succumb to his will and he would reward her with more opportunities to see Mary. However, the Queen would remain firm in her resolve that she was his lawfully wedded wife, regardless of personal cost, until her death in 1536.

The King also began to push harder for national and international recognition of Anne as his future Queen. On September 1, 1532 he invested Anne with the title of Marquess of Pembroke, in her own right, which she would be able to pass on to her offspring who were "heirs male of her body" -- whether or not they were legitimate (Lindsey, 1995:88-89). Henry also decided that Anne should have the jewels designated for the Queen of England. Katherina and her supporters were certain that Henry only demanded the jewelry because he was under pressure from Anne's unceasing avarice. Katherina initially refused to relinquish the royal ornaments, but after she received direct orders from the King she had no choice but to give them up. The Queen understandably resented this attack on her dignity and property, and bitterly protested that her gems would go to adorn the "scandal of Christendom" (Starkey, 2003:459). Katherina endured a further emotional blow from her husband when he took Anne with him to elaborately choreographed and very important peace talks with the French in Calais, just as if she were already Queen.

Katherina may have been mollified when she learned that taking Anne with him to the parley didn't work out as well as Henry had hoped it would, since all the French women who had enough rank to formally "receive" Anne were either mysteriously indisposed or adamantly refused to socialize with her (Lindsey, 1995:89). Marriage was one of the few forms of security that women of the Tudor era could count on, and marriages among the peerage were often more about strategic alliances than romantic unions. To break the social and political bonds of matrimony for mere passion was, at best, selfish stupidity. The idea that a Queen would be cast off in favor of a mistress was abhorrent to them, and they were not about to welcome Henry's trollop with open arms.

Of course, no one was rude to the man who had created the entire situation; as King he was powerful in a way his inamorata was not, and could not be insulted even by proxy. Although she had been slighted by all the Frenchwomen in the upper nobility, Anne was able to attend all of the feasts and pageants that were sponsored by Henry in Calais, which meant she was able to formally meet the King of France as though she were already England's Queen.

After the peace talks were finished, Henry decided to marry Anne, with the benefit of clergy and a full ceremony, even though the Pope had not yet granted his request for an annulment. Evidently, the King had tired of waiting for a Papal blessing on the new union. Henry and Anne were likely married in a small, secret ceremony in Dover on November 14, 1532, right after they returned from Calais (Starkey, 2003:463). They did not advertise this wedding, not only because of its presumptive bigamy, but also because the repairs Henry had ordered be made to the Tower of London had not yet been completed and custom demanded that a new Queen reside there for two days before her coronation (Starkey, 2003:464-465).

Anne's presence at Henry's side during the Anglo-French peace talks was hard enough for Katherina to bear, but it was nothing compared to the shock she felt when she received information from her loyalist grapevine that the King had actually committed the grave sin of bigamy by marrying his courtesan. The news did not take long to get to her, either. Less than two weeks after Henry and Anne's semi-secret wedding, Katherina sent a letter to Chapuys. She wanted to vent some of her emotional anguish in regards to both Henry's treatment of her and the Curia's lack of a definitive response to her plight, and she wanted Chapuys to send the Emperor information attesting to her misery and suffering, so Charles V would subsequently prod the Pope into action. She wrote,

> "there is no justice for me or my daughter. It is withheld from us for political considerations. I do not ask his Holiness to declare war -- a war I would rather die than provoke; but I have been appealing to the Vicar of God for justice for six years, and I cannot have it. I refused proposals made to me two years ago by the King and Council. Must I accept them now? Since then I have received fresh injuries. I am separated from my lord, and he has married another woman without obtaining a divorce; and this last act has been done while the suit is still pending, in defiance of him who has the power of God upon earth. I cover these lines with my tears as I write. I confide in you as my friend. Help me to bear the cross of my tribulation. Write to the Emperor. Bid him to insist that judgement be pronounced. The next Parliament, I am told, will decide if I or my daughter will suffer martyrdom. I hope God will accept it as an act of merit by us, as we shall suffer for the sake of the truth." (Froude, 1891:197-198:1891)

Katherina was not only convinced she was in the right and was the King's lawful wife, she was sure there was no other way the Pope could decide but in her favor. Furthermore, she was willing to die rather than be cast aside and be told that she had been an incestuous concubine for the decades of her marriage to Henry. She was so determined to have her marriage recognized as legitimate she was even willing to risk her life, and the life of her only surviving child. Apparently she feared Mary's displacement even more than Mary's death. While her determination demonstrates a great deal of courage and fortitude, it does not provide evidence of the maternal concern to which Katherina's resistance is often ascribed. Without doubt she loved her daughter and was committed to keeping her in the line of succession, but her top priority seems to have been to establish that her marriage was a valid one.

While the King's first wife waited in misery to hear if the Pope would decree that her marriage was valid, the King's new wife spent time choosing the plate and other accouterments to outfit her household in a manner which would reflect its new status (Starkey, 2003:465-466). The fact that Henry and Anne were openly behaving as though they were man and wife outraged Katherina's supporters. Many of them vented their anger by suggesting, in secret, that England would turn against Henry in the event of an invasion by Charles V, and that such an invasion would probably occur. Dr. Pedro Ortiz, the Imperial Representative to the Pope and Katherina's ardent supporter, wrote to Empress Isabella of Portugal, the wife of Charles V, in January of 1533 to say that he hoped that Henry would one day,

"acknowledge the error into which the Enemy of Mankind has led him, and amend his past conduct;

otherwise it must follow that his disobedience to the Pope's injunction and his infidelity to God once proved, he will be deprived of his kingdom and the execution of the sentence committed to his Imperial Majesty [Charles V]. This done, all those in England who fear God will rise in arms, and the King will be punished as he deserves, the present brief operating as a formal sentence against him. On the main cause, there being no one in Rome to answer for the opposite party, sentence cannot long be delayed." (Froude, 1891:199-200)

The King had good reason to be concerned, and he worried because Katherina was "of such high courage" that "with her daughter at her side, she might raise an army and take the field against me with as much spirit as her mother Isabella" (Waller, 2006:32). The Holy Roman Emperor wielded enormous power and if he could have indirectly ruled England by putting Mary on the throne as his puppet-Queen, he would have had dominion over most of Europe. Although the invasion was, in truth, unlikely, it would be a disservice to Henry to imply that he was merely being paranoid about the possibility. As intelligent as Henry was, he would have undoubtedly been aware of both the extent of popular support for Katherina and his kingdom's vulnerability to attack by foreign powers. The ambition of Charles V, and the firm resolve of Katherina, would have caused Henry real anxiety because they posed a significant danger to his crown and country.

Fortunately for Henry, Charles was not prone to being goaded into war on the say-so of his ambassadors. Nevertheless, the Emperor was still a major obstacle blocking Henry's path to an annulment. The fact that his aunt, a woman of impeccable royal bloodlines, was being replaced by the dissolute daughter of an upstart noble appears to have been deeply offensive to the Emperor's sense of decorum. Furthermore, the disrespect Henry showed Katherina hinted of disrespect for his Imperial nephew, and thus could not be borne. The distaste Charles felt for Anne Boleyn must have stiffened his resistance to the annulment, since he was more open to the nullity suit if Henry were willing to choose some other bride than a woman many considered to be no better than a common doxy. There were rumors that the Emperor was willing to let the Pope grant the annulment, even though Katherina would feel betrayed, if there were provisions made for Mary to remain in the line of succession and "if the King made a suitable marriage, and not a love-marriage" (Froude, 1891:200).

Henry did not give a fig if other rulers disapproved of his choice of a lover, no matter how many difficulties it threw in his way. He would have Anne, and those who did not like it could lump it. He and Anne were married in another small ceremony on January 25, 1533, this time in London. The nuptials were not widely announced, but the wedding was much less clandestine than the one in Dover (Strickland and Strickland, 1851:223-224). Anne's father and her uncle, the Duke of Norfolk, have frequently been portrayed as fellow-schemers who demanded that Anne get a crown from the besotted King, but in reality they were against the marriage (Froude, 1891:230). It's reasonable to think that the political situation was too delicate, and their power too tenuous, for their comfort and that they feared retribution if Katherina returned to power. Nevertheless, Anne cared no more for their opinion than the King had cared for the opinion of the other crowned heads of Europe. She, like Henry, was determined to make their marriage as binding and legal as possible. Perhaps Henry and Anne needed news of their marriage to circulate because Anne was beginning to suspect she was pregnant? Certainly, by mid-February, the King's new bride was hinting that she was with child (Ives, 2004:163).

The news of Anne's pregnancy must have broken Katherina's heart into even smaller pieces. Using Chapuys as her mouthpiece, Katherina sent a pleading message to her nephew in the desperate hope that a Papal decree would drive Henry back into her arms. On her behalf, Chapuys wrote that,

> "The Queen was thunderstruck, and complained bitterly of his Holiness. He had left her to languish for three and a half years since her appeal, and, instead of giving sentence, had now devised a scheme to prolong her misery and bastardize her daughter. She knew the King's character. If sentence was once given there would be no scandal. The King would obey, or, if he did not, which she thought impossible, she would die happy, knowing that the Pope had declared for her. Her own mind would be at rest and the Princess would not lose her right. The Pope was entirely mistaken if he thought he would induce the King to modify his action against the Church. The Lady [Anne Boleyn] and her father, who were staunch Lutherans, were urging him on. The sentence alone would make him pause. He dared not disobey, and if the people rose the Lady would find rough handling." (Froude, 1891:206-207)

As Anne became increasingly certain that she was pregnant, the urgency to obtain an annulment intensified; Henry wanted Anne to be recognized as Queen before the new Prince (for surely it was a boy) was born. At the end of March Henry therefore appointed Thomas Cranmer as the Archbishop of Canterbury (Ives, 2004:164). With Cranmer securely in office, the King could ask him to "judge" the lawfulness of Henry's first marriage. It was now just a matter of time before the King's marriage to Katherina was nullified, and the Vatican's opinion would be rendered nonessential.

The international tide had turned in Henry's favor, leaving Katherina relatively helpless. It had become obvious the Emperor was reluctant, or unable, to invade England. Without Charles V to enforce them, Papal Bulls were worthless pieces of paper. Anne was pregnant and there was hope for a son; a male heir who would spare the country the civil war that might come if a woman, such as his half-sister Mary, should inherit Henry's crown. In April of 1533 even Dr. Ortiz, always so loyal to Katherina, wrote to the Emperor that he "feared the Pope had sent, or might send, absolution to the King" (Froude, 1891:212). Katherina was now desperate and was growing steadily more angry with both the Pope and her husband. At the end of April Chapuys wrote to Charles V to report that the Queen, who had "hitherto [been] so scrupulous in her profession of respect and affection for the King that she thinks she will be damned eternally if she takes a step which may lead to war. Latterly, however, she has let me know that she would like to see some other remedy tried, though she refers everything to me" (Froude, 1891:221). Katherina had clearly reached the end of her tether, and was willing to tacitly condone a war to get rid of Anne Boleyn and force the King to acknowledge the validity of his first marriage.

That same month Chapuys wrote that the King, once so "naturally kind and generous," had changed so much that he "did not seem to be the same man," which the ambassador attributed to Anne having "so perverted him" with her influence (Froude, 1891:216). However, Anne should not have to shoulder the blame for Henry's increasingly bad temper. For one thing, Henry may have suspected, or been aware, that Katherina was now welcoming the invasion of England by a foreign power, which would have made him view her as a serious threat to his crown, not merely a thorn in his side. Her very existence was a danger to the legitimacy of his expected son, and any affection he had once felt for her had presumably dried up after years of her stubborn defiance of his will. Moreover, if the King had McLeod syndrome, it was the disease, not Anne, which instigated such a change in the formerly chivalrous and caring King. The paranoia and irrational impulses that can result from McLeod syndrome would have aggravated Henry's anger with Katherina, spurring him to act in an increasingly cruel manner.

On May 23, 1533, Cranmer obligingly declared the marriage between Katherina of Aragon and Henry, King of England, to be "null and void" (Scarisbrick, 1970:312). Less than a week after Cranmer's decision Anne came to the Tower of London from Greenwich and three days later, on June 1, 1533, she was anointed and crowned by the ever-compliant Cranmer (Scarisbrick, 1970:313).

The marriage between Henry and Anne turned out to be tumultuous, which surprised no one. Part of the reason must have been the fact that, as a wife, Anne was no longer a mysterious object to pursue; she was caught. That meant that Henry, ever the hunter, had started looking for other game. This sent Anne into a frenzied rage. This time, instead of placating her ire as he had done so often before, Henry told her she had to put up with his infidelity, advising her to "shut her eyes, and endure as her betters had done" and warned her that he "could humble her again in a moment" (Starkey, 2003:508). The new Queen must have been stunned by this change in his attitude. If nothing else, her anger should have been met with attempts at appeasement because emotional upset was considered to be a real threat to an unborn baby, since to aggravate a gravid woman was believed to be capable of causing fetal death and miscarriage (Cressy, 1997:46). However, the reality Anne had to adjust to was that her power was *lessened* by the fact that the King had become her husband, and he could now command her affection whereas in the past he had had to entreat her for it. Anne was now his property, as well as his Queen, and he was well aware of it.

There may have been another reason for his sudden disregard for the heavily pregnant Anne's happiness. McLeod syndrome was possibly altering how Henry treated everyone around him, not just his recently acquired bride. Although McLeod syndrome did not affect him severely enough to actually make him a killer until 1535, it did make him very disagreeable to live with in the years leading up to his more drastic changes in behavior.

The birth of a son would have put Anne on a more equal footing with her increasingly difficult husband. However, on September 7, 1533 Anne gave birth to her first and only surviving child, a daughter who was named Elizabeth. Although this newborn girl would eventually become one of England's most revered monarchs, the birth of a daughter was a serious disappointment to both Henry and Anne. Nevertheless, Henry took the bad news of another daughter with apparent calm. A hearty baby was an important sign that the King was capable of producing healthy offspring, which would place on Katherina the sole 'blame' for her long string of miscarriages and still-born infants and counter the suspicions that Henry was the cause of his reproductive woes. Speculation that the King could not breed strong sons was clearly making the rounds, since a close friend of the Duke of Norfolk, a man named De Gambaro, wrote to the Duke that Anne's expected "child would be weak, owing to his father's condition" (Froude, 1891:239). With a robust infant to prove his virility, the King was sanguine about his daughter's arrival, considering her birth to be a good omen, indicating that he and Anne would also have healthy sons (Lindsey, 1995:99).

Although it was not as painful to her as the birth of a son would have been, the arrival of a rosy-cheeked daughter to the King and Anne must have driven Katherina nearly demented with vexation and sadness. She wrote to the Pope again in October of 1533 to beg him to encourage Charles V to forcibly restore Catholicism to England and herself to the throne, warning his Holiness that,

> "If a remedy be not applied shortly, there will be no end to ruined souls and martyred saints. The good will be firm and will suffer. The lukewarm will fail if they find none to help them, and the rest will stray out of the way like sheep that have lost their shepherd … I write frankly to your Holiness, for the discharge of my own soul, as to one who, I hope, can feel with me and my daughter for the martyrdoms of these admirable persons. I have a mournful pleasure in expecting that we shall follow them in the manner of their torments. And so I end, waiting for the remedy from God and from your Holiness. May it come speedily. If not, the time will be past." (Froude, 256-257:1891)

There would, however, be no invasion to aid Katherina; any momentum in that direction had long since dissipated. The former Queen had to deal with yet more emotional pain when, a few months later, Henry seemed to be proven correct in his prediction of future children with Anne. The new Queen was known to be pregnant again by February of 1534, when Chapuys wrote to inform Charles V of the matter; further evidence for this pregnancy appears in a letter from George Taylor written to Lady Lisle in April of that same year describing Anne as having "a goodly belly" and again when Chapuys mentions the Queen's "condition" at the end of July (Dewhurst, 1984:54). Oddly, there is never any further mention of this pregnancy after that; it is as though it evaporated. Some historians assume that the baby was either stillborn or died shortly after the birth, and the royal couple never made a formal announcement about their loss because the infant was another girl (Fraser, 1994:219). There is also an alternative explanation: if the fetus miscarried before Anne felt it move, or "quicken," it would have been considered that the fetus had not yet been given a soul (Hull, 1996:105). As such, it would not have required baptism, and the loss would not have been discussed publicly. If, however, the Queen was pregnant in February, the pregnancy would almost certainly have been past the point of quickening, so the idea of a late term miscarriage that was treated as a private matter seems the most plausible. Fetal loss happened with distressing regularity in the Tudor era, so even though Anne was the Queen it may have been considered bad form to discuss her loss. At the end of September of 1534 Chapuys again mentioned Anne's possible pregnancy, but in the context that the King did not believe she was actually with child (Dewhurst, 1984:55). Had Anne miscarried in early August, and then erroneously thought herself to be pregnant again in

September? Or had she had a "phantom pregnancy" -- wanting a baby so desperately her mind created the false symptoms of a normal gestation -- the entire time? A similar mystery possibly occurred the next year. In June of 1535 William Kingston wrote to Lord Lisle that Anne was once again in possession of "as fair a belly as I have ever seen," but no miscarriage or birth was ever recorded and the letter may have actually been written in 1533 or 1534, which means there was probably no pregnancy before the autumn of 1535 (Dewhurst, 1984:55). What is certain is that the lack of a successful pregnancy was undermining Anne's power at court, and causing her faction considerable distress.

    Catholics were becoming increasingly aggrieved by the King's separation from the Church, and many of them blamed Anne's Protestant-leaning influence. In November of 1534 Parliament passed the Act of Supremacy, which declared that Henry was the head of the Church of England. This was almost too much for Papal loyalists to endure. Katherina and her supporters renewed their efforts to persuade Charles V to invade England in order to restore both Katherina and the Church's authority to their rightful place.

    Henry was, in a way, justified in his growing paranoia; even those he trusted were often in league with Katherina, and therefore his secret enemies. For example, in April of 1535 one of Henry's personal physicians, Dr. Butts, who was a secret supporter of traditional Catholicism, had an opportunity to communicate with Katherina's physician. Of course, Katherina's doctor immediately shared anything Dr. Butts had told him with Katherina and Chapuys. The ambassador quickly wrote to Charles V, telling him that Butts had said, "there are but two ways of assisting the Queen and Princess, and of setting right the affairs of the realm: one would be if it pleased God to visit the King with some little malady. The second method was force, of which, he said, the King and his Ministers were in marvellous fear. If it came to a war, he thought the King would be especially careful of the Queen and Princess, meaning to use them, should things turn to the worst, as mediators for peace. But if neither of these means were made use of, he really believed they were in danger of their lives. He considered it was lucky for the King that the emperor did not know how easy the enterprise of England would be; and the present, he said, was the right time for it." (Froude, 1891:323)

Moreover, that same Dr. Butts also sent Chapuys a covert message that several nobles were secretly ready to join the Emperor's cause during an invasion (Froude, 324:1891). Dr. Butts was a man whom Henry trusted, literally, with his life. It would have been easy for a royal physician to poison or weaken the King ahead of an invasion. Is it any wonder that Henry's fears and suspicions became steadily worse with so much skullduggery going on behind his back, even among his personal attendants? The Duke of Norfolk allegedly said that Henry was so "troubled in his brain" about the circumstances of the Great Matter "that he does not trust anyone alive" (Haile, 1910:115). Although McLeod syndrome could have caused him to become paranoid, being surrounded by such duplicity fed his distrust and doubtlessly heightened its effects.

Although many historians consider 1536 to be the year in which Henry's behavior changed so significantly, it was only the year that the alteration in his conduct became *dramatically* apparent. As early as 1532 he became less and less kind and respectful toward Katherina of Aragon, moving into outright viciousness toward her by 1534. The King's increasing ruthlessness toward everyone around him soon became undeniable. As a younger man Henry ordered executions only as a last recourse against a significant danger to his crown, especially if he was familiar with the condemned. In contrast, after 1535, executions were precipitately ordered with frightening regularity.

One of the clearest signs of Henry's increasing violence was the execution of three Carthusian priests and a Bridgettine monk on May 4, 1535 (Starkey, 2003:523; Bernard, 2007:167-168). Their only 'crime' was their steadfast belief that the Pope was the Holy Father and head of the Church, which was now treason in England. Their deaths were by hanging, drawing and quartering, a nasty business involving being hung, then let down from the noose before they died from lack of oxygen, then being disemboweled and castrated while still conscious, before having their entrails burnt in front of their faces. Once they were dead their bodies were cut into quarters and beheaded. There is even a rumor that their castrated privates were stuffed into their mouths to stop their ceaseless prayers, but historians are not sure whether this is the truth, or merely a rumor to further strengthen Henry's reputation for barbarism. The executions must have given Henry some form of gratification, because on June 19 he sent three more Carthusians to the same hideous death, including one named Sebastian Newdigate, who had once been one of Henry's courtiers before he renounced his earthly wealth and joined the religious order (Marshall, 2006:27). Newdigate appears to have been the first of the King's friends or acquaintances to be executed in connection with Henry's Great Matter. The King tried, in person, to persuade Newdigate to change his mind about the Pope's supremacy. According to the *Catholic Encyclopedia* of 1913, Newdigate "was thrown into the Marshalsea prison, where he was kept for fourteen days bound to a pillar, standing upright, with iron rings round his neck, hands, and feet. There he was visited by the King, who offered to load him with riches and honours if he would conform. He was then brought before the Council, and sent to the Tower, where Henry visited him again" (1913:630). Newdigate refused to acquiesce to Henry's wishes or accept the validity of Henry's arguments and died with his fellow Carthusians.

    Having now killed someone with whom he was familiar, the King subsequently found it easier to send his friends to their deaths. Henry ordered the beheading of Bishop John Fisher three days later, on June 22. To be honest, there was at least some legal reasoning behind Fisher's execution. If the King had always been a ruthless, bloodthirsty monster he would have executed the Bishop long before. Fisher had been openly defying Henry for eight years, and the King had stood by while Fisher actively preached against him and penned books defending the validity of Katherina's marriage (Bernard, 2005:111). If Henry had been a brutal tyrant prior to his fortieth birthday, he would have had Fisher arrested and executed in 1529, after the defiant Bishop preached a sermon in support of Katherina's marriage to the King, in which he compared Henry to the evil biblical monarch Herod (Scarisbrick, 1970:225). Since the Bible depicted King Herod as a savage madman who murdered his wife and family members, as well as ordering the slaughter of male infants in Bethlehem, to associate him with Henry was so insulting it could be considered treasonous. In 1533 Fisher had given Henry even more of an excuse to execute him when he appealed to other European rulers to invade England and depose Henry, an act of blatant and indisputable treason (Scarisbrick, 1970:331). Yet the King still spared Fisher's life because the prelate had always been an important and respected member of Henry's court. It was not until McLeod syndrome would have begun to affect Henry, causing the previously egotistical yet well-meaning King to become irrational and savage, that Fisher was finally condemned to be beheaded. Just a few weeks before his execution the Pope elevated Fisher to the rank of a Cardinal, signaling the Curia's support of Fisher's stance. Henry was understandably incensed by the Papacy's attempt to reward his enemy, and refused to allow the Cardinal's hat to be brought into England from Rome. The King was unfaltering in his intention to show that he, not the Pope, determined the course of the Church in his own country, so Fisher's promotion did nothing to save him from Henry's wrath. After the Cardinal's death, comparisons were made between Fisher and John the Baptist, who had likewise had his head cut off for criticizing the marital practices of his King (*Catholic Encyclopedia*, 1913:462).This is perhaps an unjust comparison since Fisher had also appealed to other rulers to overthrow his King, and any monarch of the Renaissance era would have considered this behavior treasonous and therefore deserving of execution.

    Regardless of whether or not Fisher's execution was justified (within the legal system of the time period), Henry now seemed to have very few scruples about killing learned men he had once befriended and esteemed. He had Thomas More beheaded on July 6. More's death made much less sense than the execution of Fisher. Fisher had been publicly deriding Henry, whereas More had not. It was also a foolish political move on

Henry's part, especially after the incredibly unpopular beheading of John Fisher. Renowned for his piety and learning, More was esteemed all across Europe; there would only be a universal denouncement of Henry if he ordered More's judicial murder (Smith, 1982:174). As could have been expected there was widespread public condemnation of More's death, both domestically and abroad. It was pointed out that the former Chancellor had never given the King an excuse to kill him, since he had never openly rebelled against Henry's commands. Therefore, More's beheading served only to make Henry look like a degenerate fool. If nothing else, Henry had always been profoundly concerned with his reputation, and was careful to behave in a manner he felt was befitting for a great King so this sudden disregard for public opinion seems to be as much of a radical departure from the King's earlier behavior as the execution itself.

Henry was fast gaining a reputation as a despot and murderer who killed anyone who disagreed with him, no matter if that person had been a confederate, or was a well-loved public figure, or was innocent of the charges brought against them. Caught up in Henry's gory new policy of demanding blood and death, people rapidly forgot that the King had once been very different.

How different had Henry become? The King's behavior preceding the point where McLeod syndrome made him vicious is illustrated by his reaction to other well-known priests who sided against him in his Great Matter. Only three years earlier, in 1532, a priest named William Peto preached an Easter sermon in which he asserted that the King, who was in the congregation *listening*, would meet his end just like the Old Testament tyrant Ahab (Bernard, 2005:152). He warned the King that if he didn't mend his ways, dogs would lick his blood from the stones just as they had licked Ahab's after his death in battle. Peto also strongly implied that Anne was Jezebel reborn. Considering that Jezebel was considered to be a harlot who had slaughtered prophets and replaced them with idol worshipers, this was a thundering theological condemnation of Anne. Henry was enraged, but he didn't have Peto's head cut off. He looked for other solutions or punishments. First, he had one of the theologians who was on his side, a priest named Curwin, preach the following Sunday. Peto was away at the time, so it seemed like a choice opportunity to refute him. Things did not go according to Henry's plans, however, since another friar, who was named Elstow, stood up from among the assembled listeners and began loudly refuting Curwin (Bernard, 2005:152-153). Unsurprisingly, Peto and Elstow were called up in front of the King's council, where Henry and his chief ministers castigated the pair soundly. The friars stood their ground. When the Earl of Essex told them they should be stuffed into a sack and dropped into the Thames to drown, Elstow told Essex "Threaten these things to rich and dainty folk who are clothed in purple, fare delicately, and have their chiefest hope in this world, for we esteem them not, but are joyful that for the discharge of our duties we are driven hence. With thanks to God we know the way to Heaven to be as ready by water as by land, and therefore we care not which way we go" (Stone, 1904:277). In spite of the flagrant disrespect they showed for the King and his courtiers, the friars were not executed. Instead, Peto and Elstow were freed and sent into exile (Bernard, 2005:153). They emigrated to Antwerp, where Peto continued to needle Henry by publishing a book defending the legitimacy of Katherina's marriage to the King.

Once the King's mind had been so affected by McLeod syndrome that his personality changed and his anger became precipitate and indomitable, Henry became nearly unrecognizable from the man he was when he was younger.

The year 1536 has been identified as a pivotal one because so many events occurred which highlighted Henry's metamorphosis, not the least of which was the King's ruthless beheading of an obviously innocent Anne Boleyn.

Katherina, who had suffered so much and had received so little from Henry in return, died on January 7, 1536. Even at the last, Henry refused to let Mary go to see her dying mother (Lindsey, 1995:112). The spitefulness of this act, to both his daughter and to the woman who loved him so faithfully for so long, appears to beggar belief. But was he really trying to be cruel? Was this one of the manifestations of McLeod syndrome? Or did Henry keep Katherina away from Mary because he was sincerely worried about invasion by the Emperor? The King knew that Charles V would have a massive advantage if he could use Mary to symbolically head his troops. What if Mary used the visit to her mother in order to escape to her allies in Spain?

Invasion was certainly still a threat, especially with the possibility of armed insurrection by Henry's Catholic subjects. Chapuys had written to a minister of the Imperial court as recently as October of 1535 to confidently assure him that an invasion of England "would be easy, for everyone was irritated. The King's treasure would pay for all, and would help, besides, for the enterprise against the Turk. It was time to punish him [Henry VIII] for his folly and impiety" (Froude, 1891:360). So not only were there plots afoot to overrun England for religious reasons, the pot was sweetened by the large store of wealth

Henry had accumulated from dissolving the monasteries. It can only be assumed that not even Chapuys believed that Charles V was a good enough Catholic to return all that money to the coffers of the Church. Instead, the rewards of Henry's impiety would go to line the Emperor's pockets. While the effects of McLeod syndrome would doubtlessly have increased Henry's fears and driven him into paranoid agitation, Henry had good reason to worry about his daughter and his nephew.

Chapuys had also encouraged the Emperor to invade by implying, or stating outright, that Henry might murder Katherina and Mary. Was Henry really planning to execute them? It seems unlikely, but it is not outside the realm of possibility. However, it should be remembered that a lot of what is known about Henry, the Great Matter, and Anne Boleyn is the result of letters written by Chapuys. These letters are certainly valuable, in that they often give a first person account of what was happening in Henry's court, but they are not without flaws. For one thing, Chapuys was a devoted friend of Katherina's, and as such he was angry with Henry and detested Anne Boleyn. There was little he would not accuse them of doing, thinking, or saying. He also seemed to feel there was a pressing need for Charles V to invade England in order to put Mary on the throne and restore Catholicism, and he therefore provided the information that would be most likely to induce the Emperor to act. Even the ambassador admitted that much of his information was hearsay and rumors. Clearly the letters written by Chapuys cannot be taken as gospel, even though they have provided a wealth of useful data for historians.

In spite of Chapuys reports, Charles V didn't think Henry would kill his first wife and eldest daughter. However, the Emperor wasn't sure enough about the matter to risk the lives of

Katherina and Mary, so he wrote to Chapuys to tell him that Henry "cannot be so unnatural as to put to death his own wife and daughter. The threats you speak of can only be designed to terrify them. They must not give way, if it can be avoided; but, if they are really in danger, and there is no alternative, they must yield. A submission so made cannot injure their rights. They can protest they are acting under compulsion, in fear for their lives. I will take care that their protestation is duly ratified by their protectors at Rome" (Froude,1891:365-366).

      Whether or not Henry would execute Katherina became moot upon her death. The fact that Katherina passed away without seeing her only child one more time was tragic, but at least she didn't die completely alone. Her closest friend, Maria de Salinas, hearing that the Queen's health had taken a marked downturn, violated the King's orders and rushed to Katherina's side. Maria had come to England with Katherina in 1501, and she had stood by the Queen throughout the hardship of the years following Arthur's death. Maria made an excellent marriage to William Willoughby, who was the 11th Baron of Willoughby de Eresby, and remained a loyal Lady-in-Waiting to the Queen. This brave and true friend rode sixty miles in freezing weather to reach Katherina before her death (Lindsey, 1995:113). At some point in her journey Maria, who was in her mid-to-late 40s and would have been considered an elderly woman, was thrown off her horse. Being a very smart and determined woman, Maria turned this accident to her advantage, and used the stains on her dress to convince Katherina's steward, who was acting as the Queen's jailer on Henry's orders, that she had "lost" the papers giving her permission to see her dying friend (Lindsey, 1995:113). Her ploy worked. Once Maria was safely inside, she went to Katherina's room, locked the door, and then refused to come out again. Therefore, despite the King's attempts to keep Katherina from any personal comfort, her dearest friend was able to be by the Queen's side when she passed away.

Maria got away with her impudent defiance of the King's commands, probably because her daughter, Catherine Willoughby, was married to Henry's closest friend, Charles Brandon the 1st Duke of Suffolk. Catherine Willoughby would marry again after Suffolk's death, to a man named Robert Bertie with whom she had two children, Susan and Peregrine Bertie. Peregrine Bertie was an ancestor of Lady Diana Spencer, who married Charles, the current Prince of Wales, and was the mother of Princes William and Harry, who are 2nd and 3rd in line for the throne of England. Thus, Maria De Salinas was, in a manner of speaking, revenged on Henry VIII for her friend's death. It is Maria's descendants, not Henry's, who will sit on the English throne.

Chapuys, who had held Katherina in the highest regard, also came to see the dying Queen. He kindly told her a white lie, informing her that Henry was tiring of Anne, and was already planning to reunite with Katherina (Lindsey, 1995:113). Before she died, Katherina wrote one last letter to Henry. In it she forgave him for his sins against her and begged him to take care of Mary. She ended the letter heartrendingly, telling Henry that, "Lastly I make this vow, that mine eyes desire you above all things" (Porter, 2007:106). She still loved him, in spite of all he had done to her. Then she signed it, "Katherina, the Queen of England" (Lindsey, 1995:113-114). In death, as in life, Katherina maintained that her marriage was valid, and managed to have the last word on the Great Matter.

When the news that Katherina had died reached Henry, his behavior was grotesque. He shouted, "God be praised that we are free from all suspicion of war," which was, to say the least, an inappropriate thing to say when notified of a death in the family (Starkey, 2003:549). In spite of his legitimate fear of an invasion and the justifiable relief he would have felt that such a serious threat had been removed, the fact he spent the next day rejoicing over Katherina's death with Anne is, frankly, repulsive. They dressed completely in yellow, which some historians argue was a mark of respect because it was the color of mourning in Spain, but the fact that he and Anne celebrated with feasts, dancing, and jousting indicates that they were jubilant about Katherina's death, and makes the color yellow appear chosen for its cheerfulness (Lipscomb, 2009:52-53). He also confiscated Katherina's estate for himself, ignoring her last will and testament by keeping the goods and money for his own purposes (Starkey, 2003:550-551).

  How did Mary handle this insult to her mother? How much did Henry's vicious disdain for Catherine's passing add to the agony of losing the mother to whom, in spite of their years of forced separation, she was still very close emotionally? How could Mary reconcile the King's behavior with that of the father she had once known and continued to love? It seems as though Mary built an emotional fortress for herself by blaming Anne for all of Henry's malevolent deeds. Did she, perhaps, believe the rumors that the King had literally been 'bewitched' by Anne (Lindsey, 1995:117)? In the Tudor time period accusations of witchcraft were no laughing matter (Gifford, 2007:xi). People truly believed that witches could summon Satan, have sex with Prince of Darkness, and then use the powers he gave them to perform acts of evil against the innocent. There was also the belief that ill wish charms and medallions could be used to inflict harm. Mary's loving father had changed, in a very short space of time, into a monster who rejoiced at her mother's death. Did she and her friends whisper to each other that Anne Boleyn was not just a harlot, but a witch as well? Was it from these whispers that the myths that she had six fingers, large moles, and a goiter were created (Ives, 2004:39-41)?

Anne was not a witch, of course, and in the end she was kinder than Henry. She at least began to feel sorrow about Katherina's death, and more importantly, remorse about how Katherina had been treated (Starkey, 2003:551). After all, Anne had once served the Queen as a Lady-in-Waiting. She had known Katherina, and may have genuinely liked her at one time. Now that Katherina was no longer a threat, she might have been able to embrace the remembrance of that past affection. While the King crowed his delight at the passing of his first Queen, his second Queen may have wondered if the same treatment was in store for her. Anne was pregnant again at the time, so she should have felt more secure, yet she must have noticed that Henry had grown erratic and strange. Did she fear this change was the result of his growing dissatisfaction with her? What if he turned on her as he had done to Katherina? Anne had no powerful nephew to aid her. She was helpless without Henry's protection. Did she have any inkling of the fate that was in store for her?

After Katherina's death Anne attempted to reconcile with Mary. As would be expected, she was soundly rebuffed by the grief-stricken and angry Princess. Even though the understandably bitter Mary had not appreciated her stepmother's gesture, Anne still tried to apprise Mary of how much danger she was in from her father's anger. The Queen wrote a letter to her aunt, Mrs. Anne Shelton, who was serving as Mary's de facto warden, and the letter was left (conveniently) for Mary to find. In it Anne stated:

> "My pleasure is that you seek to go no further to move the Lady Mary towards the King's grace, other than as he himself directed in his own words to her. What I have done myself has been more for charity than because the King or I care what course she takes, or whether she will change or not change her purpose. When I shall have a son, as soon I look to have, I know what then will come to her. Remembering the word of God, that we should do good to our enemies, I have wished to give her notice before the time, because by my daily experience I know the wisdom of the King to be such that he will not value her repentance or the cessation of her madness and unnatural obstinacy when she has no longer power to choose. She would acknowledge her errors and evil conscience by the law of God and the King if blind affection had not so sealed her eyes that she will not see but what she pleases. Mrs. Shelton, I beseech you, trouble not yourself to turn her from any of her wilful ways, for to me she can do neither good nor ill. Do your own duty towards her, following the King's commandment, as I am assured that you do and will do, and you shall find me your good lady, whatever comes." (Froude, 1891:388)

Anne was clearly exasperated by Mary's behavior, but was still benevolent enough to caution the young woman on her perilous position if the Queen's baby was the son Henry wanted.

Henry was not only changing mentally, he was also losing the brawny physique of his youth. Among people of Henry's era, forty was generally considered to be the start of 'old age' (Lipscomb, 2009:62-63). Regardless of the fact he had now reached the advanced age of forty-four, the King still insisted on jousting. On January 24, 1536 Henry's athletic prowess finally failed him. During one of the tournaments he held to celebrate Katherina's death, Henry was unhorsed. He was wearing full tournament armor that probably weighed 50 pounds or more, and his horse, which was also in full armor, reportedly fell on top of him. The horses they used in jousting were not small animals. Taking into account the amount of force that would have hit Henry, it is plain that his accident was a serious one, bad enough that the King was unconscious for more than two hours (Lipscomb, 2009:58).

Some people have theorized that he sustained brain damage in this jousting accident, and it was the resulting intracranial hemorrhage that cause his personality to alter so drastically. It is possible that a strong blow to the head, sustained during the accident, caused a blood clot that created intracranial pressure which then pushed his brain forward in his skull, squashing the frontal lobe against the inside of his forehead. The frontal lobe of the brain is considered to be the center of an individual's personality. Although an injury like this would not necessarily impair his motor functions, it could have caused serious psychological problems. Some symptoms of a brain injury are lethargy, difficulty in concentrating, memory issues, bad judgment, depression, irrationally moody behavior, emotional outbursts, insomnia, a low sex drive, and radical personality changes (Cifu and Caruso, 2010:52). The personality changes can be so severe that it is comparable to having schizophrenia.

Although such an injury could potentially be the cause of a personality change such as Henry's, he was already exhibiting signs of mental change *before* his accident. He was definitely becoming irascible as early as 1532, and he started his first judicial killing spree in 1535. Prior to 1535 he seldom executed one of his familiars, only pursuing such extreme measures if there was a clear and present danger to his throne. Yet, after 1535, he began executing a great number of people every year, even when the victims were among his family members and closest friends. It is possible that the jousting accident caused a brain injury that *exacerbated* the mental deterioration begun by McLeod syndrome. There is no medical reason why Henry could only have one ailment at a time.

In addition, the accident could have been precipitated by the muscular deterioration that is a consequence of McLeod syndrome. If the King's nerves and muscles had been sufficiently compromised by his illness, this could have slowed his once agile reflexes, making it much harder for him to remain on a horse while in full armor. Regardless of the reason for his accident, Henry's jousting days were over.

Anne miscarried a male fetus on January 29, just a few days after Henry's accident. This also happened to be the day of Katherina's insultingly small funeral (Lindsey, 1995:115). Anne was most likely into the second trimester when the fetus spontaneously aborted. In spite of continued speculation to the contrary, there is no real evidence that the fetus was deformed (Ives, 2004:297). The couple was, of course, distraught. Henry visited Anne in her chamber and lamented, "I see that God will not give me male children" (Ives, 2004:299). His comment understandably upset Anne, who told him that she had lost the baby because his fall from his horse had scared her so badly, and because he had broken her heart by loving other women

(Lipscomb, 2009:70). This was a completely reasonable explanation for miscarriage in this era (Cressy, 1997:46). It was also a brilliant argument by Anne, since it repositioned the miscarriage as the result of a shock, not as the Queen's personal failing, as well as getting in a telling blow against Henry's wandering fancy. A flash of the younger Henry reemerged after Anne's accusation that his actions had caused their misfortune. He was "much grieved," or ashamed that his behavior had caused Anne to miscarry, and stayed with the Queen for a while in order to comfort her (Walker, 2002:13).

Putting together the reproductive records of Henry's first two Queens, they had at least nine, and possibly even thirteen, pregnancies between them. It is blatantly obvious that they, and Henry, were fertile. Yet very few pregnancies ended successfully and only two of the babies who were born alive survived infancy. Given the relative rarity of this type of obstetrical history (even in the Tudor era, most pregnancies that carried to term produced children who lived for at least a few months; repeated stillbirths and neonatal deaths were uncommon) it seems likely that the King was the source of their troubles. If he was Kell positive, it would explain all the reproductive misfortune he and his wives endured. Perhaps if Anne hadn't been murdered she might have eventually been lucky and had more healthy children, provided that any of the potential offspring had received a Kell negative gene from Henry. Unfortunately, the King would behead his wife in the very near future and she would therefore never be given the chance to have more children.

Was the fact she lost a son in January the reason Henry killed Anne in May? It is a matter of great debate among historians. Certainly the miscarriage can be considered a strong motivation for the King to annul his marriage to Anne. Some historians think that he may have already been debating getting rid of her (Starkey, 2003:551). This argument certainly has merit. After Katherina's death, Charles V began extending diplomatic olive branches toward England. The Emperor made it clear that if Henry would set Anne aside and make a "fit" marriage, there would be a complete reconciliation between their realms (Froude, 1891:398). This would have been a strong inducement to cast off a Queen who may have begun to bore Henry. Furthermore, there was no son and no guarantee of a male heir in the near future. She was a commoner and had no powerful connections to give him aid. Anne was pro-French, while most of the English were in favor of an Imperial alliance. She was still very unpopular with the Catholics in his kingdom. He could replace her with a young and welcomed aristocrat from another country, who would be embraced by his people. Nevertheless, the King did not act like a man who was tired of his wife. Henry continued to vigorously fight to have Anne recognized as Queen by Charles V, and was thus still committed to his Queen just weeks before her death (Ives, 2004:300). Moreover, Henry was not about to back down from his decision to sever the English ties to the Catholic Church.

On April 25, 1536 the King wrote to his representatives at the Imperial court to inform them of the developments:

> "The Emperor's Ambassador has been with us at Greenwich with offers to renew the alliance, the conditions being that he would allow the Emperor to reconcile us with the Pope, that we will declare our daughter Mary legitimate and give her a place in the succession, that we will help him against the Turks, and

declare war against France should France invade Milan. Our answer was that the breach of amity came first from the Emperor himself. We gave him the Imperial crown when it lay with us to dispose of. We lent him money in his difficulties, etc. In return he has shown us nothing but ingratitude, stirring the Bishop of Rome to do us injury. If he will by express writing desire us to forget his unkind doings, or will declare that what we consider unkindness has been wrongly imputed to him, we will gladly embrace his overtures; but as we have sustained the wrong we will not be suitors for reconciliation. As to the Bishop of Rome, we have not proceeded on such slight grounds as we would revoke or alter any part of out doings, having laid our foundation on the Law of God, nature, and honesty, and established our work thereupon with the consent of the Estates of the Realm in open and high court of Parliament. A proposal has been made to us by the Bishop himself which we have not yet embraced, nor would it be expedient that a reconciliation should be compassed by any other means. We should not think the Emperor earnestly desired a reconciliation with us, if he desired us to alter anything for the satisfaction of the Bishop of Rome, our enemy. As to our daughter Mary, if she will submit to the laws we will acknowledge and use her as our daughter; but we will not be directed or pressed therein. It is as meet for us to order things here without search for foreign advice as for the Emperor to determine his affairs without our counsel. About the Turks we can come to no certain resolution; but if a reconciliation of the affairs of Christendom ensue, we will not fail to do our duty. Before we can treat of aid against the French

King the amity with the Emperor must first be renewed."
(Froude, 1891:410-411)

Was the King defending his break from Rome, and thus his marriage to Anne, simply from pride? Or did he still love her, and their shared adversity had merely strengthened his attachment to her? Did he still expect to have more children with the Queen? It was, after all, a reasonable assumption. She had proved herself to be fertile, in that she had produced a thriving daughter, and had gotten pregnant again easily. Considering the fact that at least half of all pregnancies miscarried during this era, her obstetrical difficulties were not *necessarily* considered unusual or insurmountable (Cressy, 1997:47). Neither Henry nor Anne could have known that he probably had Kell positive blood, which seriously lowered their chances of a healthy offspring. They had only been married for a little over three years, and she had already given him one healthy child, and was thought to have only lost the boy the King had hoped for due to the shock of his jousting accident, which would have been acknowledged as bad luck and proof of her love for Henry.

So, did Henry still love Anne, or was he already plotting her legal murder? There is a good chance that if McLeod syndrome had made him irrational and erratic, he would have alternated between grumbling about getting rid of Anne and declaring she was his Queen, depending on which mood he was in and who he was with.

One historian, Greg Walker, argues that Anne's downfall was actually due not to her miscarriages, but to some hasty words she said to one of the King's courtiers, a man named Henry Norris, at the end of April (Walker, 2002). If the King was suffering from paranoia induced by McLeod syndrome, then he could have turned violently and suddenly against Anne, and his abrupt anger could have been the result of a minor argument she had with Norris, as Walker has suggested. Anne was hot-tempered and often seems to have spoken without considering the consequences of her words. Her status as Queen was unlikely to have helped her learn discretion, except perhaps around her husband. One day in late April, the Queen spoke hastily while vexed, and it may have cost her everything. Anne asked Henry Norris, who was a groom of the stool and engaged to her cousin Madge Shelton, when he planned to wed. Norris hedged that he would wait just a bit longer. This irritated Anne. In her anger she told him he was looking for "dead men's shoes, for if ought came to the King but good, you would look to have me" (Walker, 2002:21). This was a major blunder. It was treason to even think about the death of the King, let alone to talk about whom his Queen might marry after his demise. Anne knew almost immediately that she had said something dangerous. She sent Norris to her chaplain, John Skyp, to swear she was faithful to the King, or "a good woman" (Lindsey, 1995:122).

    The theory that her conversation with Norris led to her execution has widespread support among historians, for good reasons. After all, Anne was on shaky ground; her enemies were awaiting an opportunity to dispose of her, and may have turned her hasty comment into her death warrant. The Catholic faction at court, which hated Anne with a passion, was always eager to drag her down. Henry had recently started to woo Jane Seymour, a member of a Catholic-supporting family, and the pro-Catholic courtiers hoped to use the King's mystifying lust for plain Jane to at least get Princess Mary reinstated in the line of succession, even if they could not overthrow Anne herself. The ranks of those enemies had grown and now included Thomas Cromwell, a former ally who had helped craft Henry's divorce from Katherina and was the King's current Chancellor of the Exchequer. Both the Queen and Cromwell were Protestants, but they had lately begun to differ on the direction the Reformation should take. This came to a head in a battle over the smaller monasteries. Cromwell, possibly motivated by religious hatred of Catholics and certainly by the desire to fill the King's coffers, wanted to destroy every monastery and confiscate their riches for the Crown. In contrast, Anne wanted them left intact and used to promote learning and produce scholars who would spread the Gospel throughout England (Starkey, 2003:554-558).

  Cromwell had enjoyed a ringside seat for Anne's destruction of Cardinal Wolsey. He was too wise to underestimate Anne, and knew she was a formidable obstacle in the way of his plans to line his pockets with a share of the expropriated monastic goods. Working under the timeless assumption that "the enemy of my enemy is my friend," Cromwell began to help the Catholic faction, and Jane Seymour, gain more of Henry's favor. Thus, when Anne told Norris he looked for "dead men's shoes," her enemies made sure that the news, on which they placed the worst possible interpretation, quickly reached the King's ear.

  The first real sign of trouble came when one of the Queen's musicians, Mark Smeaton, was arrested on the last day of April. He was of low rank, and the only one of the men accused of having sexual intercourse with Anne to confess to the crime. Some historians speculate that his low social status made him a target for torture. There were rumors in London that Smeaton had been "grievously racked" (Ives, 2004:326). If an interrogator is willing to seriously hurt someone, the accused will, almost 100% of the time, confess to anything. Smeaton never recanted his confession, but it is easy to understand why he would rather die a quick death by beheading than be tortured indefinitely, so his testimony remains questionable. Even if he had recanted, it wouldn't have saved Anne. By the time Anne was brought to trial it was clear to the whole court that the King who had loved her so fiercely now wanted her dead, and what Henry wanted, he got.

    The next major sign that Anne's end was approaching occurred the next afternoon, when the King questioned Henry Norris after a May Day tournament. The King apparently offered Norris a full pardon if he would confess, but Norris steadfastly maintained his innocence (Lipscomb, 2009:81). Norris had been one of Henry's closest friends for more than two decades. Therefore, Henry was determined to destroy his wife and a dear friend on the basis of a rumor concerning a single imprudent conversation. One would need to think of Henry as clinically paranoid to understand what would motivate him to do such a thing. Even if he wanted to cast Anne aside, he didn't need to judicially murder one of his most loyal friends to do it, so Norris' death is senseless. If Henry had McLeod syndrome, then he was possibly suffering from episodes of extreme paranoia. It is likely that it was the delusional paranoia that Henry was experiencing, when fed by the smallest morsel of doubt that Anne might want him gone, which caused Henry to develop a passionate and irrational hatred of her. It is almost certain that Cromwell, and her other powerful enemies, fostered the King's growing suspicions of her. What should have been a tempest in a teapot blew up into a hurricane, and Henry had Anne arrested on May 2.

It was reported, by Chapuys, that "On the evening of the day on which the Concubine was sent to the Tower, the Duke of Richmond went to his father to ask his blessing, according to the English custom. The King said, in tears, that he, and his sister the Princess, ought to thank God for having escaped the hands of that woman, who had planned to poison them" (Froude, 1891:418). He also seemed to believe, despite the ludicrousness of it, that Anne had betrayed him with more than a hundred men (Lindsey, 1995:128). The implausibility of her crimes did not matter anymore. Once the King had resolved to believe that Anne had betrayed him, he was willing to believe the worst of her, no matter how far-fetched the accusation.

Henry was not alone in this, however: the whole of Europe seemed to be enthralled by the scandal of Anne's fall, and the tales grew with the telling. The Imperial ambassador to the French court wrote that the King had actually caught Anne in bed with the royal organist (Froude, 1891:419). On May 13, John Husee, a friend of Lord and Lady Lisle, wrote them with the latest news from London about Anne's trial. To Lady Lisle he wrote,

> "Madame, I think verily if all the books and chronicles were totally revolved and to the uttermost persecuted and tried, which against women has been penned, contrived, and written since Adam and Eve, those same were, I think, verily nothing in comparison of that which hath been done and committed by Anne the Queen, which though I presume be not all things as it is now rumored, yet that which hath been by her confessed, and other offenders with her, by her own alluring, procurement, and instigation, is so abominable and detestable, that I am ashamed that any good woman

should give ear thereunto. I pray God give her grace to repent while she now liveth. I think not the contrary but she and all they shall suffer." (Froude, 1891:422-423)

Husee likewise sent a letter to Lord Lisle, declaring "Here are so many tales I cannot tell what to write. Some say young Weston shall scape, and some that none shall die but the Queen and her brother; others that Wyatt and Mr. Page are as like to suffer as the rest. If any escape, it will be young Weston, for whom importunate suit is made" (Froude, 1891:423).

Why were the King and his court so willing to believe such exaggerated and baseless accusations against the Queen? Even if McLeod syndrome had made Henry nearly insane with unreasonable distrust, why did other people glom on to the outlandish tales with such evident credulity and glee? The answer may lie in the era's conceptualization of witchcraft.

For the Tudors, witches were indisputably real. Witches were devil worshipers who performed monstrous acts for no logical reason or motivation other than the enjoyment of doing evil. Moreover, like all devil worshipers, witches were also thought to have extreme sexual appetites that induced them to experiment with homosexuality and bestiality (Warnicke, 1991:192-193). The men who had been accused of having sex with Anne were all either well-known Romeos, or were accused of having committed sodomy, or were perhaps a little too loyal to the Queen for Cromwell's comfort (Starkey, 2003:572; Denny, 2006:288). Court rumors had already suggested that the King had begun to suspect he had been "seduced by witchcraft" into marriage with Anne (Starkey, 2003:551). If Henry could be convinced that his wife was truly a witch, then any calumny could be laid at her door. Absolute belief in witches would also encourage others, both noblemen and commoners, to be willing to entertain the notion that Anne wanted to poison her stepchildren, had indulged in wanton carnality with a variety of lovers, and had even enjoyed an incestuous affair with her brother. Everyone "knew" witches did these sorts of things (Warnicke, 1991:4). If Anne was a witch, then she must have done these things, and if she had done these things, then she must be a witch. As is usual with public opinion, there was an assumption that she would not have been accused of such awful behavior unless she had done something to arouse suspicion. Anne's enemies must have rejoiced in this perfect catch 22 that assured her destruction.

Some historians believe the accusations of witchcraft were a result of her miscarriage of a malformed fetus, since the birth of a malformed baby was considered by the people of the Tudor era to be God's punishment for the "unnatural" sexual acts practiced by devil worshipers (Warnicke, 1991:195). However, most historians disagree, and think that the idea that Anne was a witch spurred the rumor her stillborn son was deformed, rather than the reverse, since there was no such accusation made at the time of the miscarriage (Loades, 2009:125). While evidence lies primarily with the academics who believe the Queen's loss was normal, and only rendered 'monstrous' after the fact, there may have been some kernel of truth in the rumors. If the Queen's pregnancy was lost as result of her body rejecting a Kell positive fetus, then the fetus may have been swollen and discolored. Given the ease with which "false memories" can be created after the fact in order to fit in with more recently acquired knowledge, the accusations of witchcraft could have caused details about the fetus's color or size to be reconfigured as a deformity (Comer, 2004:179).

After a brief trial whose outcome was clearly predetermined, the Queen and the innocent men (including her own brother) with whom she was formally accused of having committed adultery, were all put to death. The men were executed on May 17, and Anne's reaction to Smeaton's death, the only one of the accused to have pleaded guilty, is a good indicator of her innocence. On hearing he had died without recanting his confession she said, "Did he not acquit me of the infamy he has laid on me? Alas, I fear his soul will suffer for it!" (Froude, 1891:430). The Queen herself was likewise legally murdered on May 19.

Even ambassador Chapuys, whose animosity toward and loathing of Anne is well-documented, thought she was innocent of the crimes of which she was accused (Starkey, 2003:578). Anne herself swore, on her hope of salvation, both before and after receiving the sacrament, that she was innocent (Lipscomb, 2009:86). There have been strong arguments made that Thomas Cromwell, not Henry, was the bloodthirsty plotter who orchestrated the deaths of Anne Boleyn and many other court members, while the King himself was a victim of Cromwell's duplicity (Fraser, 1994:245-246). However, even if Cromwell was feeding Henry false information in the hopes of inspiring Henry's wrath toward particular individuals, such as Anne Boleyn and her friends, it still required the King to turn abruptly and forcibly against those he had loved, which indicates that Henry was experiencing paranoia and excessive mood swings. Thus, Cromwell might have been exploiting the King's weaknesses, but that hardly makes Henry blameless. However, utilizing a King's paranoia could be a dangerous tactic, and Cromwell himself was later executed as a result of Henry's irrational fury.

Henry was already engaged to his third wife, Jane Seymour, before Anne had been dead twenty-four hours, and they were married a mere eleven days later. Jane is one of the most ambiguous of Henry's wives, since her personality is frequently obscured by that of the more powerful people who surrounded her. She seemed to have very little will of her own, and appeared, with few exceptions, to be content to do as she was told by the authority figures in her life. It has frequently been charged that, on the orders of her family and their allies at court, she set out to make herself pleasing to the King once he showed his interest in her (Starkey, 2003:590). All of her coy refusals of Henry's pursuit lack the authenticity of Anne's noncompliance. Anne left court and avoided Henry. In contrast, Jane stayed at court, right under the King's nose. In March, when Henry sent her a bag of money and a personal letter, she threw herself down on her knees and begged the messenger to remind the King that she was "without reproach" and if he wanted to give her money he could give it as a wedding gift when she had made "some honorable match" (Starkey, 2003:589). She had just declared, in the coded language of chivalry, that she was virgin who was saving herself for marriage. Henry was entranced by the idea of having a new maiden to woo.

For many people, including most historians, the biggest mystery about Jane Seymour is what Henry found so captivating about her in the first place. There is no telling what goes on in the human heart, and why people fall in love, but Kings, like other powerful and wealthy people, typically pick an exceptionally attractive or charismatic person to partner them. Thanks to the extreme talent of Henry's portrait artist, Hans Holbein, we have a very good idea of what Jane looked like. Holbein's portraits are thought to have been almost photographic in their accuracy. Jane had, at best, mediocre looks. An ungenerous person could reasonably call her plain, or even ugly. Neither was she witty. She had nothing to recommend her. She wasn't beautiful, and she wasn't smart. She could in fairness be described as 'drab'. Hers was not a powerful family. When the King married her he gained "one brother-in-law who bore the name of Smith, and another whose grandfather was a blacksmith at Putney" (Ives, 2004:4). After years of living with the sizzle of Anne Boleyn, what was it about Jane that attracted the King?

Maybe Jane's charm came from the fact she was not beautiful, not smart, not vibrant, and not from a powerful family. Henry seemed to be well and truly tired of strong, beautiful women who outsmarted him (Starkey, 20003:585). Jane's passive and nearly nonexistent personality must have been a gentle rain on the scorched earth of his ego. She would never best him in a mental battle. Other men would never covet her for her comeliness. She would never match her will to his, since she was amazingly docile. She would never take attention away from Henry. The King would always shine in comparison with her. If, by any chance, he became weary of her, leaving her would be simple, since her relatives were all completely dependent on Henry's graces. She was as exciting, and as comforting, as a glass of warm milk.

Chapuys was certainly not impressed with her. Although he hated Anne fiercely and might therefore have been expected to be kinder when describing any woman who supplanted her in Henry's affections, his reports on Jane were scathing. According to the sharp-eyed ambassador she had little personal beauty, being pale to the point that she looked washed out and faded, and she was "not a woman of great wit" (Starkey, 2003:584). The cynically-minded Chapuys, familiar with the attitudes and behaviors of the English court, seriously doubted she was really a virgin. In fact, Jane was so obviously lacking in attractions that the ambassador speculated that perhaps she had a "fine *enigme*," which was a euphemism for the mysterious and secret place between a woman's legs, that was the source of the King's infatuation (Starkey, 2003:584). However, it turns out that Henry could not have been snared by her fine *enigme* because Chapuys later reported that Jane "had been well taught … that she must by no means comply with the King's wishes except by way of marriage" (Starkey, 2003:590). Henry liked her 'maidenly modesty' so well that he promised not to be with her without a chaperone present. Although still married to Anne, he had Jane installed in Cromwell's apartments in the palace. Cromwell, ever eager to please his King and undermine Anne, moved elsewhere. Now all that Jane, and more importantly her male family members, had to do was wait and see if Henry would divorce Anne on some pretext.

Perhaps Jane's family wasn't expecting Henry to kill Anne, but it clearly did not trouble them when he did so. It did not seem to bother Jane much, either. She waited complacently while another woman was destroyed to make way for her. It could be said that Anne had done the same thing, but that is inaccurate. She fled from Henry until it became clear that he was looking for an annulment and had separated from Katherina; only then did she submit to his courtship. Anne and Henry were very much married when Jane let him woo her, so much so that Anne was pregnant. Neither Jane, nor her ambitious family, seems to have been worried that she might be marrying a psychopath. Henry was King. That was all that mattered.

The average English subject was repulsed by Jane and Henry's behavior. Many of them may not have liked Anne, but Henry's rush to marry, and Jane's willingness to become Henry's consort so soon after Anne's death, looked deeply suspicious. Henry was forced to write Jane and warn her that "a ballad made lately of great derision against us" was circulating (Lindsey, 1995:124). The disapproval of the commoners was certainly not going to stop Henry, but he did care about his reputation enough that he had his Chancellor publicly plead with him, on behalf of the nobility, to remarry for the good of the country (Lindsey, 1995:130). Graciously, the King agreed to wed again, for the sake of his beloved Kingdom. He and Jane married quietly, one could almost say furtively, on May 30, 1536. Anne had been dead for a little over a week.

The year was only half over, but Henry had already had his first wife die, he had almost been killed himself in a jousting accident, his second Queen had miscarried a longed-for boy, he had beheaded that Queen, and he had married a third wife. Moreover, there was also a great deal of political turmoil, both in England and in Europe. The new Anglican Church was starting to take shape, and many loyal Catholics were unhappy that so many aspects of their religion were being forcibly taken from them. Protestants were no more content since the religious beliefs that Henry embraced, and thus regarded as true and worthy enough to be believed by all of his people, were a strange mishmash of Reformation ideas and deep-rooted Catholic dogma. His rejection of the Pope, and his stubborn adherence to the doctrine that the body and blood of Jesus were *literally* present in the communion bread and wine once a priest had blessed it, drove both Catholics and Protestants insane. This would later allow Henry to execute Catholics who maintained that the Pope was the head of the Church, while also allowing him to kill Protestants for believing that the body and blood of Christ was a metaphor, not a real presence in the communion host. Henry's parliament had also passed Cromwell's pet legislation, the Act for the Dissolution of Monasteries, which was tearing apart religious Orders and transferring their wealth into to the royal treasury, as well as to those the King wished to reward (Scarisbrick, 1970:337-338).

Henry had become draconian and intractable in his beliefs. Even though Katherina was dead, he was still adamant that the invalidity of their marriage be universally acknowledged. When Anne Boleyn was executed on May 19, 1536, Mary thought she was safe, and that her father would allow her to return to court and to his affections (Starkey, 2003:597). As recently as February, Henry had displayed a real hope that his daughter would come around to his way of thinking, and as a sign of his continued affection for her, the King sent his eldest daughter a crucifix that had belonged to Katherina, which was believed to contain a piece of the True Cross (Froude, 1891:395-396). With Katherina's death, Henry appeared to believe that Mary would have no other loyalties except to himself. It was the common expectation of the time period that a child would obey his or her parents, regardless of circumstances. Even as an adult, a child was considered to be 'naturally' obedient to their mother and father. Mary's rebellion against her father was somewhat mitigated by her loyalty to her mother, but after Katherina's demise Henry would have probably assumed that Mary would now be compliant to his wishes, even if they were contrary to her best interests. To do otherwise would mark Mary as having an appalling disregard for God's ordained hierarchy.

Mary, however, spurned these overtures as much as she was able. From a modern perspective it seems very reasonable for an adult daughter to be unwilling to kowtow to the father who wanted to declare her the illegitimate product of incest, especially so soon after the loss of her mother. Nevertheless, people in the sixteenth century would have seen the situation rather differently. Mary's refusal to do her father's bidding was, pure and simple, a rebellion against both a parent and the Crown, and such grave offenses merited harsh retribution. Yet even by the norms of the time, it would have been considered an obscenity for a father to have his child killed. Unfortunately for Mary, the King was now mentally unstable enough to set in motion plans to try her, his own daughter, for treason if she refused to agree with his claims about her mother and his right to be supreme head of the Church (Scarisbrick, 1970:353). The King was actually threatening to behead his own child because she maintained he had been married to her mother. This aggression toward his oldest daughter appears to be ample evidence of a decisive emotional shift and a loss of reason. But was his wrath completely the result of his erratic temper? Although his reactions were, in all likelihood, affected by McLeod syndrome, Henry was nevertheless probably right to fear his eldest daughter and to be angry with her.

Less than a year before Anne's death, Mary had been actively encouraging Charles V to invade England to restore Katherina to the throne and to punish the heresy of Protestantism. Mary wrote to Chapuys, imploring him to tell the Emperor that,

"The condition of things is worse than wretched. The realm will fall into ruin unless his majesty, for the service of God, the welfare of Christendom, the honor of the King my father, and compassion for the afflicted souls in this country, will take pity on us and apply the remedy. [The remedy of which she spoke was the invasion of England by a foreign power to force the monarch, Henry VIII, to submit to the judgement of the Pope.] This I hope and feel assured he will do if he is rightly informed of what is taking place … The whole truth cannot be conveyed in letters. I would, therefore, have you dispatch one of your own people to inform him of everything, and to supplicate him on the part of the Queen my mother and myself for the honor of God and for other respects to attend to and provide for us. In so acting he will accomplish a service most agreeable to almighty God." (Froude, 1891:355)

Calling for her father's overthrow was clearly insubordination that would have sent anyone else posthaste to the chopping block.

Aware that Mary was in real danger, Chapuys frantically tried to figure a way to smuggle her out of the country if needs be, in a desperate attempt to save her from being murdered by her father (Scarisbrick, 1970:352). Chapuys begged her to submit to the King's will, promising that no one would hold her accountable for what she had to do under duress, and that the Pope would later absolve her (Scarisbrick, 1970:352-353). Under extreme pressure, Mary finally gave in and capitulated to her father's demands. She had to sign a document that, in essence, declared that she agreed with the premise that she was the illegitimate product of incest, since her mother had been her father's sister-in-law, and that she also denied the Pope was the head of the Church, which was a repudiation of one of the keystones of her Catholic faith. She always felt guilty she had succumbed to Henry's threats, and never forgave herself for signing it, even though it saved her life (Lindsey, 1995:132).

Once Mary had surrendered to his will, the King welcomed her back to court. Although the King's umbrage toward his daughter may have been explained by her treasonous actions, his irrational behavior when she returned to his court calls for a different explanation. When Mary presented herself to him, Henry embraced her and told her that she should no longer be worried, since his relentless persecution of her was all Anne Boleyn's fault (Lindsey, 1995:133). He made this claim in spite of the fact that when Henry forced Mary to sign the document declaring herself illegitimate, Anne had already been dead for weeks! Then the King, who had apparently forgotten that he was the main author of the threats against Mary, turned to his courtiers and accusingly said, "Some of you were desirous that I should put this jewel to death," whereupon Jane, in one of the few acts that make her at all memorable, told the King, "That had been a great pity, to have lost your chiefest jewel in England" (Lindsey, 1995:133).

Jane was always kind to Mary. It would be more to her credit if her family hadn't been Catholic sympathizers who doubtlessly directed her to help Mary in every way she could. It is impossible to tell when Jane was doing something for herself or when she was following orders. If she had gone out of her way to be nice to Elizabeth, or to improve Elizabeth's situation, even though Jane's faction loathed the little girl as the daughter of a

Protestant usurper, it would be clearer that her charity to Mary was simply the impulse of a kind heart.

Henry's children were a great source of worry, both to the King and the kingdom. The lack of a son born in lawful wedlock meant there was no suitable heir. Henry had recently declared both Mary and Elizabeth illegitimate, so the King had only illegitimate children from which to choose his successor. His illegitimate son, Henry Fitzroy, had a chance of inheriting the throne, due to a strong preference for male rulers, whereas an illegitimate daughter would almost certainly not have the same opportunity to ascend the throne. However, the King had grown so paranoid that he was afraid to declare any of his children his heir, in case they tried to claim their inheritance before it was due. It is unclear whether or not he was thinking specifically of Fitzroy, who was an intelligent and strapping young man, much as Henry himself had been. Did the King fear his son would depose him, if given a chance? Did he fear the Catholic loyalists would depose him in favor of Mary? In the King's extreme state of paranoia, everyone may have been suspected.

Fear that his son would depose him was soon needless. Henry Fitzroy died on July 23, 1536 from what has commonly been reported to have been tuberculosis (Lipscomb, 2009:93). There had been no sign that Fitzroy had been unwell in the spring, so it was more likely to have been a relatively quick illness rather than the long, drawn-out decline suffered by those with tuberculosis. The King ordered the Duke of Norfolk to bury the young man in secret, since the succession was in grave doubt, and Fitzroy had been a possible heir. The King may have wished to keep Fitzroy's death a secret until he had impregnated the new Queen, so that the loss of one potential male heir was offset by the possible arrival of another. Whatever the King's motives,

Norfolk tried to follow Henry's directions. Fitzroy's body was covered in straw and transported on a wagon, which was followed only by two mourners, then quietly interred at Thetford Priory (Lipscomb, 2009:94). When the King heard the details about the small funeral he flew into a rage. In one of the lightening-fast shifts of mood that can occur with sufferers of McLeod syndrome, Henry seems to have forgotten that he himself had ordered a furtive burial and became furious that his son had not been given a more lavish service. He threatened to imprison Norfolk in the Tower, much to the dumbfounded Duke's fear and consternation (Erickson, 1980:272). Norfolk first wrote his will, because Henry's anger was not conducive to longevity, and then he wrote to Cromwell to insist that he was not a traitor. Fortunately for Norfolk, the King's vexation waned, and the Duke was spared.

  Norfolk was not the only one of Henry's subjects who was exasperated and afraid. Many of the English commoners were very unhappy with their King as well. His untoward behavior, combined the prevailing bad harvests in England that year, fueled the supposition that Henry was the "mouldwarp" of ancient prophecy (Lipscomb, 1936:148). Although the word looks sinister, it is actually just the older English word for "mole". Many people believed that Merlin, the wizard who had served King Arthur in the myths and legends, had prophesied there would one day be an evil King, whom would be known as the mouldwarp. The mouldwarp would seem good at first, but then be revealed as an agent of the Devil. Rumors of what would happen to England under the rule of the mouldwarp spread throughout the kingdom. People said that Henry was cursed by God, and that Charles V would invade and drive Henry off the throne. Henry was called a fool, and a beast, and was accused of being a lustful buffoon who only wanted food and women (Scarisbrick, 1970:354). The King who was once hailed as a flower of chivalry was now scorned as a profoundly unpopular and gross tyrant.

Even the new Queen was suffering from Henry's authoritarianism. Jane made the error of pleading with Henry to leave at least a few of the religious Orders intact. She was, after all, a Catholic. More importantly, her family and court allies were also Catholic. This might have been an attempt by the anti-Reformation faction at court to see if she could sway the King, in the hopes that she would be able to intercede for the traditional faith in other matters as well. If so, it failed spectacularly. Instead of being influenced by the Queen, Henry told his bride of just a few months not to interfere in his affairs, and reminded her of what had happened to the last Queen who had been so foolish as to meddle in affairs of state (Starkey, 2003:602). This is usually interpreted as a reference to Anne Boleyn, whom he had so recently executed. However, it could have meant either Katherina or Anne, since both had been women of strong opinions who were now no longer Queen. Regardless of which ex-wife Henry was referring to, it is plain that Jane's position was far from secure. Henry did not appear to be as enamored of her as he had been of Anne Boleyn. He and Jane had been wedded only a week when Henry, after meeting two new lovely ladies at court, expressed regret that he had not met them before his nuptials (Starkey, 2003:602). How the Queen felt about Henry's brusque treatment of her will remain a mystery, but it would be very surprising if she were not frightened and intimidated by her husband, which is hardly a recipe for marital felicity.

Although the King could bully his spouse into

submission, his tremendously unpopular laws and actions were making it very difficult for him to keep his other subjects compliant. The north of England broke out in rebellion. The most famous rebellion is the one centered in Yorkshire, called the Pilgrimage of Grace. There were a plethora of reasons, religious and economic, why the King's subjects would want to revolt, but a significant motivation for the uprising was simply that a great many Englishmen and women preferred to remain Catholic and were disgusted by Henry's marital transgressions. The rebels, led by Robert Aske, wanted some of the changes forced upon them to be abolished. They wanted, among other things, for the monasteries be restored, for Mary to be recognized as Henry's legitimate heir, and they especially wanted the officials whom they saw as responsible for the enforced alteration of their religious life to be punished (Starkey, 2003:602).

    Henry's crown was in real jeopardy. The rebels could have won; they certainly had enough popular support. The only reason why they did not oust Henry and place Mary on the throne was that their leader, Robert Aske, didn't really want to topple the King. It troubled his conscience to overthrow God's anointed sovereign. When the King invited Aske to London to discuss the rebellion, Aske did so with the utmost trust that Henry would be willing to address the needs of his people. Henry, who was completely disingenuous, agreed that they should have justice. He promised a general pardon, among other things. Aske, believing the King, disbanded his followers and told them the problems would be addressed. The noted historian, J. J. Scarisbrick wrote in his book *Henry VIII* that "Aske was Henry's most loyal, as well as most critical subject" and it was Aske's "faith that the King would not break his word nor wreak bloody revenge which really defeated the Pilgrimage" (1968:342).

    The physical discomfort that Henry was suffering doubtlessly exacerbated his irritability and poor policy-making decisions. Henry was plagued with chronic and agonising ulcers on his legs. It is suspected that Henry had osteomyelitis (Ives, 2004:190), or venous ulcers (Keynes, 2007:180-1). Osteomyelitis is an infection of the bone. Some of the symptoms of this kind of infection are bone pain, swelling that can occur in just a small spot or that can puff up a patient's whole leg, redness near the affected area, fever, nausea, chills, sweating, and in general you feel like you are death on toast. Osteomyelitis can last the patient's whole life if not properly treated. Henry probably got it when he fell off a horse while hunting or jousting. If he hurt his bone, even if it hadn't been broken, the injury could have caused it to become infected. When osteomyelitis is severe, little splinters of bone can break away and start working up through the muscle and into the skin, creating a large and painful weeping ulcer. These ulcers are disgustingly smelly as well as agonising for the patient. Henry must have hated them, not just because of the discomfort, but also because having a pus-oozing sore didn't jibe with the athletic youth that he once was. In a time period where good legs were a hallmark of male beauty, having ulcerous limbs would have seriously detracted from the King's attractiveness. Henry, even when he was still a good-natured young man, was vain. How emotionally painful those blights on his legs must have been for him!

    With the King deteriorating rapidly, both physically and emotionally, what could Tudor medicine do to heal him or alleviate his symptoms?

Chapter Five
Tudor Medicine: Horoscopes, Humors, Herbs, and Health

The medical professionals at Henry's court would have included physicians, apothecaries, and surgeons. The very best healers in England would all have been at the King's disposal for any of his medical requirements. However, during the first four decades of his life he had little need for any of them, except in small matters. The King was a robust and vigorous athlete until he was middle-aged. His constitution did not begin its serious downturn until after his fortieth birthday, but his deterioration from that point on was fairly rapid. By the time the King was forty-five, he was decidedly unhealthy.

There have been numerous theories about the health and fertility of Henry VIII, from many academic quarters. The King had certainly developed enough health problems after middle age to warrant multiple theories, so it is hardly surprising his illnesses have prompted so much speculation. A few of the most documented of his problems were obesity, ulcers on his legs, depression, mood swings, loss of mobility, recurrent headaches, fevers, and a general malaise. Doctors, amateur historical sleuths, and professional historians have all tried to figure out why Henry was in such poor health. Some of these theories are extremely plausible, and others have been thoroughly disproved.

Surprisingly, theories about the King's health seldom link Henry's illnesses to his Queens' obstetrical problems; the majority of the hypotheses focus only on his *personal* physical ailments. Only a very few recognize that his health issues may be the root cause of his checkered reproductive history. In contrast, the theory that Henry had a Kell positive blood type and resulting McLeod's syndrome explains both his difficulty in begetting an heir and his extreme psychological alteration in middle age. Although it is a reasonable possibility that a Kell positive blood type was the cause of Henry's reproductive problems, and the concurrent McLeod syndrome caused many of his other disorders, it is doubtful that they can be blamed for *everything* that went wrong with Henry's health. Any additional conditions or illnesses would not mean that he was not also Kell positive, or that he did not also have McLeod syndrome. People can certainly have more than one ailment at a time. While there is strong evidence that Henry became mentally unbalanced and paranoid after the age of forty because of McLeod syndrome, it probably did not cause his fevers and leg ulcers. The King's leg ulcers were most likely the result of osteomyelitis, as was discussed in the previous chapter, and had nothing to do with his blood type.

Another of the ailments which Henry might have had is myxedema (Murphy, 2001). Myxedema is a byproduct of hypothyroidism, a medical condition in which the thyroid gland doesn't make enough of the hormones it is supposed to produce. Myxedema could certainly have caused some of Henry's physical problems, including weight gain, constipation, muscle pains, and possibly even impotence. The presence of this illness would also explain a few of his psychological ailments, such as his chronic depression, mental abstractions, irritability, and mood instability. Nevertheless, it does not explain why his Queens had so much trouble bringing a baby to full term. Furthermore, Henry did not appear to show other signs of myxedema, such as brittle nails, intolerance of the cold, slurred speech, or a goiter. It is also the case that myxedema is more common in women over fifty years of age than it is in men. Although this does not mean a younger man could *not* have this condition, it does lower the *likelihood* that he had it.

Another disease involving the endocrine system, called Cushing's syndrome, has been offered by historian Robert Hutchinson as a possible cause of Henry VIII's mental and emotional deterioration (Hutchinson, 2005). Henry indisputably displayed some of the symptoms of Cushing's syndrome, including rapid weight gain, particularly in the torso and face, muscle weakness that especially affects the hips and shoulders, slower healing of wounds and skin abrasions, fatigue, headaches, and probably impotence. It could have also caused some of his psychological disturbances, including depression, paranoia and anxiety. Additionally, he may have experienced the growth of a "buffalo hump" and a "moon face", where fat pads along the collarbone and on the back of the neck swell to unnatural proportions. Hutchinson also argues that Cushing's syndrome could explain the ulcers on Henry's legs: Cushing's can cause hypercalcemia, which is an elevated level of calcium in the blood that can lead to the death of the skin tissue, also known as skin necrosis. However, hypercalcemia is a rare complication of Cushing's, so this seems unlikely. Furthermore, Cushing's syndrome cannot account for Henry's reproductive history before his fourth marriage. Neither does it explain why his personality altered *before* he began to put on so much additional weight. A diagnosis of Cushing's syndrome could not completely solve the puzzle of Henry VIII's reproductive history and behavioral change.

It is also possible that Henry had type II diabetes. Unlike type I (juvenile) diabetes, type II diabetes usually presents in adulthood and is associated with being overweight, although thin people certainly develop it as well. The King became monumentally obese in the last dozen years of his life, so he certainly had one of the risk factors for acquiring Type II diabetes. However, while Type II diabetes might provide an explanation for some aspects of his midlife personality change, infertility and ill health, it cannot explain why his wives suffered so many fetal losses. When male patients with Type II diabetes have fertility problems it is often because of erectile dysfunction and/or low sperm count, which could explain the lack of pregnancies for his fifth and sixth wives, but not the reproductive troubles of his first and second wives. A man cannot get a pair of women pregnant as frequently as Henry did his first two Queens if he suffers from either chronic erectile dysfunction or low sperm quality. It is true that defects in the sperm of male diabetics, caused by varying blood glucose levels, can decrease the chances of conception, or increase the chances of miscarriage, but miscarriages caused by defective sperm are typically the spontaneous abortion of a 'nonviable' embryo. An embryo conceived with defective sperm would not have progressed to the fetal stage, let alone survived to the third trimester of pregnancy. This is quite unlike the reproductive issues experienced by Henry's first two Queens: Katherina and Anne conceived fairly quickly and miscarried late in their pregnancies. Thus, Type II diabetes does not fit as the cause of Henry's reproductive troubles.

      Given the vast number of Henry's symptoms, how is it possible to determine which might have been caused by McLeod's syndrome? Complicating the diagnosis is the fact that people did not record whether Henry ever showed certain physical signs of McLeod syndrome, such as dystonia (sustained muscle contractions which may be seen as tics, cramps or spasms) or hyperkinesia (an abnormal increase in muscle activity, such as twitching or hyperactivity). Nevertheless, that does not necessarily mean they were not present. If the tics were small then people may not have noticed them or supposed them worth recording in their letters or journals. In addition, it is impossible to confirm that he had an enlarged liver or abnormalities of his blood cells, which are often the clearest signs of McLeod syndrome. Tudor medicine was not sophisticated enough to permit the kinds of tests that would have identified these symptoms. It is obvious that the *physical* symptoms which might be attributed to McLeod syndrome, when taken alone, can not conclusively prove that Henry had the disease. Instead, the theory that Henry had McLeod syndrome largely relies on his radical personality shift to make a convincing argument that McLeod syndrome had affected his brain.

McLeod syndrome almost always starts when a person turns forty, then continues to get worse as the patient ages. This description fits Henry's slow but progressive personality alteration like a glove. The only problem is that even Henry's psychological symptoms have a co-morbidity of sorts, in that it is hard to conclusively demonstrate where McLeod syndrome began and the King's natural egocentrism left off. Even when he was perfectly sane Henry was extremely self-centered and self-aggrandizing. Everybody in the Tudor court knew the quickest way to worm oneself into Henry's favor was to agree with everything he said and act like he was the best athlete, the best warrior, the most chivalrous knight, and the most handsome monarch in Christendom. The King was deeply religious, but he really seemed to think that God agreed with him on every topic, and that the Almighty wanted his happiness above all other earthly things. Lacey Baldwin Smith points out that when Henry became enamored of Anne Boleyn it was "clear he thought the deity might be successfully petitioned to act the role of a divine pimp" (1982:121), and prayed that God would inspire Anne to want to satisfy the royal lust.

    As knowledgeable and learned as the King was, in some ways his theological beliefs were very childlike. Henry apparently treated religion like it was a magic spell; if he said the right prayer with the right incense at the right shrine then, presto! God would give him what he wanted. Henry was also a hypochondriac, and feared illness the way a small tot fears the possible bogeyman in his closet. In fact, the King's personality as a whole often seems to be that of a man-child. He had the wants, needs, and intelligence of a grown man, but the same intense yearning and tantrum-throwing tendencies as a young boy. On the one hand he loved people and gave them gifts with the sweet generosity of an easy-going youngster; on the other hand, if he did not get what he wanted he assumed that someone had done something wrong and ought to be punished. Since he seemed to feel Heaven was always on his side, the person spoiling his plans could not be God, but it was open season on his courtiers to discover who was the 'cause' of Henry's unhappiness. Like any overindulged tyke, his sense of entitlement was astounding.

After his fortieth birthday it appears that he shifted from being a good-natured but overly pampered and occasionally bratty man into a cruel tyrant, and by the time he hit his fifties he had transformed into a completely psychopathic despot.

How can one distinguish between the King's innate narcissistic tendencies and his changed mental state after McLeod syndrome had begun? It is possible by looking at the motivations for his actions before and after the illness changed him. Henry did not lose his intelligence to McLeod syndrome; he lost his ability to reason. His illness caused Henry to be increasingly paranoid, depressed, and gripped by strange mental fluctuations. It was the paranoia that was the most dangerous to the people around Henry. Although the term paranoia is bandied about in everyday conversation, in its true clinical manifestation paranoia causes anxiety and fear strong enough to engender delusions. The fear, anxiety, and delusions then provoke the patient to exhibit irrational, or even violent, behavior. One minute Henry would be fine, then a fit of paranoia would grab him, making him think someone was 'out to get him', and the result would be that innocent someone losing his or her head.

The King also seemed to have more temper tantrums and less impulse control as he aged and the disease progressed. The last thing anyone wants is an absolute monarch who gets angry easily and orders a beheading during an aberrant snit. Even before the onset of McLeod syndrome Henry was often stubborn, and once he had reached a decision, he seldom changed his mind. It's true that he would indulge in fads and had the occasional wild idea when he was younger, like any normal person, but in general he was a slow, methodical, and cagey thinker. His circumspection was a good thing, considering that it was nearly *impossible* to change his mind. Cardinal Wolsey cautioned that once Henry got an idea into his head, nothing in heaven or on earth could get it out again (Smith, 1982:107). In important matters, such as policy, the King tended to make his decisions especially cautiously, so that he felt secure in the path he had chosen. Unfortunately, even as Henry became completely irrational, he remained stubborn. During the last dozen or so years of his life he would doggedly cling to a decision he had made hastily and made from the perspective of a paranoid mental state.

    It was even worse whenever the King did not display a pigheaded determination to maintain an erroneous course of action. As he aged he grew quick-tempered and erratic, demanding things be done and then becoming enraged when his orders were carried out. As Henry approached his fifties, the once steadfast King became dangerously capricious. His escalating paranoia meant that the people who dealt with him the most were in constant jeopardy. Eventually his paranoia grew to the point he trusted no one, not even his closest advisors and oldest friends. It was noticeable to Charles de Marillac, the French ambassador to Henry's court, who wrote to Francis I in 1541 that the King had begun to have "a sinister opinion of some of his chief men" (Fraser, 1994:336). Henry's courtiers knew something was very wrong with their ruler, and they were justifiably afraid of his rage. Lord Montague (Henry Pole), a member of Henry's court who was eventually executed unjustly at the behest of his monarch, said that Henry would "be out of his wits one day ... for when he came into his chamber he would look angrily, and after fall to fighting" (Erickson, 1980:288). Imagine what it must have been like to be at the mercy of such a person, knowing that a madman had absolute control over your life.

If the King were alive today, there are technological advances that would offer him some relief from his illnesses, but in his own time his medical options were much more limited. How would the Tudor physicians have dealt with their monarch's mysterious maladies?

Tudor medical practices seem extraordinarily odd when compared to modern Western ideas about science and health. For one thing, there was no understanding of germ theory or 'medicine' as we know it. Instead, health was thought to be influenced by four mysterious liquids in the body, called humors, which could be thrown out of balance and cause "dis-ease". These humors were believed to be affected by the foods a person ate, what they drank, and the seasons. Moreover, the movement of celestial bodies, like the sun, moon, and stars, were assumed to have direct ramifications on people's health, because they affected the body's humors. Today 31% of Americans still believe in astrology and another 18% are at least willing to entertain the idea that it may be accurate; the vast majority of the scientific community, however, regards it as nothing more than superstition. In the Tudor era, though, astrology was still considered to be a science and was a crucial part of a medical education. In fact, the average Tudor physician was as much an astrologer as he was a doctor.

How did these theories and beliefs about astrology and humors come to influence 16th-century English medicine so heavily? Oddly enough, Tudor medical philosophy was a gift of the ancient Greeks, by way of the Muslim occupation of the Iberian Peninsula.

Medicine, and the Greek ideologies of science and philosophy, came back into Western Europe via Islamic scholars. The Islamic era began in 622, and shortly thereafter the religion, and the military and political dominance of Arabic Muslims, began to spread rapidly throughout the Middle East. Between 637 and 670 Islamic forces conquered Syria, Egypt, Persia, and large sections of Northwest Africa (Freely, 2010:72). While Jewish and Christian minorities in Islamic countries were discriminated against in some ways, for the most part they were tolerated rather than persecuted, and were even able to excel in certain professions, like medicine (Khanbaghi, 2006:15-16). Eventually a medical school was established in the Judeo-Christian intellectual stronghold of Gundishapur (in what is now Iran), which achieved great renown and produced doctors who were well respected throughout the Middle East (Khanbaghi, 2006:15).

Jewish and Christians doctors became so famous for their medical skills during the early centuries of Islamic growth that when Al-Mansur, a prominent Arab Caliph, became ill he requested the services of the head of the medical school in Gundishapur, a Christian physician named Gurgis ibn Buhtisu (Freely, 2010:75). Fortunately, Buhtisu was able to heal the ailing Caliph. It is probably safe to assume that Gurgis used astrology to help him find a cure for Al-Mansur. Medical tradition in Gundishapur borrowed from Persian, Greek, and possibly even Chinese and Indian medical theories, all of which were often influenced by astrological thinking (Frye, 1975:397). Persians were skilled astronomers and this no doubt shaped their medical practice since a horoscope is supposed to show predictions of an individual's health (Wright, 2002: 108-109). What is known for certain is that it was around this time that Al-Mansur became a devoted follower of astrology, which obviously provides circumstantial evidence that the Caliph believed astrological information played a part in his recovery.

    Al-Mansur was not the first Muslim to embrace the Zodiac. Islamic culture had previously been exposed to astrology via Persian, Indian, and even Roman authors (North, 2008:187). However, it was Al-Mansur's interest in astrology which *legitimized* it as a science (Gutas, 1998:33). Al-Mansur was keen to learn more about the subject of astrology. To this end, the Caliph requested copies of Greek mathematical writings from the Byzantine Emperor, who was a very powerful Christian in possession of these texts. In a display of interfaith Christian-Muslim cooperation, one that would be wonderful if emulated in today's political climate, the Emperor generously sent him Euclid's works (Gutas, 1998:32-33).

    It is almost impossible to overestimate the value of this gift. Euclid is acknowledged as one of the most influential people in the history of mathematics, and as the "Father of Geometry" his concepts are still used today, over 2300 years after he first formulated his theories (Smith, 1958:103-107). The worth of the information he had received was not lost on Al-Mansur, who initiated a "translation movement" that brought other Greek works of physics and philosophy, as well as the intellectual writings of Christian and Jewish savants, into use in the Islamic world (Gutas, 1998:31-33). Al-Mansur had Gurgis ibn Buhtisu, whom the Caliph had established as the court physician, personally translate many Greek medical texts into Arabic (Khanbaghi, 2006:47). Many other Christians were also recruited from Gundishapur to help with the translation of both Syrian and Greek works for the edification of Islamic academics (Kaser, 2010:137). The Caliph's desire for learning and education was both eager and multifaceted. In an effort to acquire as much knowledge as possible, Al-Mansur even had Indian ambassadors translate astrological and astronomical works from Sanskrit into Arabic for use by his court scholars (North 2008:188). The importance of Al-Mansur's dissemination of multicultural sciences and beliefs cannot be exaggerated in terms of its effect on the Islamic world.

In his quest for deeper astrological understanding, Al-Mansur obtained the services of a Jewish astrologer named Mash'allah, whose writing on astrology and astronomy were so influential that he was even referred to centuries later by Copernicus (Freely, 2010:74). On the advice of Mash'allah and other astrologers, Al-Mansur founded the city of Baghdad, which became the epicenter of learning, science, and culture for Islamic scholars (Freely, 2010:72-74). Thus, it was a combination of enthusiasm for astrology and the help of Judeo-Christian scholars which allowed Al-Mansur to spark an intellectual awakening in the Islamic world more than 700 years before a similar Renaissance would occur in Europe.

The Muslim world's knowledge of science and astrology came to Western Europe following the Muslim conquest and occupation of south-western parts of the continent. During the seventh and eighth centuries Islamic rulers sent their troops into Europe, taking almost the whole of what is now Spain and advancing into France until they were halted in 732 by Charles Martel at the Battle of Tours (Freely, 2010:72). For several hundred years, Muslims controlled most of the Iberian Peninsula (Chejne, 1983:2). Under Islamic auspices, the city of Toledo, which is located in present day Spain, became a prominent center for the study of literature and the sciences (Al-Andalusi et al, 1996:xi-xii). A lot of this knowledge was reintroduced to the West when Spaniards captured Toledo from its Islamic rulers in 1085, during the early years of the Christian reconquest of the Iberian Peninsula.

There was a great hunger in medieval Europe for the new and rediscovered Islamic knowledge, including the sciences of physics, astronomy, mathematics, medicine, philosophy, and logic (Shora, 2008:156). In the 1140s a scholar named Gerard of Cremona made his way to Toledo to study the materials Islamic scholars had stored and translated. After he arrived in Toledo, Gerard met and befriended an Islamic scholar, Ghalib the Mozarab. Together they began the work of translating Arabic texts into Latin, which was the language of European academics. First, Ghalib would translate the Islamic writings into Castilian Spanish, which Gerard would then copy into Latin (Shora, 2008:156). Among the many writings they translated were the works of Greek scientists and philosophers. In this manner, the works of Ptolemy, Euclid, Aristotle, and Plato were reintroduced to Western Europe (Shora, 2008:156). Gerard and Ghalib collaborated on eighty-eight translations of Arabic works, and thus provided the intellectual tinder for the fire of the twelfth-century Renaissance (Shora, 2008:156).

One of the most significant medical texts in medieval and Renaissance Europe, the Persian physician Avicenna's *Canon of Medicine*, was among the writings translated into Latin and disseminated by Gerard of Cremona (Deming, 2010:134). Equally influential was Gerard's translation of the work of the Greek physician, Galen, who maintained that human health was based on the four liquid elements, or humors, in the body (Glick, 2005:191). Galen was considered the "Prince of Physicians" and was such a revered medical authority that to contradict him bordered on sacrilege (Lutz, 2002:47). For example, when Dr. John Geynes, a member of the London College of Physicians, dared to openly disagreed with Galen in 1559 he was vilified by his fellows and forced to recant (Ball, 2006:56). European medicine would be based on Galen's theories until the discovery of the microscope in the seventeenth century and the advent of modern germ theory.

      Islamic and ancient Greek medical theories were not just coming into Western Europe via the Iberian Peninsula. Scientific theories were also flowing along a more direct route from Northern Africa, across the Mediterranean, and into Italy. Two of the most prominent centers for the introduction of Greek and Arabic scholarship were Salerno and Sicily, which are both located in what is now modern day Italy, and thus close to Islamic North Africa (Shora, 2008:157). Salerno was already an established center of medical learning in Europe by the 10th century, renowned for producing both male practitioners and famous female physicians known as the "women of Salerno" (Siraisi, 1990:13). Prior to the infusion of Greek and Arabic ideas, writings about the Salernite physicians emphasized that they were skilled at healing, but not necessarily well versed in the theoretical aspects of medicine (Siraisi, 1990:13). With the introduction of Greco/Arabic knowledge, physicians became more focused on the academic aspects of their work, transforming the science of medicine in Europe. As a result of the conceptual shift that transformed medicine from a skill or healing art into a science, women were driven out of public practice and medicine became an almost exclusively masculine profession. However, the actual nitty-gritty work of nursing the sick continued to be done by women since housewives or other older women in the family were the ones expected to look after ill or injured members of the household (Sim, 1996:89).

Astrology and medicine were almost inextricably entwined in the new medical ideology learned from the texts translated out of Arabic. Healing was assumed to be effected by bringing the humors back into balance, and it was conjectured that there could be no internal harmony of the various fluids unless the physician could read the various astrological forces acting on his patient (Dixon, 2004:10). Catholic Christians in Europe, unlike their Eastern Christian counterparts, had vigorously suppressed astrology for hundreds of years based on the writings of St. Augustine, who viewed astrology as demonic and asserted that it threatened the individual's free-will (North, 2008:122). This created a quandary for Western physicians: how could Christian doctors use astrology to cure people and not be guilty of committing a grave sin? Would the Church allow this new medicine to be practiced, or would physicians be condemned as heretics?

Daniel of Morley went to study under Gerard of Cremona in Toledo, in the hopes of finding the answer to the dilemma that Christians faced when studying and using the sciences of the pagan ancient Greeks. Daniel believed he had found a solution for Christian scholars and doctors. He wrote that pagan knowledge was "like the gold that the Jews had borrowed from the Egyptians before the exodus; it was not holy, but it was useful" (French, 1994:31). This idea increased the acceptability of astrology and other pagan concepts as legitimate areas of study for Christians, but Church consent was patchy and uncertain for centuries. In the early 1300s Italian astrologer Cecco d'Ascoli, who lectured at the University of Bologna, was burned at the stake, most likely for his belief in astrological determinism (Siraisi, 1990:68). However, other astrologers who were his contemporaries were more lucky. This may have been because they asserted that the planets were instruments of God's will, an idea found in Dante's famous early 14th century epic poem, *The Divine Comedy* (North, 2008:249).

Astrology had also crossed over into wider popular culture, as evinced by the fact that Chaucer, who was another famous 14th century author, wove allegories of astrological lore into his famous opus, *The Canterbury Tales* (North, 2008:251). Clearly his readers were expected to be conversant enough with astrology to understand them. Astrology was becoming mainstream and was practically required for all academic study, but practitioners still had to be careful not to come into conflict with Church doctrines. By the time Henry VIII was born, astrology and humoral theory were well and truly entrenched in English medicine, and both concepts had become commonplace knowledge within English culture.

The humoral theory of medicine seems simple, at first glance. The human body was presumed to be made up of four elements, earth, air, water, and fire, each element having its own substances and attributes (Dixon, 2004:10). Earth was cold and dry, air was warm and wet, water was cold and wet, and fire was hot and dry. Each element made a different kind of humor, or fluid, in the body. Earth made black bile, air made blood, water made phlegm, and fire made yellow bile. People's health depended on the mixtures of humors inside of them, which doctors often referred to as a patient's "complexion", since the coloration of the skin was believed to be an invaluable diagnostic tool (Sim, 2005:80-84).

A doctor was expected to diagnose a patient's humoral balance based on their appearance, their astrological horoscope, and their urine. For example, the physician would diagnose an individual with an excess yellow bile if his or her physical and emotional attributes of indicated a "choleric complexion", such as "leanness of body; costiveness [constipation]; hair black or dark auburn, curled; visage and skin red as fire or sallow; little sleep; dreams of fire, fighting or anger; wit sharp and quick; hardy and fighting; pulse swift and strange; urine highly coloured and clear; voice sharp" (Sim, 1997:81-82).

A physician's goal was to help people achieve "eukrasia", or the perfect balance of humors for perfect health (Albala, 2002:49). Humoral balance was achieved when certain ratios of blood to other humors were met. Ideally a person would only have ¼ as much phlegm as blood, only 1/16 as much yellow bile as blood, and a mere 1/64 as much black bile as blood (Albala, 2002:49). If an individual had more blood than was ideal when compared to the other humors, then they were deemed to be sanguine, which was manifested as an easy-going and jolly personality. If the imbalance was too much in favor of blood, the sanguine person would become impulsive and pleasure-seeking to the point of shamelessness. If an individual had too much phlegm, he or she was classified as phlegmatic, and thus calm and kind with the risk of becoming slothful or idle. Too much yellow bile made a person choleric, which was more problematic than having too much blood or phlegm, since choleric individuals were easily irritated and prone to aggression and sharp mood swings. Those with too much black bile were considered melancholy, or introverted, thoughtful, and prone to depression. Individuals with humoral balance were an ideal mix of all attributes, with no particular risk of immoderate forays into any particular emotion or behavior.

Humors were seen not as static, but as in constant need of adjustment. There were several ways in which the physician hoped to balance his patient's humors. The *Tancuinum Sanitatis*, a medical textbook written by an Arab physician, Ibn Botlan, prior to 1100 AD and copied into Latin for use by European scholars, was a very influential work that discussed the "six things that are necessary for every man in the daily preservation of his health" (Arano, 1976: Preface). Ibn Botlan wrote that,

> "The first is the treatment of air, which concerns the heart. The second is the right use of food and drinks. The third is the correct use of movement and rest. The fourth is the problem of prohibition of the body from sleep, or excessive wakefulness. The fifth is the correct use of elimination and retention of the humours. The sixth is the regulating of the person by moderating joy, anger, fear, and distress." (Arano. 1976:Preface)

Rather than being simplistic, humoral medical theories were immensely complex. Of course, modern understandings of health and the body render most of these ideas null and void, but that does not mean that the physicians of this era did not study their craft carefully, or that it was easy to learn. A physician was expected to not only deal with the symptoms of illness, but also have knowledge of all the variables which could potentially affect his patient before creating a unique course of treatment for that person's ailment. Just looking at the various factors physicians were expected to take into account is enough to demonstrate the labyrinth that Tudor doctors had to negotiate.

Food was a particularly potent form of medicine for the Tudors. Avicenna wrote that when something was eaten it was first turned into "chyle" in the stomach, and was then transported to the liver where it was 'cooked' into blood, phlegm, black bile, and yellow bile (Siraisi, 1990:106). Since everything a person ate or drank were aspects of an element, a person's diet would strongly affect the balance of their humors. The belief that some foods have a medicinal value has in fact made a comeback in recent years, albeit in a modified form, and with a very different scientific basis. Tudor physicians often tried to ensure that the people under their care ate 'healthy' foods, or foods that would make "good juice and good blood" in the body (Sim, 1997:86). These would not necessarily be the same foods that are considered 'healthy' by the modern medical community, but there were some dietary recommendations that are still accepted today. For example, sixteenth-century doctors, just like many of their modern counterparts, found that people who drank a moderate amount of red wine enjoyed better health (Sim, 1997:86). Other foods that were judged to be particularly beneficial during Henry's reign included fresh bread made with pure flour, the meat of pigeons or red deer, good beer or ale that was approximately 6 days old, and milk with sugar or mint leaves added (Sim, 1997:86). Many foods were only 'good' if eaten by a person of the correct complexion. Pork was good for people with very robust systems, yet was thought to cause 'raw humors' in individuals of lesser hardiness, while chicken was good for the more delicate individual but might ignite in the belly of a stronger person, leading to 'burnt' or 'adust' humors (Albala, 2002:49). Some foods, such as most raw fruits and vegetables, were supposed to be too hard to digest and were only good when they were properly cooked. Other foods that were considered likely to make "ill juice", or bad blood, if eaten too frequently were hard cheeses, mutton or swan butchered when the animal was too old, black puddings, and all uncooked herbs except for lettuce, borage and chicory (Sim, 1997:86).

Adding to the intricacy of the humors was the fact that the element of a food could change depending on the season or the method of preparation (Sim, 2005:85-87). For instance, it was believed that meat that was boiled was 'cooler' than meat that had been roasted (Albala, 2002:129-130). Moreover, foods were conceptualized as having different 'degrees' of a humor, so that both quinces and mulberries were cold and dry, but quinces were of the second degree and mulberries edged up against the third degree (Sim, 2005:85). Millet was cold and dry to the second degree, and could help "dry out superfluous humors" (Arano, 1976:XXII). Bread made from wheat was deemed to be the most nutritious, while rye bread made "weak" blood, and barley bread was too "cold" to be very healthy (Adamson, 2004:3).

Unsurprisingly, breads made of coarser and lesser grains were considered acceptable for the poor and the working classes, while the wealthy and the nobility were presumed to need finer breads just to survive, since their bodies were inherently more delicate and their stomachs could not digest anything but the best. This did not mean, however, that lesser grains were never ingested by the upper classes. Because barley was 'cold', it was administered to feverish patients in the form of barley water, which was made by boiling pearl barley and then straining it to retain only the broth (Adamson, 2004:3). Barley water, sweetened with fruit and sugar, is still served in England to this day. Those who could afford it ate rice cooked in milk while they were convalescing, since it was supposed to fortify and increase one's blood (Adamson, 2004:4).

    Emotions, called 'passions' were also understood to affect the temperature of the body and the humors; grief and envy were cold, dry passions that would cause the heart to shrink, while love and joy were warm, moist passions that would expand the heart (Dixon, 2004:11). It was accepted that someone who experienced a great shock, or grief, or unrequited love, would manifest physical symptoms of their emotional state. This conceptualization of the emotions as feelings which could affect one's health meant that mental and physical illness were both potentially the result of some internal imbalance or the natural result of a some personal upheaval, and allowed both the patient and the physician to see the mind and body as a unified whole (Simon, 2008:182). A patient suffering from depression could be thought of as having too much black bile in his body, which in turn gave him other physical symptoms of illness, or it could be that some ailment had caused his levels of black bile to rise, which had caused him to feel despondent. Only a doctor could figure out the chicken-or-the-egg question of which came first, the passion or the humoral imbalance. Regardless of the origin of the illness, a person suffering from mental anguish should avoid food that would exacerbate unhappy passions, such as rabbit meat, garlic, red wine, leeks, and onions (Woodford, 2004:46-47).

It was also recommended that people change their diets in order to adjust their bodies to the seasonal effects of the weather. In summer the diet should emphasize cooling foods, like lettuce and lamb, while in winter people were cautioned to eat foods that would heat them up on frosty days, such as beef and pork, served with warm drinks and a final course of pears and cheese (Adamson, 2004:213). Sauces served with foods in warm weather should be made with cooling ingredients, such as rosewater, lemon and other citrus juices, or vinegar, with hot spices, such as mustard, ginger, pepper, cinnamon, and cloves being reserved to flavor foods during the colder months (Bober, 2001:242).

Some humoral theory lingers in the cultural consciousness, since even today some flavors are associated with certain seasons or seasonal events. For instance, foods traditionally served during fall and winter holidays are usually liberally flavored with "warm" spices. Pumpkin pie and hot mulled apple cider are both redolent of the cinnamon, cloves, and nutmeg they are infused with, while Christmas is often linked in the public mind with gingerbread men and gingerbread houses. In contrast, lemonade, which is simply water flavored with lemon juice and sugar, is considered a wonderfully refreshing beverage for summertime.

A person's humors were also thought to vary according to nationality. The Spanish and Italians were more 'hot-blooded' than the English or the Dutch, and doctors had to adjust their humors accordingly; vinegar was regarded as a delightfully cooling condiment for Italians' digestion while hot spices were best for the chilly English (Albala, 2002:128-129). Henry often blamed the "hot Spanish blood" of his first wife for her resistance to their divorce and the obstinacy of their daughter,

Mary (Edwards, 2011:36; Starkey, 2003:517). The medieval belief that the Spanish were a hot-blooded race was also echoed by the King of France, who complained, after he was forced to marry a Spanish princess as part of a peace treaty with Charles V, that his new wife was "very hot in bed and desireth to be too much embraced" (Starkey, 2003:458).

Age was also a factor in humoral medical theory. Children were presumed to be hot and moist, and as a person aged he or she would become more hot and dry, before finally turning cold and dry with the onset of old age (Sim, 2005:84). Children and adolescents were reckoned to be impossible to actually bring into "eukrasia", or humoral balance, because of their excessive wetness and heat, qualities that became particularly intense during puberty and then gradually became more manageable as the cold and dry aspects of maturity readjusted the individual's internal climate (Shepard, 2006:56).

Men and women were also believed to have inherently different humors. Women were the 'colder' gender, which made them less rational, but more compassionate than men (Schaus, 2006:309). The medical problem represented by gender was a matter of great interest to Tudor physicians. Reproduction was largely mysterious and misunderstood, apart from the very obvious relationship between intercourse and procreation. Much of the prevailing wisdom about gynecology and obstetrics relied not on anatomical dissection or observation, but instead, like all other matters of health, depended on the writings of the ancient Greeks, particularly Galen. Galen surmised that the reason women were not men was because their colder natures had prevented them from extruding their genitalia before their birth. Galen conceptualized the vagina as an inverted, inside-out penis still trapped in the body, while the ovaries were feminine testicles and the uterus was the equivalent of the scrotum (Thompson, 199:34). Women were also known to produce 'seed', or semen, and if they went without sex, especially if they were accustomed to coitus and then had to go without it (as in the case of widows), it was imagined that the build up and spoiling of their seed could cause them to become hysterical (Thompson, 1999:34-35). Both Galen and the Islamic physician Avicenna recommended masturbation in order to prevent a buildup of "superfluities", and while men were thought to be naturally handy at this task, some women, particularly virgins, might require the assistance of a midwife who would stimulate them to orgasm as a method of preventing ill-health from sexual frustration (Bullough, 1996:58). This was in direct conflict with the Church's stance on masturbation as a sin. However, solitary masturbation was the least serious offence in the hierarchy of sexual misdeeds, so it probably didn't generate much punishment for the penitent Christian who confessed it to his or her priest (Brundage, 1990:174). Moreover, the cost of the sin had to be weighed against the cost that refraining from sin would have on one's health, which doubtlessly provided a reason to indulge in the minor spiritual infraction now and then.

Galen also believed that a woman's seed was necessary to reproduction, and that if a woman did not achieve an orgasm during sexual intercourse, there could be no pregnancy (Kandeel, 2007:6). This had some clear advantages for women. Obviously husbands would have been very interested in making sure their wives enjoyed the sex act, since female pleasure was required in order to produce an heir, so women would have been given their due attention in the bedroom. However, it has left a lingering belief that pregnancy cannot result from rape (Constantine, 2006:1-2).

These ideas about women were accepted without question by the scientific and medical community for hundreds of years. Galen's theory was one of the strongest rationales used to bolster the belief that women were inferior to men; since men had been strong and 'hot' enough to have been able to successfully produce a penis and testicles they were clearly and without question better than women (Thompson, 1999:34). Aristotle's writings further cemented European opinions of women as the inferior sex, since he argued that women were deformed, or mutilated, males and were thus inherently monsters (Hartel, 1993:93). This was also in line with the teachings of the Church, which insisted that because Eve had tempted Adam to sin all women were also prone to embracing evil (especially lust) and leading their masculine superiors astray (Schaus, 2006:267).

In light of medieval theories about gender, is it really surprising that Henry VIII was afraid to leave his throne to a female heir? After all, no matter how much he loved a daughter, or how smart she was, she was still a 'monster' who was weaker and less logical than the men of her court. How could a woman, by nature a 'mutilated man' and who was furthermore cursed by the sins of Eve, rule England? Moreover, from both a medical and social standpoint the act of producing a male heir was a crucial part of kingship. Not only did a man need to be a good lover to get a woman pregnant, it was also assumed that a man's sperm directly reflected his own strength and virility. Strong men would make strong sperm, which would beget male babies, while weaker men made weak sperm that produced daughters, or worse -- no offspring at all. Powerful men who were able to satisfy their wives' carnal appetites were thus able to produce many sons (Kandeel, 2007:6). If the King had only daughters, then QED he was not powerful. He was not manly. It was possible he was weak, and could therefore be overthrown by a mightier rival.

Tudor physicians were aware of sperm's social importance, as well as its importance in reproduction, and could give medical advice on how to invigorate and enhance the supply of semen. For example, turnips were credited with the ability to bolster sperm production, and were best when eaten "stewed twice and consumed with very fat meats" (Arano, 1976:XXIII). Onions were also believed to increase the amount of semen a man produced, while garlic, leeks, and asparagus were all conjectured to increase the sex drive (Adamson, 2004:6-11).

Clearly, in the medical ideology of the Tudor era, food played a crucial role in health. More recently, it has been suggested that food played a significant role in causing some of the many problems Henry faced during his reign. About twenty years ago historian Susan Maclean Kybett (1989) suggested that Henry VIII had land-bound scurvy because the foods he usually ate lacked, or were extremely low in, vitamin C. She argues his low levels of vitamin C would have accounted for his mood swings and physical deterioration, and for the reproductive troubles that plagued his wives. However, there are several significant problems with the scurvy hypothesis, including the fact that for the wealthy there was a year-round availability of foods rich in vitamin C. Moreover, doctors emphasized the need to eat citrus fruits, such as oranges and lemons, in order to maintain a proper humoral balance, so these foodstuffs would have been consumed whenever possible by anyone who could afford them (Adamson, 2004:227). In general, even moderately wealthy people consumed a fair amount of vitamin C, if not from exotic fruits like lemons, then from produce commonly grown in England. For example, the Tudors were fond of desserts made of gooseberries, which have a significant amount of vitamin C in them. Better yet, they frequently put currants in meat dishes and desserts, and just one cup of black European currants contains 338% of the recommended daily amount of vitamin C. There is also evidence that people ate fruits throughout the winter months, as well as in summer. For example, it was considered medically sound for a meal to end with pears, which are a decent source of vitamin C, during wintry weather.

In light of the fact that medical wisdom of the time postulated that an individual's diet was one of the principal influences on a person's humors, it can safely be assumed the King's food intake was of particular concern to his staff of royal doctors. For example, when Henry was feeling ill or out of sorts his physicians often stuffed him with rhubarb (Smith, 1982:12). A cup of chopped rhubarb has a significant amount of vitamin K in it and is a reasonably good source of vitamin C. Modern clinical trials have indicated that English rhubarb may fight cancer, lower cholesterol, act as a laxative, as well as having anti-inflammatory effects (Tillotson et al, 2001:190-192). Therefore, rhubarb might have alleviated some of the King's chronic complaints. Just because sixteenth-century doctors could not explain *why* something was good for the patient in a way that is credible according to modern science does not mean that they were too ignorant to observe that it was effective in restoring health. If nothing else, the fiber in rhubarb would have provided the King with some relief from his persistent constipation.

Food was not the only medicine available to the Tudors, of course. While some remedies, like ground up animal parts or charms, were probably useless or even harmful, herbal medicine might have been more efficacious than has previously been thought. Garlic, which was plentiful and therefore cheap, was accepted as such a potent medicinal herb that it became known as "the poor man's physic" (Wilson, 1991:361). Scientific research has shown that garlic does indeed have many medical applications, since it is a natural antibiotic, anti-fungal agent, and kills intestinal parasites, among other things (Block, 2010). In contrast, there is no evidence that some of the medical charms, such as hanging a peony root around your neck to ward off epilepsy, might have actually worked (Jones, 2008:175).

    There were two sources of helpful herbs. First, there was the housewife's garden. Part of a housewife's 'job' was to treat any illness or infirmity her family experienced. Doctors were expensive and relatively rare, so most people were treated at home by their wife, mother, or other older female relative. It was so common for women to be healers that the English government stepped in to prevent them from encroaching on the trade of male physicians. In 1512 a law was passed to keep unauthorized people, such as "women that boldly and customarily take upon them great cures and things of great difficulty", from practicing medicine, but in 1542 this law was softened to allow women to dispense medical aid, provided they did not compete with "real" doctors by requesting a fee for their services (Sim, 1996:88-89). Most women would have had a small garden so that they could cultivate herbs which had both culinary and medicinal properties. The second source of herbal remedies was the local apothecary. Apothecaries were the pharmacists of the Tudor world. They would make "simples" by taking herbs and preparing them by drying, distillation, or extracting the oil from them, and would use the simples to create compounds called "Galenicals", which were considered sophisticated medicine (Porter, 1999:190-191).

Although the products are very different, apothecary shops were, in many ways, much like modern pharmacies. If you pop into your local pharmacy you can find "over the counter" medicines, and prescription medicines that are only dispensed on the orders of a physician. Unlike today, there was nothing to stop the apothecary from creating and dispensing his own cures, but he also filled a doctor's 'prescriptions' just like his modern counterpart (Given-Wilson, 1996:96). Physicians would diagnose disease and recommend a medication, called a "physic" for a patient, but often the apothecary would be the one who actually concocted the remedy, since such mundane labor would probably be seen as unworthy of a doctor's talents. The apothecary also sold things, like rosewater and spices, that were understood to have medical properties but were used so frequently that pharmacists dispensed them directly to customers, much as hydrogen peroxide or aspirin are available today (Given-Wilson, 1996:96).

Sugar was also supplied by the local apothecary. It was considered both a 'spice' and a 'medicine' in the Tudor world. It was believed that sugar could cure everything from headaches to childbirth pains, and it became so ubiquitous in pharmacies that the phrase "like an apothecary without sugar" became a way of saying that something was useless (Feltoe, 1991:13). Since sugar was known to be both tasty and to possess amazing curative powers, it was used liberally in both food preparation and medicines. Often apothecaries sold medical candies which were sugar syrups or pastes that were mixed with things like spices, nuts, berries, or fruits, which were presumed to aid in digestion and to provide health benefits inherent in the ingredients themselves (Richardson, 2003:165-166).

Food and herbs were tangible aspects of Tudor medicine, but there were also astrological ailments that a physician needed to address. To deal with astrologically-based ailments the physician needed to be able to cast a patient's horoscope, in order to ensure an accurate diagnosis. Medical authorities were united in their belief that "everything relating to times, the air, and waters, and complexions, and diseases is changed by the motion of the planets" (Siraisi, 1990:123). Even the herbal cures a doctor prescribed, as well as much of the patient's diet, were incorporated into medical astrology theories, since plants were presumed to be under the influence of certain heavenly bodies (Voigts, 2008:31).

A patient's astrological ills would have been hard for a physician to treat. Even today, it is very difficult to move things around in the solar system. For one thing, there are no convenient ways to grasp most planets. For another, it's a real challenge to find oven mitts large enough to grasp the sun. The best a Tudor physician could do was to recommend the patient ingest food and medicine which might counteract the effects of the celestial events.

Astrology was somewhat different during the Tudor era than from the kind of astrology practiced now. While there were 12 houses of the Zodiac, just as today, there are planets used in modern astrology that had not yet been discovered in the 16th century. Astrologers would plot the five known planets -- Mercury, Mars, Venus, Jupiter, and Saturn -- as well as the locations of the sun and moon, within each of the twelve houses of the Zodiac at the time an individual was born. This would create a 'natal chart' or horoscope, which could be used to diagnose a patient's illness or give a prognosis of their health outcomes. For example, Saturn was the planet that exerted the strongest forces on the earth element, and was thus likely to influence a melancholic disposition if prominent in a person's horoscope, while the moon was associated with water, and thus phlegm and the phlegmatic personality traits (Dixon and Weisberg, 2004:10). Moreover, Mars and Saturn were considered to be very negative influences, and were called the "Infortunes" (French, 1994:42). If the Infortunes were in the wrong aspect to the moon when the patient became ill then they were thought to cause serious illness, or even predict death (French, 1994:42).

The physicians of the Tudor time period believed that the macrocosmic was reflected in the microcosmic (French 1994:47). In other words, what was occurring in the heavens was also occurring at the level of the human body. Therefore the patient's horoscope, and the planetary influences, could also be aligned with the parts of the body affected by the houses of the Zodiac. Each house of the Zodiac ruled different body parts, and this was frequently illustrated in medical texts by the Zodiac Man.

(See Image on page 201)

Zodiac Man
This image of L'Homme Zodiacal was published between 1411
and 1416 in Très Riches Heures du Duc de Berry

The Zodiac Man showed only the major correlations between the heavens and the body, since the the astrological signs were presumed to control more aspects of health than was easily seen in the illustration. For example, Aquarius was believed to "rule" the ankles, calves, tibia and fibula, which is clear from a quick glance at the Zodiac Man, but Aquarius was also understood to affect the patient's airways, or 'breath'. Since there were only five known planets, the signs had to "share" ruling celestial bodies, but the influences on health would differ depending on which house the shared planet was positioned in. Venus ruled both Libra and Taurus, but Libra was surmised to be an influence on the kidneys and urine, while Taurus affected the neck and shoulders. To make matters more complex, Libra was regarded as a "co-ruler" of the skin, along with Capricorn. Capricorn was also accepted as the ruler of the knees, the skeletal system, and all its joints.

What about Cancer, the sign under which Henry VIII was born? Cancer is ruled by the moon, is the cardinal (or first) water sign of the Zodiac, and was considered cold and moist by nature. Cancer was thought to rule the thoracic organs, with the exception of the heart, which was in Leo's bailiwick. Any imbalance in Henry's humors would, in theory, cause problems in the organs ruled by his natal sign. Thus, Henry's physicians would have contextually situated his digestive issues and constipation within the natural vulnerabilities of his birth sign. Furthermore, his increasingly bad temper and headaches would be ascribed to the fact that the moon, which affected his emotional landscape, was in the volatile house of Aries.

Doctors needed to be fairly competent astronomers so they could keep track of the celestial movements that would affect their patients. They needed to be able to tell where every planet was in each house of the Zodiac not only at the time of the patient's birth, but also at the onset of the patient's illness. Physicians especially needed to know how the planets and the astrological houses affected the three main parts of their patient's horoscope, the ascendant, sun sign, and moon sign, as well as the major "nodes", which are mathematical points based on the relative positions of the sun, moon, and planets in the natal chart. Doctors would then combine the astrological information with their diagnosis of an individual's humors, and try to formulate treatments or lifestyle modifications that would restore, or keep, their patient in good health.

So what would a Tudor physician do for a patient who was born under the sun sign Aries and was suffering from anxiety and a fever? The ill person would be diagnosed as having too much choler, and would be prescribed "bed rest, light clothing (preferably colored white or light blue), cooling baths, and the juice of citrus fruits, aimed at medicating the patient's hot, dry conditions with cold, wet applications, much as a bucket of water douses a fire. Such an approach might well have done the trick, though early physicians knew nothing of the health benefits of vitamin C" (Dixon, 2004:10).

There were other types of professional health care during the Tudor era, not just physician/astrologers and apothecaries. While doctors were charged with helping the patient maintain health and fight disease, surgeons, or barber-surgeons, were responsible for external medical needs, such as the treatments of burns, cuts, boils, bites, stings, and anything else which might require cutting into the body or patching up a wound (Wear, 2000:210-211). Surgeons and barber-surgeons, no matter how skilled, were generally felt to be inferior to physicians, since physicians were trained at prestigious universities and surgeons tended to learn their trade as apprentices (Watson, 2009:6). However, the common idea that Tudor surgeons were fools who indulged in unbridled bloodletting is undeserved. Surgeons had strict rules and procedures for why, how, and when a patient should be bled, and actively discouraged bloodletting for children, pregnant women, the elderly, and the very ill (Whitney, 2004:100).

Lacking modern medical knowledge and equipment, the physicians of Henry's court would have sought the answers to the King's medical problems in his natal horoscope and by examining the tell-tale signs of his humoral imbalance. Although they could do nothing about the movement of the stars, whenever Henry was ill his royal physicians would have tried to put his humors back into balance by using dietary recommendations and herbal remedies, and would have employed surgeons for more extreme measures, such as blood-letting or the cauterization of his leg ulcers. All of their efforts would be increasingly futile during the last decade of Henry's reign.

Chapter Six
Tyranny Unchecked: Rebellion, Birth, Death, and a New Bride

The King's physical and mental illnesses continued to worsen over time and Henry apparently crossed some sort of internal Rubicon in 1536, after which it seems that he was no longer able to fight the impulses of his paranoia. His reign from this point onward is marked by ever-increasing oppression and unreasonableness. No one was safe. It is around this time that the King gained his reputation of employing a crab-like attack, in that he appeared to be moving diagonally toward one goal, then diagonally toward another goal, yet all the while moving forward toward his real object without anyone being the wiser until it was too late to divert him. He appears to have enjoyed making his chosen victim feel special and safe right up until the moment before he struck, frequently catching the person so off guard that they were utterly shocked when they were imprisoned in the Tower, where there was every likelihood that they were doomed to be executed for crimes that existed mainly in Henry's mind.

It has frequently been assumed he behaved this way from a combination of a cruel pleasure in trapping his victims and for ruthless political advantages. However, this villainous and backstabbing behavior may not have been a vicious caprice on the King's part, or part of any larger stratagem. Henry may not even have been fully aware of what he was doing. The mental symptoms of McLeod syndrome would have made him sincerely erratic. Thus, he was not *planning* on killing the person that he had just raised within the peerage or conferred special favors on, it just so happened that soon after their elevation or reward his paranoia inspired him to believe his former favourite was actually a mortal enemy to be eliminated. Another argument against the idea that Henry plotted the annihilation of his victims for sadistic reasons is the fact that he never stayed around to watch the execution of his victims; he was typically off hunting or gone on some other pretext when the deaths actually occurred. The King did not appear to demand the judicial murders for personal enjoyment. Rather, it seems that he just wanted people executed as a punishment for their (largely imaginary) treason. It is very possible that he felt he had no choice in the matter, or at least that justice was being served.

It was not just a new-found penchant for executions that marks the change in the King's personality. Henry's courage and honor, attributes that had once been so precious to him, fell by the wayside without him appearing to notice. He could no longer be trusted to keep his word, no matter how openly he made his promises. When the rebels who had participated in the Pilgrimage of Grace realized that Henry intended to renege on the guarantees he had given them, they revolted again, in January of 1537. Henry was unable to see that he had contributed to their discontent, and instead used their renewed uprising as an convenient excuse to exterminate them. Henry, apparently afraid to face the ire of his subjects, sent the Duke of Norfolk to lead the troops to put down the rebellion, while the King himself stayed in safety (Scarisbrick, 1970:346). Since the King was still physically healthy enough to go hunting for long hours, many historians have assumed it could only have been cowardice that kept the once warlike Henry away from the front lines.

    Norfolk and his troops captured all the leaders of the rebellion, including Aske. Aske's capture was unjust, since he was only there because he was trying to stop the rebellion. He had been trying to talk the rebels out of fighting because he was sure that the King, who had said with his "own mouth" that the needs of the people would be met, would keep his word (Benard, 2007:381). His faith in Henry was, in hindsight, particularly misplaced. Not only was Aske still treated as a rebel in spite of his efforts on the King's behalf, but Henry went out of his way to ensure that Aske died in a painful way. Once Aske was condemned to a traitor's death, which would involve hanging from the neck until nearly strangled and being eviscerated while still alive, he pleaded with his King to be "full dead ere I be dismembered" (Starkey, 2003:605). Henry consented to Aske's entreaty, but it was very like the way in which the Devil is said to make a bargain; no matter what you ask or how you ask, the granted request will not go well for you. In this case, Henry was indeed the Devil. Aske was promised he would be dead before he was torn apart, but instead of the quick demise by beheading or hanging that he was expecting, he was given a slow, excruciating, and horrible death. Aske was hung up in chains over the ramparts of York castle until he died of starvation, dehydration, and exposure several days later, and only after this agonizing death was he dismembered (Starkey, 2003:605).

Henry's response to the rebellious leaders, although appearing to be barbarically ruthless and spiteful, was not necessarily indicative of an inherently vicious streak in his character. For people of the Tudor era, God had ordained a perfect hierarchy among all things on the earth, called the great chain of being, which included people, plants, animals, and even minerals (Lovejoy, 1976). The King was the absolute pinnacle of the human pyramid, and his place there was ordained by God. Since he was given his status by the Almighty, to rebel against the King was, *de facto*, a rebellion against God's divine plan. This was, then, not only treason, but also heresy. Even the most moderate and respected of humanists, such as Thomas More, advocated horribly painful deaths for all those who were so wicked as to commit heresy. Nevertheless, the savage death of Aske, which had extended his agony for days instead of the hours a traditional traitor's death would have meant, was a prelude to what was to come. Henry would grow increasingly merciless as McLeod syndrome continued to eat away at his mental faculties. The once magnanimous King would eventually become a volatile and brutal tyrant.

The rebellion of his unhappy subjects and their abject suppression aside, there was a good reason for Henry to be a happy man in 1537. His most recent Queen was pregnant. This was joyous news for the King, Jane's family, the political faction that supported the Seymours, and for Jane herself. Until she gave

Henry a son – not just a child, it had to be a son – Jane was in danger. Henry's eye had started wandering almost as soon as the wedding bells had stopped ringing. Shortly after his marriage Henry saw two beautiful ladies, who must have been new to his court, and openly lamented that he was "sorry he had not seen them before he was married" (Starkey, 2003:602). In order to protect herself, Jane was careful to remain meek and docile around Henry, only rarely hazarding disagreement with her husband. On one such occasion she begged the King to return Mary to court, in order to try to reconcile him with his eldest daughter, even though Mary was still in disfavor and such a request might have ignited his temper. As mentioned previously, taking this risk on Mary's behalf would be more impressive if it had not been the primary goal of the political faction backing Jane. Henry was an old man from the point of view of his contemporaries, and therefore the succession to the throne could have become a pressing issue at any time. Those who remained loyal to Catholicism couldn't be sure Jane would have a boy who could be reared as a loyal son of the Church, so the best hope available to try to stop the Reformation in England was to make sure Mary was heir to the throne. It is difficult to truly give Jane credit as an altruistic family peacemaker when she was doing exactly what her supporters would have wanted her to do.

There are other reasons to be skeptical of Jane's supposed kindness. In the few areas where the new Queen could have her own way, she seemed obsessed with petty micromanagement, to the point it almost looks like bullying. When the Queen was craving fat quails during her pregnancy, Lord and Lady Lisle had made sure that she got them in the hopes that she would remember them favorably (Lindsey, 1995:134). Knowing that Lady Lisle had requested that her daughters be allowed to be

Ladies-in-Waiting to the Queen, Jane could have simply welcomed them both as a sign of her appreciation for the quails. Instead the Queen told their mother to bring both her daughters to court, so Jane could pick the one she liked best. In fairness, the pain a young girl would feel when she was sent home as the least attractive sister was not a matter of great concern to adults in that era. In any event, Jane picked Lady Lisle's daughter Anne to serve as a Lady-in-Waiting, most likely because she was the prettier of the sisters. However, the Queen then made her new Lady-in-Waiting change almost her entire wardrobe because of a dislike of the French-styled apparel the girl had brought (Lindsey, 1995:133). Many historians speculate that Jane did not want to see French fashions because that style reminded her of Anne Boleyn's fashion preferences, and that may have been a contributing factor, but it looks suspiciously as though the Queen did not want her Ladies to look *too* pretty. There is some fairly convincing corroboration for the idea that Anne was less attractive in her new outfits. The King himself commented in a letter he wrote to Lady Lisle that her daughter's new headdress "became her nothing so well as the French hood" (Starkey, 2003:606). A less attractive Lady-in-Waiting probably pleased Jane very much. It was important to Jane's status to have lovely Ladies-in-Waiting, yet important to her marriage that they not be so lovely as to catch the King's attention. Having done it to her predecessor, Jane was well aware that if Henry took a fancy for one of her Ladies, then he could easily get rid of an old Queen to make way for a fresh one.

Jane's pregnancy was her best hope for security. If she had a son, it wouldn't matter if the King's eye wandered over the lovely Ladies of the court: Jane would remain Queen. Henry would never do anything to jeopardize the legitimacy of his heir, so he would never repudiate the woman who had borne him a son. Sadly, it would cost the Queen dearly to give Henry his greatest wish. The birth of Henry's only legitimate male heir was far from easy. Jane's labor was a hellish three days long. It was so difficult that the whole court made a procession to St. Paul's church in order to pray for her and the child. Everyone hoped their prayers were answered when Jane delivered a healthy baby boy in the early hours of October 12, much to Henry's gratification and joy. With a seemingly supernatural compliance to her husband's desires, Jane had given birth to the boy expected of her. They called the newborn Edward, a name shared with some of England's greatest kings, and made even more auspicious by the fact he was born on the Eve of the Feast of St. Edward, a saint who had once been an British monarch.

  To say London celebrated the birth of the new Prince of Wales would be a gargantuan understatement. There were processions, special masses sung in churches, bonfires, free food and wine for all, and a volley of 2000 guns were fired from atop the Tower of London (Starkey, 2003:607). Prince Edward was christened on October 15, and his older sister Mary, whom the King had made quasi-legitimate by reinstating into the succession, was his godmother. All seemed to be going very well. Jane was apparently recovering and was able to receive guests in her chamber. Unfortunately, Jane's health did not last; she became ill with what was probably puerperal fever, also known as childbed fever, an infection that was a common cause of postpartum deaths during this time period (Lindsey, 1995:135). The Queen's decline was rapid and she died either late in the evening of October 24, or the very early morning of October 25, less than two weeks after her greatest triumph (Starkey, 2003:608). Despite his later protestations that Jane was his favorite wife and his dearest love, there is no record to indicate that Henry had even bothered to be with her when she died. He was a serious hypochondriac even as a young man, and if McLeod syndrome had affected his brain it certainly wouldn't have made him more rational about illness. Thus, he would have likely avoided even his dying Queen's sickbed.

In fact, Henry behaved so oddly during Jane's illness that historians are hard pressed to find a reasonable explanation for his behavior. The King had decided he wanted to go to Esher by October 25, even if the Queen "amend not" (Starkey, 2003:608). He was openly, and obviously, more concerned with hunting than with Jane's health. When he was younger, Henry seemed to feel genuine love and concern for those close to him. Why would he suddenly be so heartless when his wife, the woman who had borne him the son he was desperate for, was dying? If nothing else, the King should have known to put on a good show of grief. Thus, his behavior seems to be a clear sign that McLeod syndrome was affecting his mental state, since it was out of character with Henry's behavior prior to 1530 and showed a new unawareness of social niceties.

No one can really know how the King felt when Jane died, and he may have endured genuine and profound grief, but it is almost certain her loss caused him a least one novel discomfort. He had always been in love with a new woman before he had separated from a former wife, so he was adrift after Jane's death. For the first time since his teens Henry had no one to consider his true love. Cromwell and the King's other ministers knew that this was a golden opportunity for Henry to make an alliance with a powerful European court. The King's last two wives had brought him no large dowry, no property, no influence and no alliances. They weren't royalty; they were merely court ladies of whom he had become enamored. Now that he had no fixed interest in any woman, he could finally be coaxed into a marriage with strategic importance. He could be persuaded to marry for the same reasons everyone else in royal courts married --- money and power. However, there was a significant problem facing his future wedding plans. Henry, who was devoted to the concept of love, wanted to marry for money and power only if it were certain that the bride was young and beautiful, so that he could love her (Lindsey, 1995:138). He took it for granted that she would love him.

  His ministers, and his courtiers, were not foolish enough to tell him that he no longer possessed the personal beauty that he could have once counted on to charm a new bride. He had once been a splendid athlete with a god-like face and body, but he was now an obese and unhealthy middle-aged man with recurrent ulcers on both of his legs, which stank and wept pus. To make him even less appealing, half of Europe thought him a heretic and the other half thought him an enemy of the Reformation. They were both right, as it happens.

  Moreover, Henry did not seem to understand that very few people, if anyone, saw his marriages in the same pious and necessary light that he did, but rather saw the deaths of his multiple wives as an exercise in opportunistic murder or willful neglect. Even if the royal and noble families of other countries had been prepared to marry their kinswomen to an aged apostate with oozing legs, they would have been reluctant to pledge them to a man who was thought to have murdered Queen Katherina with poison, known to have executed the probably innocent Queen Anne, and was accused of letting Queen Jane die from lack of proper medical care. The King's reputation of callousness toward his wives was so great that a rumor had circulated that when he was asked who should be saved during a dangerous moment in Edward's birth, the baby or Jane, he had demanded that they save the baby since he could "always get another wife" (Lindsey, 1995:137). By this point Henry was more minotaur than man in the eyes of the public, having been mythologized as a dangerous beast who sacrificed women to his own monstrous appetites. Some prominent historians wonder why the King waited so long to marry again after Jane's death, or credit his hesitation to his mourning for Jane, but perhaps he waited because no one would consent to send him a bride.

Given that he was a viewed throughout Europe as a physically repulsive murderer, the King's hubris with regards to his desirability seems astounding. For example, when he was toying with the idea of marrying a French noblewomen he was very worried that he would be betrothed to a lady who was not beautiful enough to please him, so he told the French ambassador that he'd like a selection of beautiful ladies sent to Calais so that they could be inspected for suitability. The King was adamant this was necessary because he needed to make the choice himself, since "marriage touches a man too closely" (Smith, 1973:72). The ambassador, offended at the thought of French ladies being displayed as though they were pets to be bought, sarcastically asked Henry if he "would perhaps like to try them all, one after the other, and keep for yourself the one who seems the sweetest", and reminded the King that, "It was not thus, Sire, that the Knights of the Round Table treated their ladies in old times in this country" (Smith, 1973:72).

Henry's blunt pursuit of a pretty bride was somewhat shocking even to other royals. Although the King of France was one of the most notorious womanizers in Christendom, he was repulsed to think of women being treated like commodities so blatantly and sent word that the ladies of his court were not to be treated like "horses trotted out at a fair" (Lindsey, 1995:138). Henry realized that he'd have little chance of seeing his future Queen in person before the wedding, so he would have to preview his prospective brides another way.

Fortunately for Henry, the portrait painter at his court was Hans Holbein, who was extremely talented. In the absence of photography, one of Holbein's paintings was the surest guarantee of an accurate likeness. So the King decided that once marriage negotiations reached a promising stage, he would send Holbein to visit and paint the lady in question, giving Henry the opportunity to back out of the union in time if she was not attractive enough to suit him.

Negotiations did not always reach the point at which Holbein would be dispatched. For a while Henry was trying to entice Marie of Guise, a tall and beautiful young woman from a hugely powerful French family, into an engagement. There's a story, which has not been confirmed by historians and thus may just be a rumor that was passed around as a good joke on the much disliked Henry, that Marie strenuously opposed the match, claiming that she was tall but her neck was small, clearly implying that she didn't want to risk her little neck to Henry's axe. True or not, Marie wisely decided to marry a monarch with a less fearsome reputation, King James V of Scotland.

Thwarted in his pursuit of a French bride, Henry started looking for an alliance with the Holy Roman Empire. His fancy soon alighted on the sixteen-year-old niece of Charles V, Christina the Duchess of Milan. She was everything he was looking for in a prospective spouse; she was famous for her beauty, would bring a rich dowry, and was well connected politically. There was the problem that she was the grand-niece of his first wife, Katherina of Aragon, but although that would have deterred a less egocentric man, it was only a minor impediment in Henry's opinion. Although Charles V did not want the marriage between his kinswoman and the English sovereign to proceed, it was not diplomatically prudent to acknowledge this too openly. The lack of flagrant resistance was taken as a an endorsement by the once astute, but now undiscerning, Henry. In fact, the King thought negotiations were going so well that he sent Holbein to paint Christina's portrait. After all, Henry had to make sure her beauty had not been exaggerated before he could judge her as worthy of becoming his consort. Christina agreed to sit for the painting, but seems to have been determined to do everything in her power to avoid meeting Henry at the altar. She made it very clear that she was "not minded to fix her heart that way", and would only marry under a direct order from the Emperor (Lindsey, 1995:139). There is a reasonable likelihood that Henry would have seen her resistance as coy flirtation. Even if he had not become mentally ill as a result of McLeod's syndrome, his ego was such that it probably did not occur to him that a pretty teenager with many marriage prospects before her would not consider his suit the best option. When the King finally got her portrait, he became even more smitten with the lovely Duchess. It took Henry several months to finally come to terms with the fact that Charles V did not really favor the marriage, and to accept that Christina would never be his bride.

    There is an anecdotal tale about Christina's rejection of Henry which is similar to the tale involving Marie of Guise, and just as unproven. Christina is rumored to have told Henry's ambassadors that if she had two heads, she would be glad to give one to the King (Lindsey, 1995:139). Once again, Henry's judicial murder of Anne Boleyn was coming back to haunt him.

Even if Duchess Christina and Marie of Guise never actually made snide comments implying that Henry was someone who routinely beheaded his wives, the fact the semi-slander was widely reported and believed demonstrates how unpopular and untrusted Henry had become, both domestically and abroad.

Although some historians speculate that Henry waited almost three years before marrying again because of his enduring love for Jane Seymour, the King's vigorous search for a bride appears to indicate that he wanted to enjoy connubial felicity again, but had difficulty in locating a suitable partner. At one point in the summer of 1538 the King had sent Holbein to France to paint the portraits of no less than five women whom he was negotiating to marry. This included the two sisters of Marie of Guise, Renee and Louise, as well as Marie Vendome, Anne of Lorraine, and the King of France's sister (Scarisbrick, 1970:359). While negotiating for the hands of the five Frenchwomen, Henry was still hopeful that his suit for the Duchess of Milan would be accepted. Moreover, his chief minister, Cromwell, continued to suss out possible consorts from among the ruling families of the Germanic states. The King was clearly a man who preferred to live within the bonds of holy wedlock.

During Henry's fruitless search for a wife he also began to indulge in more brutal policies to secure his throne from those he perceived as threats. To that end, he had most of his maternal kindred executed for various implausible reasons. This is a good example of Henry's personality change and possible madness, but it simultaneously demonstrates how hard it can be to distinguish between madness and valid political strategies. Henry, when he was a freshly crowned monarch, eagerly tried to mend the rift between the Tudors and his mother's family. In a reversal of his father's policy, the new King offered his Plantagenet kinfolk places at court, honored them, and showed them royal favor (Starkey, 2009:306). Only one family member, the Duke of Buckingham, was stupid enough to be anything but grateful for Henry's favors. Buckingham didn't just want the King's friendship, he wanted the King's crown. The Duke was so candid about his desire for the throne that it is somewhat mind-boggling. Buckingham bragged about prophecies which foretold that he would one day rule England, saying that God had killed the infant son born to Henry and Katherina of Aragon in order to punish the King and to pave the way for Buckingham's ascent. The Duke also declared, openly, that the King would never have an heir. Buckingham's actions were brazenly treasonous. Henry, who had been incredibly patient in the matter, had no choice but to have his cousin executed in 1521, but he clearly did not enjoy the prospect (Scarisbrick, 1970:118-120).

  Sadly, the older Henry seemed to positively relish beheading his family members. As McLeod syndrome continued to make the King more and more mentally unbalanced, Henry no longer wanted peace with his relatives: in his paranoia he could see them only as a threat to his throne and dynastic ambitions. The King arrested his Plantagenet cousins, Henry Courtenay, Henry Pole, and Edward Neville, found them all guilty of what were obviously trumped up charges, and ordered them killed a few weeks before Christmas in 1538 (Scarisbrick, 1970:364). Henry Courtenay was the King's maternal first cousin and had "been brought up of a child with his grace in his chamber" (Ives, 2004:105). Courtenay remained a friend and favorite of Henry's until shortly before his death. This means that the King ordered the legal murder of a man who had been raised as though he were Henry's brother, and had been a member of Henry's intimate circle all his life. Henry also had Courtenay's son, who was named Edward, thrown into the Tower. The unfortunate Edward Courtenay was held in the Tower until 1553, when Henry died. After Mary became Queen of England, she gave Edward his freedom (Whitelock, 2010:192). As unjust as the treatment of Edward Courtenay was, at least he survived, which is more than can be said for Henry Pole's son. After the King beheaded Henry Pole, he sent Pole's son to the Tower, where the young man simply disappeared (Scarisbrick, 1970:364). When and how he died remains unknown. The King also arrested Pole's mother, the Countess of Salisbury, who was his eldest daughter's godmother, and threw her into the Tower as well. Edward Neville had also been one of the King's friends and had served him faithfully as an Esquire of the Body. Thus, the King was not just murdering men who were alternative possible heirs to his throne, he was murdering men that he had known all his life as his closest friends and companions. His unjustifiable attacks must have bewildered and terrified them all.

It is likely that Henry's growing paranoia could not allow men to live if he perceived them as threats to Prince Edward's inheritance. There may, however, have been other, more rational, reasons for their deaths. Many historians believe that the possibility of a foreign invasion influenced his decision-making. The King's biggest enemies, France and the Holy Roman Empire, had formed an alliance. The monarchs of both France and the Holy Roman Empire were loyal to Catholicism, and Henry knew there was a chance they would invade England and give the throne to his eldest daughter, Mary, who was a zealous adherent of the old faith. Moreover, France was closely allied with Scotland, and the Scots would have gladly allowed the French to amass troops along the Scottish-English border. There was therefore a very real possibility that England would be invaded on multiple fronts: by a Franco-Scots alliance from the north and by the armies of Charles V from the south. Henry's kingdom would be "but a morsel amongst these choppers", and would be eaten up accordingly (Scarisbrick, 1970:362). England needed clear leadership and a clear succession. Was the King displaying mental instability when he executed so many of his kinsmen? Or was he just securing his throne for his infant heir?

Henry desperately needed a political alliance that he could call on for aid should England be forced into a war with multiple opponents. If he was successful in his attempt to marry a woman from a powerful French family, or a wealthy relative of Charles V, then he might be able to drive a wedge between France and the Empire, thus preventing them from carrying out a joint invasion. There were also advantages to allying himself with one of the ruling houses of the Schmalkaldic League, which was an alliance of Lutheran principalities within the Holy Roman Empire. The Schmalkaldic League was a strong military power that would be a valuable ally for England should Charles V declare war. The dire need to forge a political alliance does, however, make Henry's requirement that his bride be beautiful, and the consequent delay caused by his insistence on commissioning and inspecting portraits of the candidates, seem more than self-centered: it borders on madness. If Henry was not actually being influenced by the mental deterioration resulting from McLeod syndrome, his hesitation in favor of personal happiness would be, at minimum, egotism run amok. A good or reasonable monarch would have been willing to marry anyone who could help him survive such a severe threat to his kingdom, regardless of his personal preferences. After all, it is not as if a King would be discouraged from having a mistress to provide emotional and physical satisfaction. However, if he was suffering from mental instability as a result of McLeod syndrome, it would explain why he was unable to be rational about the urgency of the situation and the unreasonableness of his demand for a pretty bride.

Frankly, the King was doing very few things rationally after the mid 1530s. This supports the theory that his mind was negatively affected by McLeod syndrome, inasmuch as it is hard to image anyone, especially a person who was once known for his intelligence, being so inept without some kind of mental deterioration. For example, it was important that he resolve some of the religious differences in his own country, which would hopefully keep social unrest from exploding while he was distracted by a war. Instead of building a consensus, however, the King seemed to go out of his way to make the situation worse. Henry had been excommunicated in 1538, right around the time he was executing Courtenay, Pole, and Neville, but he was still faithful to the majority of Catholic dogma. If he returned to the religion of his birth he would be reinstated in communion, and there would no longer be such a strong threat of rebellion from within his own borders, since there was still a Catholic majority at the time, especially in the northern counties. If he rejected Catholicism and became a Protestant, then he would have allies in the German principalities and would be supported by those who had become disillusioned by Papal practices. His personal faith would matter less if he openly promoted religious tolerance, quit destroying monasteries, and stopped the practice of burning reformers alive. Free from persecution, his subjects would be much less likely to rise up against him from either side.

Rather than take any of these approaches, in late spring of 1539 he pushed the Six Articles through Parliament. These laid out the six key beliefs which were to be embraced by English subjects. Based on Henry's own beliefs, the Six Articles refuted the key ideas of the Reformation (Smith, 1982:157). The Six Articles were often referred to as "the whip with six strings" (Lindsey, 1995:140). They reinforced some of the basic tenets of Catholicism, including the belief in transubstantiation, that were anathema to Protestants. One of the most significant issues for the Reformation was the rejection of transubstantiation, or the belief that the bread and wine of the communion were literally transformed into the body and blood of Christ during communion (Bernard, 2007:499-502). Reformers, in general, insisted the transformation was only symbolic. However, after the Six Articles passed, a person who openly expressed a doubt that the bread and wine actually transformed into the flesh and blood of Jesus could be burned at the stake as a punishment for their disbelief. The Six Articles also declared that priests could not marry, which was contrary to another significant aspect of the Protestant movement (Smith, 1982:157). As a result of the Six Articles, the Reformers were in great danger. Since all the King's subjects were expected to adhere to the doctrines espoused by the Six Articles or risk execution, devout Protestants could be martyred at the King's command if they should persevere in their faith. When lawmakers realized what a powerful weapon they had placed in the hands of "zealots", the Six Articles were modified to allow people a chance to recant their reformist views and avoid being burned at the stake (Smith, 1982:159). However, the new laws remained a formidable legal cudgel to be used against the Reformation, and inspired Martin Luther to insist "the devil sits astride [Henry] so that he vexes and plagues Christ" (Smith, 1982:157).

The Six Articles were no friend to Protestants, but the Henrician church also denied Papal authority, a key piece of Catholic dogma. Thus, all those who wished to remain firm in their traditional faith were in just as much danger as the Protestants who wished to leave it. To consider the Pope the head of the universal church was, in Henry's opinion, treason against the right and true supreme head of the church, the King himself. As many loyal Catholics could attest, believing that the Pope was the heir to St Peter could be a quick route to martyrdom in Henry's England (Bernard, 2007:167-168). The passage of the Six Articles, together with the denial of Papal authority, meant that almost everyone in England, except the King himself, was in danger of being burned at the stake as a heretic. Henry had, lamented one reformer, "destroyed the Pope, but not popery" (Smith, 2009:99).

This muddled line between Protestantism and Catholicism was a foolish stance, almost certain to create dissension in his subjects, and seems incongruous given that Henry had not been a foolish man. It is possible that his narcissism made him believe that his personal interpretation of faith was, axiomatically, the True Faith. However, if his personal faith aligned so closely with Catholicism, why didn't the King just return to the Church and make a great many of his subjects happy and safe? After all, the Pope who had vexed him was dead. Katherina of Aragon had passed on as well. He had already made sure his marriage to Anne Boleyn was declared unlawful and had proclaimed that Elizabeth was a bastard. There was no reason why Henry couldn't have at least made overtures to the new Pope, who would have surely wished to reconcile England to the Mother Church again. The fact that Henry had created an untenable religious climate in his country, practically guaranteeing civil unrest at a time when there was a danger of invasion by multiple forces, was asinine to the point it could be thought of as insane. This could be a strong indication that Henry was suffering from mental impairment as a result of McLeod syndrome. It is hard to believe he would have made such bad decisions otherwise. Even if he hadn't been particularly interested in policy as a young man, he had at least been smart enough to listen to Wolsey and other able ministers. Why, except for a medical reason, would Henry have started to suddenly govern so poorly after the early 1530s?

Some historians argue that, rather than making a mistaken mixture of neither true reformation nor true orthodoxy, Henry was deliberately choosing a "middle way" between Protestantism and Catholicism (Bernard, 2007:578). This may be so, but Henry's middle way appealed mainly to himself, since it repulsed both devoted Catholics who were determined to remain faithful to the Church and the passionate Reformers who were committed to spreading the Gospel. Furthermore, the middle way changed with Henry's moods. Ceremonies and rites which had been sacred to the King, and thus to the neoteric Anglican Church, such as covering statues for Lent and crawling to the cross on Good Friday, would suddenly be forbidden as Henry lost his taste for them (Scarisbrick, 1970:422). When the initial draft of the Bishop's Book, which would be the defining doctrines of the Henrician church, included a list of theologically unsound traditions or practices that should be eschewed, Henry crossed out any that he personally indulged in, such as astrology or 'lucky' days, meaning that his particular superstitions would still be held as Godly (Scarisbrick, 1970:406). Rather than being a rational appeal for religious moderation, the King's middle way simply tried to force his subjects to conform to his personal beliefs. Parliament was informed that "his majesty desires above all things that diversity of religious opinion be banished from his dominion" (Smith, 1982:156), and Henry seemed determined to convert the English people to his way of thinking -- even if it killed them. Many years later, his daughter Elizabeth would say that she had "no desire to make windows into men's souls" (Loads, 2006:137), but Henry appeared convinced he could not only make windows into a person's soul, he could also ascertain the correct beliefs that should be contained therein. This kind of stubborn, and undeniably egotistical, belief that it was his right to command his subjects' innermost thoughts seems indicative of a psychological malady, such as narcissism, but could also be a result of the lessened rationality that results from the onset of McLeod syndrome. At any rate, a middle way was a dangerous theology to foist on a country that was in desperate need of stability, not further agitation.

Ironically, at the same time that Henry was ratifying the Six Articles, which basically made Lutheranism punishable by death, he was trying to make alliances with Lutheran strongholds. This may appear hypocritical but it was probably not an aberration caused by Henry's erratic mental state. It comes down to the fact that there was another very powerful man shaping England's policies. While the Six Articles expressed the King's personal faith, the olive branch extended to the Protestant rulers was no doubt held by Thomas Cromwell, whose power as Chancellor had grown even stronger after he helped orchestrate Anne Boleyn's death. Cromwell wanted to find allies within the Schmalkaldic League in order to strengthen England's position in case of war, and to make the Reformation more tempting to Henry. It is likely that Cromwell had to coax his stubborn and reluctant monarch into seeing the advantages of making a marriage with a highborn lady from a powerful Protestant duchy. Henry eventually became resigned to making an alliance with the Lutheran princes. However, this does not mean that the members of the Schmalkaldic League were resigned to an alliance with Henry (Loads, 2009:109). Quite the reverse in fact.

Henry, or it is probably more accurate to say Cromwell, made diplomatic attempts to build ties with the King of Denmark and Norway, the Duke of Saxony, the Duke of Urbino, and the Landgrave of Hesse. Wisely, the Lutheran states didn't believe that Henry was serious in his attempt to ally himself with them or the new faith. They therefore ignored his demands and pleas when they made their political decisions. Unjustly and irrationally, Henry took this as a betrayal, even though his Six Articles proved that he was completely disingenuous when he professed an interest in embracing Lutheran doctrine (Scarisbrick, 1970:366).

Still nursing his hurt feelings, Henry then reached out to William, Duke of Cleves, to try to make an alliance by marrying one of the Duke's two unmarried sisters. William of Cleves was not a Lutheran, but he was not a hard-line Catholic either. William was also fighting both Charles V and the Papacy, so he was more likely to be sympathetic to Henry's side of any argument with their mutual enemies. Although the Duke was not a member of the Schmalkaldic League, he had family ties to it, since his sister Sybille was married to the Elector of Saxony, who was the head of the Protestant Confederation of Germany. This would tie Henry to the Lutherans without the King having to convert to Lutheranism himself (Scarisbrick, 1970:368-369). Clearly an alliance with Cleves was the best political move the King could make, and it is likely that Cromwell arranged it and coaxed Henry into agreement.

No matter how many political or military advantages a match with one of the Duke's sisters would bring Henry still had to make sure she was suitably lovely in order to proceed with the final marriage negotiations. Thus, he sent Holbein off to Cleves to paint the portraits of both the Duke's sisters, Anna and Amelia. Since she was the older sister and the logical choice for Henry's bride, Anna's picture was the most important. Nicholas Wotton, who had actually met Anna of Cleves, assured the King that the portraits Holbein had painted "expressed their images very lively"(Strickland and Strickland, 1851:86). Wotton was therefore of the opinion that the painting was a lifelike portrayal of Anna's appearance. To the modern viewer, Anna's portrait shows a woman who was at least as handsome as Henry's first two wives, and arguably more attractive than his third. Henry must have found her visage appealing, since she was chosen to be Henry's fourth bride. The marriage contract was signed on October 4, 1539, and Anna of Cleves began her journey to England a few weeks thereafter (Starkey, 2003:625).

Chapter Seven
The Great Flanders Mare: A Bad Impression, a Fleeting Marriage, and a Lasting Slander

Henry, regardless of how far he might have progressed into mental instability as a result of McLeod syndrome, was a romantic. He had to believe himself in love. Therefore, when he was assured that Anna of Cleves, his soon-to-be Queen, was on her way to England, the King began to wax eloquent about his forthcoming nuptials. He was completely prepared to "nourish love," and ready to adore his new bride (Scarisbrick, 1970:370). More importantly for a man of Henry's undeniably robust ego, he expected that his new wife would be utterly besotted with him.

No matter how willing Henry was to consider himself in love with her, Anna was going to have many challenges ahead of her if she wanted to keep him happy. She would have to agree with all of his opinions on every subject, since he was no longer rational enough to be able to accept contradiction of any kind. The King seemed to feel 'attacked' by anyone who expressed a contrary opinion, and was prone to extreme overreactions when faced with dissent. She would have to be quick in learning the rules of courtly romance, which were entrenched in a tradition of stylized behaviors, so that she could fulfill her role as a ladylove for Henry. Finally, she would have to be very adaptable in order to deal with her new husband's ever more frequent mood swings. His courtiers were becoming increasingly aware that their monarch was dangerously unstable. The Imperial ambassador, Chapuys, noted that the "King's fickleness" defied description (Erickson, 1980:267). Henry Pole, shortly before the King had him killed, made the accurate prediction that his sovereign would be "out of his wits one day" based on the fact that when the King "came to his chamber he would look angrily, and after fall to fighting" (Erickson, 1980:288). How would Anna feed Henry's love when his appetite was so varied and so strange? More importantly, would she survive if she did not satisfy his needs?

  Although his bride-to-be was considered by all who met her, with few exceptions, to be an attractive woman, Anna was ill equipped to enthrall the King. Her upbringing had been very strict, and as a result she did not have any abilities that would keep Henry entertained. Henry adored music, singing, dancing, hunting, and playing card games. Anna was proficient in none of these things. She was unfamiliar with the rules of courtly love so she did not know the proper behavior expected of a lady by her noble lover. Anna was unpracticed in the art of witty flirtation, which Henry was accustomed to in the women of his acquaintance. She didn't even speak English, and had almost no way of communicating with her groom since she spoke neither the French nor the Latin which were the mark of an educated noblewoman (Starkey, 2003:601). Her main skill was needlework, which would allow her to embroider Henry's shirts but would not go far in winning his heart.

Things were not completely hopeless, however. In spite of Anna's lack of courtly accomplishments, there were other reasons to believe it could be a successful marriage. She was young, but not so young as to be immature, she was intelligent, she knew her responsibilities as a Queen, and she was reputed to have a very gentle and good-natured temperament. These qualities could be enough to entice Henry long enough for Anna to develop other means of amusing the King. After all, she could learn to play cards and dance. The main architect of the marriage, Cromwell, must have been especially eager for the union to be a happy and fruitful one.

Anna and her retinue traveled overland from Cleves to Calais. They only managed about 5 miles a day, partly because they were such a large group (there were over 260 attendants accompanying her) and partly because Anna attracted a crowd. Was it morbid curiosity that made people want to see her? It is extremely likely that people were speculating on whether or not Henry would someday kill his new bride, and many of the onlookers may have been eager to say they had seen the tragic and doomed Queen with their own eyes. No one knows what Anna herself thought about the possibility her new husband would murder her, as he had done Anne Boleyn. Did she assume that fear of reprisals would prevent Henry from killing her? After all, it was Anne Boleyn, a commoner, who had lost her head, not the royal-born Katherina of Aragon. Nevertheless, Katherina was rumored to have been poisoned at Henry's command, so even royalty might not be enough to guarantee safety. Did Anna worry that Henry would be cruel to her? Did she fear her wedding night with a middle-aged colossus? Was she hoping to be happy, or expecting to be sad? Sadly, there is no record of what she was thinking when she arrived in Calais on December 11, 1539.

Aside from how Anna might have felt about meeting Henry, the reception that greeted her at Calais undoubtedly cheered her. Lord Lisle, whose wife had sent the fat quails to Jane Seymour when she was pregnant, and the Lord High Admiral William Fitzwilliam, as well as hundreds of aristocrats, were all there to greet her. They welcomed Anna with every honor. Admiral Fitzwilliam hurried to show her the ship that would carry her to her new husband, which had been bedecked with decorations in her honor, and the future Queen was saluted with 150 guns (Lindsey, 1995:141). Unfortunately, it would be over two weeks before the festooned ship would be able to transport Anna to her waiting bridegroom. The weather was inclement, so the ships were unable to sail. There was no possibility of risking her life in a rough crossing. The enforced delay in departure meant that those who were there to meet Anna had a chance to get to know her better during the wait in Calais.

For her part, Anna seemed determined to make a good impression on her new courtiers. She asked Fitzwilliam to teach her how to play a card game the King liked. The admiral taught her to play cent, which was very similar to the card game piquet (Ridley, 1988). Fitzwilliam wrote to Henry that, in his opinion, Anna "played as pleasantly and with as good a grace and countenance as ever in all my life I saw any noblewoman" (Starkey, 2003:625). The admiral also considered the future Queen to be a woman who would appeal to Henry. It is significant that Fitzwilliam thought Henry would be pleased with

Anna's appearance. Fitzwilliam had grown up with Henry as a member of the King's household and he knew Henry as well as anyone could know him, so if the admiral thought Anna looked like the type of woman who usually interested the King, then it is almost certain that she did. This is another strong indicator that Anna was attractive, and the fact so many noblemen and women were impressed with her seems to suggest she was reasonably charming as well. Lady Lisle was enchanted with the soon-to-be Queen, and wrote to her daughter at court that Anna was good to serve and easy to please (Erickson, 1980:304).

Anna of Cleves finally made it across the channel and into England on December 27, where she was met by the Duke of Suffolk and his wife. She then journeyed on to Canterbury, where she was greeted by the mayor and other leading citizens of the town. The Archbishop of Canterbury, Thomas Cranmer, and the Bishop of Ely, Thomas Goodrich, were there to welcome her as well. She was escorted to St. Augustine's Abbey, a former Benedictine establishment whose charter had been dissolved by Henry and which had been seized as a royal property in 1538, where a feast and a reception were held in her honor. Cranmer wrote to Cromwell that he was disappointed that no more than 120 gentleman had been able to attend the festivities (Warnicke, 2000:129). Nevertheless, Anna herself showed every sign of being satisfied, and it appears that she enjoyed the attentions given to her, inasmuch as the Duke of Suffolk recorded that she had acted "very merry at supper" (Starkey, 2003:626). Even if she was feeling any trepidation at the thought of marrying Henry, she was clearly enjoying the social aspects of being Queen, and it seems she was determined to put her best foot forward with her new subjects.

After Canterbury, the future Queen traveled to Rochester,

where New Year's entertainments would be held, arriving there on December 30. One of the diversions planned for Anna was a bull-baiting. Bull-baiting, to modern sensibilities, seems almost indescribably vile. In this 'sport', a bull was placed in the center of a ring or arena, tied around the base of the horns with a rope, and the rope was then anchored to the ground. With the rope acting like a tether to keep the bull in place, fierce dogs would be prompted to attack the fettered bull in order to subdue or immobilize the trapped animal. Like most others of her time, Anna had no moral qualms about this form of recreation. Strangely, her interest in bull-baiting would prove to be a pivotal factor in her fate.

Anna was standing at her window, watching the bull-baiting on New Year's Day with ostensible enjoyment, when something happened that altered the whole course of her life. A group of six men, 'disguised' in matching cloaks and hoods made of multi-colored patches, burst into the room, much to the consternation of Anna and her ladies. One of the men grabbed Anna and kissed her, claiming that he and his fellows had come on behalf of the King, and gave her a token of the King's affection. Anna was "abashed, not knowing who it was, thanked him, and so he communed with her; but she regarded him but little but always looked out of the window on the bull-baiting" (Warnicke, 2000:130-131). Unfortunately for Anna, this odd-acting messenger in whom she clearly had no interest was her prospective bridegroom, Henry VIII.

Henry had tried to make a romantic gesture and it had gone badly awry. It was a part of the courtly etiquette of the time to encourage a noble suitor to greet his soon-to-be-bride in disguise, allowing them the opportunity to fall madly in love with one another at first sight, as though they were star-crossed lovers in a chivalric romance (Warnicke 2000:131). Members of European courts who had access to the romantic tales were aware of this trope. As silly as the practice seems, especially since all parties involved would have known almost immediately who was disguised and why, it gave the new couple, who were forced together for diplomatic reasons, a chance to start off on the right foot and at least enjoy a pleasant fiction that they would be a happy couple. Even in a time where marriages were often arranged, it was considered common wisdom that the couple should like each other as much as possible, and it was hoped they would fall in love soon after the wedding. Therefore, the King was trying to woo his new bride, and was attempting to "nourish love". It also allowed the groom to establish himself as the knight-errant for his new lady, laying the groundwork for her subsequent 'rule' over his heart and his behavior towards her at court.

Disastrously, Anna knew nothing of this tradition, and was therefore completely baffled by the behavior of this "messenger". She had no idea that she should have reciprocated the messenger's attentions, and "when the king perceived she regarded his coming so little, he departed in [an] other chamber, and put off his cloak and came in again in a coat of purple velvet", after which all present realized he was the King of England (Warnicke, 2000:131). Anna did what she could to salvage the situation, curtsying low before him and paying him all the attention she had been remiss not to give him when he was disguised, but it was too late. Henry spoke with her a few more minutes, then said his goodbyes. His first impression of her would not be undone.

The meeting between Henry and Anna was profoundly inauspicious. The King expected Anna to behave like a lady in a romance. In the tradition of courtly love, the lady and her knight fall in love with one another because each is the idealized standard of "nobility and courtliness" (Schultz, 2006:xx). Therefore, Anna should have looked at him and known, beyond a shadow of a doubt, that he was the most noble, most handsome, most chivalrous knight she had ever seen, and she should have fallen madly in love with him as a result. Historians have pointed out that if Anna of Cleves had been French or Italian she would have known to 'fall in love' the minute the messenger burst into her room. Instead, Anna had been raised in the strict atmosphere of a German court, where reading frivolous romances was considered immodest in ladies of quality.

    The mental impairment caused by McLeod syndrome likely exacerbated Henry's response to Anna's gaffe. With his deteriorating emotional state, he was unable to separate reality from fantasy as well as he could when young. He could not make allowances for her upbringing. The same man who had rescued Katherina of Aragon when he was younger, could not see that Anna of Cleves was as dependent on his goodwill as his first wife had been. He could not see that he had unfair expectations of her.

    A noted historian, Karen Lindsey (1995), believes that narcissism alone could explain why Henry turned against his new bride. If the King was actually a narcissist, rather than merely egotistical, Anna's indifference would have enraged him, because it did not support his belief in his projected persona. Lindsey speculates that Anna of Cleves might have, even if just for a moment, looked at Henry with disdain or dismay at his appearance. At the very least she was not overwhelmed by his charms when he was dressed as a messenger. Henry had once been the handsomest man in any room, so Anna's disinterest in him while he was disguised must have been a crushing blow to his inflated vanity. The fact that she did not fall in love with him, that she ignored him as a foolish messenger instead, did more than ruin the fairy-tale of courtly love. Her indifference or apparent dislike would have also destroyed Henry's illusions of his own perfection. Anna did not know he was the King simply by the magnificence of his presence. Anna did not look at him as though he were handsome. Anna did not seek his attentions. Her lack of interest could have deeply wounded Henry's enormous ego. Moreover, she might even have done something worse than ignore the King: she might have let it show, even for a moment, that she was unhappy that she would have to marry him. What if in an unguarded moment she had revealed, through some quick expression on her face, that she was appalled by the idea of marrying the hulking and foul-smelling man announcing himself as the King? Even without McLeod syndrome to influence his behavior, this might have destroyed her forever in Henry's opinion, since his narcissism just could not handle the fact she did not want him. Lindsey (1995:146) argues that the King would have had to turn the tables, rewriting the scene in his memory so that he was the one who had been repulsed by Anna. He was not the ugly one, *she was*. When his potential irrationality as a result of McLeod syndrome is added, it is unsurprising that he developed a deep-seated revulsion towards Anna.

    Whether from ego, or from illness, or from a combination of the two, once Henry had met Anna of Cleves he decided she was a "Great Flanders Mare" and he wanted nothing more to do with her. He stormed about, declaring "I like her not!" and claiming that everyone who had told him she was pretty could not be trusted (Bernard, 2007:151-152). He swore that if he had known she was so displeasing he would never have let her come to England. Eager to please the King, his courtiers quickly 'discovered' that she was ugly. They had all been mistaken to think her attractive! For centuries many historians accepted these new reports as accurate. Anna of Cleves, a pretty and intelligent woman, was depicted in almost every history book as the Great Flanders Mare, renowned for her hideousness. This created a false history of a victimized Henry having been duped into marrying an ugly woman.

    The historical myth of Anna being plain-looking, or even grotesquely featured, is not only countered by the records of Henry's court contemporaries, but also by the King himself. Although the new Queen's manner of dress was frequently criticized as unstylish, and thus unattractive, Anna's personal appearance was praised when she was attired, "after the English fashion, with a French hood, which so set forth her beauty and good visage, that every creature rejoiced to behold her" (Strickland and Strickland, 1851:59). Henry complained that his new wife was "nothing fair," but even he was forced to admit that she was "well and seemly" (Bernard, 2007:547). Nonetheless, many historians ignored these reports in order to explain why the King took such a strong dislike to his bride. Surely there must have been some *reason*, a reason that the Queen's repellent aspect would provide, to explain Henry's feelings? The idea that Henry might have been mentally ill, or affected by a psychological disorder such as narcissism, was seldom proposed as a means of resolving the mystery of the King's loathing for the well-looking Anna of Cleves.

    Furthermore, what about her portrait? Is that not proof that she was reasonably attractive? Why did most historians assume she was as unappealing as Henry said she was? When confronted with conflicting evidence -- Henry's insistence she was grotesque versus the painting by Holbein and the initial reports of her comeliness -- most historians assumed that Henry must be the one telling the truth. Thus was born the legend that Anna of Cleves was homely, and that Holbein must have painted her in a way which made her seem more attractive than she really was.

    There are two main reasons to doubt Anna of Cleves was actually ugly or that Holbein had painted her in a way which made her appear more attractive than she was in real life. First, no one who saw both Anna and the painting ever said it was anything but a good likeness. Secondly, Holbein kept his head attached to his shoulders. If he had doctored the painting to make Anna appear pretty when she was not, if Henry could look at it and see a significant difference between Anna and her painted image, it is unlikely that Holbein would have escaped with his life. Henry was not a man to be trifled with. He had executed others for a lesser offense than that of deliberately tricking him into marrying an unappealing woman. Holbein would have been a fool to have tried to return to Henry's court with an inaccurate portrait. Yet not only was the artist not punished, the King kept Holbein at court and continued to commission him to create portraits (Lindsey, 1995:145). Furthermore, no personal or financial reason has ever been found that would account for Holbein taking such a risk on behalf of Anna. The artist did not stay behind in Cleves and retire a rich man. Clearly, there were no bribes in play. Likewise, Holbein never received special attention or favor from Anna. Therefore, it is likely that the historians who argued that Holbein's painting of Anna was indeed "very lively" are the ones who were correct.

    Nevertheless, reality in the Tudor court was whatever

Henry believed it to be, and his version of reality was that Anna of Cleves was a Great Flanders Mare and absolutely repugnant. As one contemporary noted, "it pleased his highness to mislike her grace, but to me she always appeared a brave lady" (Strickland and Strickland, 1851:59). The courtiers were wise enough to agree, at least in public, with the King's opinion of Anna, regardless of their real feelings. Certainly no one dared argue with Henry when he decided he no longer wanted to marry his betrothed. Even before McLeod syndrome had increased Henry's capriciousness, the King wasn't a man to endure what he did not wish to. Henry demanded of Cromwell, "What remedy?", but Cromwell, understanding the grave political threats facing the kingdom, had to tell the King, "I know none," and to apologize by saying "he was very sorry therefore" (Starkey, 2003:629). This is the first time Cromwell had failed to get Henry what he wanted. To the King's paranoid thought process this could mean only one thing: Cromwell was out to get him; Cromwell was now his enemy. Although the unfortunate Cromwell didn't know it, his life was rapidly drawing to a close.

    Henry, no matter how angry he was at Cromwell or how repulsed he was by the woman to whom he was betrothed, was trapped by circumstances and had to, at the very least, receive his intended bride with all due ceremony and all the necessary demonstrations expected of a betrothed couple. On January 3, 1540, he met Anna formally at Blackheath. It was a huge spectacle, staged for both courtiers and commoners. There was a magnificent tent made from cloth of gold, and the entire court was there to greet the future queen, as well as throngs of people and at least 160 alderman from London (Lindsey, 1995:147). Henry and Anna were a sight worth seeing. Anna was wearing a gown of cloth of gold, so covered in gems down the front that it "glistened all the field", and her future groom was similarly attired, wearing a purple velvet coat trimmed with gold that sported buttons made of diamonds, pearls, and rubies (Lindsey, 1995:148). The King and his bride-to-be were both escorted by footmen dressed up to the nines and pages clothed in "rich tinsel and crimson velvet" (Strickland and Strickland, 1851:51). The richly bejeweled pair made quite an impression on their audience. One witness to the meeting, Edward Hall, praised them effusively as "so goodly a prince and so noble a King" and "so fair a lady of so goodly a stature and so womanly a countenance" (Lindsey, 1995:148). Together, the King and Anna rode on decorated horses to Greenwich, where he politely escorted her to her sumptuously readied chambers, and then left.

    Henry then retreated to his council and demanded that they find a way to extricate him from the impending nuptials, which he delayed for as long as he could. He complained that he was "not well handled" by his ministers, and he frantically asked them if he "must needs, against my will, put my neck into the yoke?" (Starkey, 2003:630). In spite of his unhappy entreaties, no one could give him a way out. However, the King's ministers did try their best. They called the ambassadors from Cleves before them to swear that Anna had not been precontracted to anyone else. If she had been precontracted, then Henry would have been allowed to extricate himself from the forthcoming nuptials. Unfortunately for the King, Anna was free to make a lawful marriage. Henry had no choice. He had to marry the woman he denigrated as a Great Flanders Mare. He complained bitterly that, "If it were not that she is come so far into England [and that great preparations had been made] and for fear of making a ruffle in the world and driving her brother into the Emperor and the French King's hands, now being together, I would never have her, but now it is too far gone, wherefore I am sorry" (Bernard, 2007:550). The King lamented to Cromwell that "if it were not to satisfy the world and my realm, I would not do what I must do this day for none earthly thing" (Lindsey, 1995:149). So it was that the reluctant Henry married his fourth wife, Anna of Cleves, on January 6, 1540. As unwilling as the King was, Anna may have been no more happy about the impending marriage. There are no written records of her opinions or wishes, but an eyewitness noted that she came to her wedding "with most demure countenance and sad behavior" (Warnicke, 2000:156). Regardless of her feelings, it is Henry's unhappiness on his wedding day that is remembered.

    The wedding night was apparently every bit as dismal and unsatisfactory to the couple as the wedding itself had been. The next morning Cromwell, eager to hear any good news, asked his King if Henry were any happier with his new bride after a night with her. Cromwell's hopes of a happy union and a possible heir were dashed when Henry expostulated, "I liked her before not well, but now I like her much worse. For I have felt her belly and her breasts, and thereby, as I can judge, she should be no maid" (Starkey, 2003:632). Henry was convinced that Anna's breasts were "loose", and that this defect signaled a lack of virginity (Lindsey, 1995:50). This was not as crass a comment as it would seem to the modern eye. During the King's era, it was believed that the loss of the maidenhead wrought clear and obvious physiological changes in women, and that a virgin's body would have had "a smooth belly and tiny erect breasts" (Wernicke, 2000:166). Therefore Henry may have actually thought his bride was not 'pristine', simply because she had large breasts which felt softer and more 'slack' than smaller breasts, and a fuller midriff than was expected of a vestal bride. The King confided to Cromwell that the discovery of Anna's unchaste-feeling breasts and belly, "struck me so to the heart when I felt them that I had neither the will nor courage to proceed any farther in other matters", after which Henry left Anna "as good a maid as I found her" (Starkey, 2003:632). He furthermore assured Cromwell, "how that his nature hath abhorred her ever sithens so far that if his grace would (which he never minded nor thinketh to do) go about to have a do with her, his highness verily thinketh that his nature would not consent thereto" (Bernard, 2007:547). In short, even if Henry wanted to try to have sex with his new wife, which he certainly did not, he didn't think he could force himself to do it because she was so repulsive to him.

Cromwell was not the only person Henry in whom Henry confided his marital difficulties. The King also disclosed his problems to his royal physicians, and told them that he found his Queen's body, "in such sort disordered and indisposed to excite and provoke any lust in him" that he "could not in any wise overcome that loathesomeness, nor in her company be provoked or stirred to that act" (Starkey, 2003:632). Henry also unburdened himself to the Earl of Southampton, explaining that he had "not yet carnally known the Queen" and, considering how much he disliked her figure, he was never likely to be "provoked thereunto" (Bernard, 2007:547). Even as Henry was telling key courtiers that Anna was so disgusting to him that he could never bring himself to have sex with her, he was simultaneously making sure that his virility could not be called into question. The King maintained that while he was unable to force himself into intimacy with Anna, he was still so potent that he was experiencing "polluciones nocturnas in sommo", or ejaculation during erotic dreams, and could "perform the act with other, but not with her" (Starkey, 2003:632). Henry took some pains to assure all and sundry that he was as virile as ever, and that the lack of a sexual relationship was completely the fault of Anna's abominable and disgusting body. The man who had once striven to be a model of chivalry threw his gently-born and lawfully wedded wife to the court scandalmongers in order to salve his pride and deny his impotence.

Prior to the onset of McLeod's syndrome we can find no other evidence that Henry was ever deliberately cruel or disrespectful to the ladies of his court. For example, he never told Katherina of Aragon, "I don't want you anymore because you are no longer a pretty young woman." He always made the excuse of their 'unlawful' marriage, even to himself, to explain why he *had* to nullify their marriage. In contrast, the older King who had experienced such a radical change in personality after his fortieth birthday, the Henry who chopped off Anne Boleyn's head and had talked about going hunting while Jane Seymour died, was apparently perfectly capable of boorish and vulgar slander.

Although Henry was greatly displeased with Anna of Cleves, the people of England liked her very much. She was an immensely popular queen. Her subjects "loved and esteemed her as the sweetest, most gracious and kindest Queen they ever had or would desire" (Starkey, 2003:652). Courtiers also found her to be a truly amiable queen. How ironic that a queen who was intelligent, kind, good-natured, and beloved by her English subjects, should be so detested by her husband. Did Anna dislike Henry as much as he despised her?

With no written evidence of Anna's true thoughts, there remains argument between historians on what she probably thought of Henry and her marriage to the King. Much of the historical debate about the Queen's liking, or disdain, for her married life centers on a significant exchange between Anna and the English ladies who attended her. Her Ladies-in-Waiting were politely wishing out loud that their Queen was fortunate enough to be pregnant with the son that the King hoped for. Anna replied, adamantly, that she was most certainly not with child. One of her attendants asked her how she could "know that, and lie every night with the King?" (Lindsey, 1995:151). Anna just reiterated that she was most emphatically not pregnant. One of the Queen's attendants was Lady Rochford, who had been married to Anne Boleyn's brother George. Lady Rochford's propensity for sneakiness and lies helped get both her husband and her sister-in-law beheaded. It seems that there was nothing that Lady Rochford liked more than vicious muckraking, and it is very likely that she had heard rumors within the court that Henry was leaving his wife untouched. Never one to miss an opportunity to hurt others or obtain juicy tidbits of information, Lady Rochford slyly remarked, "I think your Grace a maid still indeed!" (Starkey, 2003:633). This was a very foolish thing for Lady Rochford to say, since it openly cast doubt on Henry's *ability* to consummate the marriage. Such an open-ended statement did not make it clear that the King was only unable to perform the sex act with his wife, but was not impotent in general. To cast aspersions on the King's virility was something that Henry would see as treason, and could easily result in execution. Anna was either truly naive, or simply smart enough to play dumb, because she demanded to know, "How can I be a maid and sleep every night with the King? When he kisses me and takes me by the hand and biddeth me, 'Goodnight sweetheart'. And in the morning, kisses me and biddeth me, 'Farewell darling'. Is this not enough?" (Lindsey, 1995:151). If Anna was not as completely unaware of marital intimacy as she seemed, then this was a very smart comment, in that it cast doubt on Anna's ability to entice the King, and left it open to question whether or not she even knew how to perform the sex act, but it did not call into question Henry's potency. She is seems to have been careful not to imply that Henry ever tried, but *failed*, to do the deed. She just seemed to imply that he never tried at all. Anna seemed determined to keep her head on her shoulders if she possibly could. When one of the Ladies-in-Waiting began to insist that there must be "more than this" if Anna were to bear a son, the Queen declared "Nay, I am content with this, for I know no more" (Starkey, 2007:633).

    Some historians theorize that Anna actually *was* completely unaware of what happened in bed between a man and a woman. Others think that Anna knew exactly what sex entailed, but was wily enough to give Henry grounds to divorce her, not kill her, which seems more likely. For one thing, it is extremely probable that one of the older females in her retinue, such as Mother Lowe, who was the Germanic 'mother' of the Ladies-in-Waiting that Anna had brought with her from Cleves, would have told her what to expect on her wedding night, rather than leave her completely unprepared. After all, wives were expected to be willing and eager participants in the bedroom, and the female orgasm was considered to be a requirement for conception. Anna seemed to seek ways to prove her lack of sexual knowledge. The Queen even refused suggestions to consult further with Mother Lowe about her marital duties to the King (Lindsey, 1995:151). Mother Lowe was clearly the person most suited to tell Anna the facts of life, or to clear up any misconceptions the Queen might have had. The fact Anna wouldn't go to Mother Lowe for help suggests that she knew the basics about the sex act, but wished to appear as though she did not in order to remain convincingly 'naive' when questioned about consummation with the potentially impotent King.

Additionally, the Queen seemed to be well aware that Henry was displeased with their marriage. Not only was he not having sex with her, he was avoiding spending much time in her company. The political situation had also changed, and the alliance with the Protestant courts was no longer as important to Henry. Anna of Cleves, now Queen of England, knew what happened to other queens that Henry no longer wanted. Being an intelligent woman, she must have been very afraid at this point.

The idea that Anna was trying to give Henry a reason to nullify their marriage, rather than behead her for some fabricated treason, is lent credence by the rumor that she explicitly told the King that she had actually been precontracted, which was almost certainly an untruth. The Queen reportedly said to her husband that, "If she had not been compelled to marry him, she might have fulfilled her engagement with another, to whom she had promised her hand" (Strickland and Strickland, 1851:67). This directly contradicts the findings of both of Henry's representatives, who were desperately looking for a way out of the marriage, and the Duke of Cleves' ambassadors, who were firm in their assertion they could provide documentation that there was no valid precontract.

If she actually told the King this prevarication, then she was smart to offer him a legal way out of the marriage. Henry was growing ever more dissatisfied with his bride. She was, among other things, failing to be as agreeable as he expected her to be, and was perhaps offering opinions of her own. Thus, the King complained that Anna had begun "to wax stubborn and willful" (Starkey, 2003:636). As far as Henry was concerned the Great Flanders Mare was not only ugly, she was offensively unfeminine and truculent. He desperately wanted out of the marriage, and despite Anna's assertions of a precontract, there was no proof it existed. A precontract would not provide him with a nullification, so the King was determined to find another way to untie the bonds of holy matrimony.

Henry gained further motivation to get rid of Anna as spring approached. He had fallen in love with someone else, and wanted to marry her. His heart was now set on Kathryn Howard, a teenaged niece of the Duke of Norfolk and a cousin of Anne Boleyn. His present Queen noticed Henry's infatuation with Kathryn, and complained about it to her brother's ambassadorial agent from Cleves, Karl Harst (Starkey, 2003:639). Although this has been interpreted by some historians as a sign that Anna was interested in maintaining her union with Henry, it is just as likely that she was simply embarrassed by his unmannerly and public preference for another woman, or perhaps she was upset because she was worried that a new amour might compel him to remove her current wife by means of a headsman's axe.

It would not, in the end, be Anna who was the recipient of the executioner's blow. Cromwell was the one whom the King would eventually put to death as punishment for orchestrating the nuptials which had proved to be a disappointment. First, however, the King needed Cromwell to find a way to annul the marriage to Anna of Cleves.

In what seemed to be a show of faith in his minister, Henry had Cromwell made the Earl of Essex, High Chamberlain of England, and the Chancellor of the Exchequer, as well as bestowing other titles and honors on him, on April 18, 1540 (Starkey, 2003:637). It is usually assumed that Henry wanted to give Cromwell a false sense of security before he struck, but that may not have been the case. If Henry was being affected by McLeod syndrome, he might well have been sincerely desirous of rewarding Cromwell for his faithful service. The abrupt about face, wherein Henry had Cromwell arrested and pitched into the Tower on June 10, less than two months after making him a nobleman, may have been uncalculated. Henry may have experienced a sudden conviction, born of paranoia, that Cromwell had arranged the alliance with Cleves as part of a plot to harm the King's peace of mind and happiness. It is also possible that Cromwell's downfall was instigated by the courtiers who surrounded Henry, rather than by the King himself. After all, there can be no doubt that the newly created Earl of Essex had many enemies at court, and those enemies encouraged Henry to destroy him. However, Cromwell had been the target of powerful enemies for years. It was only after the debacle of Henry's union to Anna of Cleves that Cromwell fell from favor. Clearly, the King's unhappiness with his marriage provoked Henry to turn arbitrarily and illogically against Cromwell. Such a strong and irrational reaction almost demands a mental illness to explain it.

  Roughly two weeks later, on June 24, Anna was sent from court to live at Richmond. On July 6, Anna was informed of the King's doubts about their marriage, and told that Henry was planning to assemble a convocation to examine her precontract with the heir to the duchy of Lorraine. Anna immediately gave her consent to the King's desire to look into the validity of the union, but she was undoubtedly worried about her fate.

  Henry's fondness for executions ensured that everyone was terrified of the King's enmity, and was therefore willing to do whatever it took to make him happy. Henry wanted an annulment from Anna. It was the job of the clergymen in the convocation to make sure that happened. Therefore, when the convocation met to discuss the annulment, it was actually to figure out how to give the King what he wanted. Their most concrete hope of annulling the marriage was based on the fact it was never consummated, and that the King had not truly given his consent. As mentioned earlier, Henry had previously declared Anna was "no maid" because her breasts and belly felt soft like those of a woman who had lost her virginity. Amazingly, her maidenhead was restored, perhaps by some supernatural means, when Henry needed it to provide a way out of the marriage. After a very short debate, Henry's marriage to Anna was annulled on July 9. The clergy made sure to emphasize that this annulment left the King free to remarry, which he would do just three weeks later.

A delegation was sent to Richmond three days after the convocation to discuss the matter with the Queen. She was so afraid that she was going to be murdered that she fainted when she saw the serious miens of the delegates (Lindsey, 1995:154). After she regained consciousness, she engaged in some well-deserved panic. Karl Harst reported that "she made such tears and bitter cries, it would break a heart of stone" (Starkey, 2003:641). Was Anna truly that unhappy to see her marriage end, or was she simply terrified Henry would have her slain? Would the King decide she had committed some 'crime' that would cost her her life? There was probably also a very natural concern that she might be sent back to Cleves in disgrace. Anna liked England, with its more relaxed attitude toward music, dancing, and card games, and did not wish to return to her former homeland. Moreover, her nebulous marital status meant she would have been unable to wed anyone else, and thus she would have been a burden and an embarrassment to her brother if she had returned to his court. In spite of her initial fears, her agitation was quickly soothed when she discovered that Henry was offering her an official position as his 'sister' if she would agree to the dissolution of their marriage. In her new role as Henry's sister, she would be allowed to visit and socialize at court, where she would take precedence over all other ladies, except for a new Queen and Henry's daughters. She would also be given manor houses, including Richmond, and a rich annuity of 4,000 pounds, provided she remained in England. Her household would be reduced, but she would be allowed to keep several of her Ladies-in-Waiting from Cleves with her, including Mother Lowe. In short, rather than banishment or death, Anna was being given a freedom few women of her time could ever hope to attain, plus lands, money, social position, and a perfect reason to remain in England. Undoubtedly relieved, Anna agreed to Henry's terms with alacrity.

Anna did everything in her power to assure Henry of her compliance with his terms. She quickly sent him notice of her agreement, wisely begging for the occasional gift of Henry's "most noble presence" and reinforcing her concurrence by addressing him as her "good Brother" as well as signing the letter as his "most humble sister" (Strickland and Strickland, 1851:75). Some historians believe that her request to see Henry occasionally possibly indicated that she loved him, and would have liked to continue as his wife. However, taking into consideration her rapid agreement to the nullification, it appears more likely to have been a wise use of flattery and meekness to keep on the good side of her new brother.

Henry didn't trust Anna's easy assent. He was expecting more resistance to the annulment from his rejected bride. He did not seem to realize that, unlike Katherina of Aragon, Anna of Cleves did not love him and was probably very content not to be his wife. Unable to believe in her indifference, he thought she might be plotting to cajole the Duke of Cleves into a war with England, and Henry made her promise that all letters to and from her family would go through royal channels, so that her correspondence could be examined for inflammatory content. The King furthermore insisted that Anna write a letter to the Duke of Cleves insisting she was happy with the annulment and the settlement she had received. Henry felt it was important to obtain a written document proving her agreement to the dissolution of the marriage, since as a woman she was naturally dishonest and incapable of maintaining a fixed opinion. He saw no irony in this. If anyone else saw the irony, they wisely didn't mention it. He admonished his ministers that without her written compliance the annulment would remain tenuous, inasmuch as the former Queen might yet "gather more stomach and stubbornness than were expedient" and rebel against the adjudication of the King's council (Strickland and Strickland, 1851:74). In order to allay Henry's fears, Anna dutifully wrote her brother in Cleves, declaring that she was happy in England and, "God willing, I purpose to live my life in the realm" (Lindsey, 1995:157). The same day she sent the letter to one brother, Anna sent her newest brother, Henry, the wedding ring he had given her just a few months earlier, "desiring that it might be broken in pieces as a thing which she knew of no force nor value" (Starkey, 2003:643). She could not have been more clear that she was very willing to be merely a sister to the King.

    Without the threat of being executed for displeasing her husband, the newly single Anna flourished in her adopted land. She was able to indulge herself in all manner of innocent pleasures so often denied her in the austere court of the Duke of Cleves, including lovely garments and musical entertainments, without the penalty of a glowering husband to dampen her enthusiasms. The French ambassador, perhaps amazed at how happy Anna was to be so ignominiously dismissed and dethroned, wrote that Henry's ex-wife was "as joyous as ever", and that she "wears new dresses every day, each more wonderful than the last. She passes all her time in sports and recreations" (Lindsey, 1995:157).

    The man who had promoted Anna's marriage to the King of England was not so lucky. Cromwell was executed on July 28, 1540. Prior to his death, Cromwell managed to perform one last service for the King, in order to guarantee that Henry obtained his much-desired annulment. The former chief minister wrote a long letter detailing everything he remembered about the marriage, and why it should be rendered void. At the bottom of the letter he wrote the personal plea, "Most gracious prince, I cry for mercy, mercy, mercy!" (Starkey, 2003:639). However, the aged King, who had once assiduously sought a way to avoid executing the Duke of Buckingham for much greater crimes, no longer had any mercy. The once rational and romantic Henry had become a victim of paranoia and impulsiveness.

    Perhaps Cromwell's downfall would generate more sympathy if he had not frequently used Henry's emotional instability for his own ends. When it had suited him, Cromwell had encouraged Henry's bloody vengeance. Cromwell had indisputably encouraged and abetted Henry's remorseless malevolence towards Anne Boleyn, as well as the innocent men who died along with her. Now, having helped create a monster, Cromwell was destroyed by it.

The swiftness of Cromwell's fall, when it is compared to the length of time it took Henry to decide to rid himself of Wolsey, again highlights how much Henry changed during the 1530s. Prior to the onset of McLeod syndrome, the King did not find it so easy to kill his ministers and closest advisors. In contrast to his precipitous imprisonment and execution of Cromwell, Henry vacillated about dismissing Wolsey, even when the Cardinal was caught aiding Henry's enemies. In contrast to Wolsey's slow and unsteady decline in the King's favor, Cromwell was legally murdered less than four months after being imprisoned. Under the influence of the paranoid delusions McLeod syndrome was probably causing, Henry had developed a pressing need to punish those around him for any difficulties he encountered. Cromwell, having been so instrumental in arranging the marriage Henry abhorred, was a natural target for the King's senseless wrath. It made no difference that Cromwell only contrived the match because he had the King's express permission to do so. Henry was not rational, and he wanted blood to appease his ill-temper. Since his power was nearly absolute within his own kingdom, Henry was able to indulge in his frustration and ire at Cromwell's expense. Unlike the hesitant dismissal of Wolsey undertaken by the younger Henry, the older Henry was able to destroy men with much less thought and much greater ease.

  Although his behavior towards Anna of Cleves could be explained by his narcissism and a lack of sexual chemistry between the betrothed couple, the King's retaliation against Cromwell for orchestrating the match is consistent with the erratic mental processes common in McLeod syndrome patients. Cromwell's execution was ordered impulsively, as a result of the paranoid conviction that any injury done to him must be deliberate, and because of frustrated pique that required an outlet. Henry no longer seemed capable of understanding the consequences of his rash actions. Like a small child crying for a toy broken in the heat of a temper-tantrum, a short time after Cromwell's death Henry wanted him back again. He raged against his councilors and Cromwell's former enemies, blaming them for having forced him to kill Cromwell over "light pretexts," and accused them of costing him "the most faithful servant he had ever had" (Scarisbrick, 1970:383). Henry appears to have been convinced he was a victim of a conspiracy to deprive him of his most able minister. He did not seem to accept his own role in Cromwell's demise. This is a strong indicator that his thought processes were both paranoid and blatantly irrational, both potential hallmarks of the mental symptoms of McLeod syndrome.

    It would be difficult to exaggerate how much Henry's actions in the last decade of his life were at odds with his behavior as a younger man. The youthful King was not prone to seeing plotters in every corner, or blaming others for his mistakes, as demonstrated by his reaction to a jousting accident in 1524. During a tournament he was inadvertently handed his lance and set on course before his visor was lowered. This error could have easily resulted in disfigurement or death. When his opponent's lance struck the King it splintered and rocketed the potentially lethal shards into Henry's face. It was almost miraculous that Henry was not, at minimum, blinded. Nonetheless, the King graciously forgave those responsible and insisted that it was all his fault for not checking his own visor. In comparison with the older King who blamed Anne Boleyn for More's death and Mary's persecution, and who blamed his ministers for Cromwell's execution, the gracious, honest and forgiving Henry of the 1520s looks like a completely different man. There is a good possibility that the King's change from knightly to nightmare was the result of McLeod syndrome altering his personality. It almost seems implausible to suggest this radical change in character could have come about as a result of anything other than a significant underlying illness.

    The King's mental status, and therefore the circumstances of the people who surrounded him, would grow steadily worse in the 1540s. Henry would not die until January of 1547. The seven years prior to his death are a long saga of bad decisions, murders only thinly veiled by the legal system, inept foreign policy, and wanton destruction. His courtiers, aware that Henry was dangerously erratic but unaware that he was probably truly insane, scrambled to gain wealth and power by exploiting Henry's weaknesses, and they often found themselves a head shorter for their efforts. Into this hellish mess would be thrown Henry's fifth and sixth wives. His last wife was a canny widow who was wise enough to act less intelligent than she truly was, but his fifth wife was a rather silly young woman with more affection than judgment. The self-deprecating and cautious widow would survive, while his impetuous and good natured young bride would be another famous victim of Henry's headsman.

Chapter Eight
Katheryn Howard: The Unfairly Reviled Rose Without a Thorn

Katheryn Howard has been maligned by many historians as, in essence, a harlot. Even those who are sympathetic to her often describe her in terms that show that fruit of 'slut-shaming'. The noted historian David Starkey maintains that he writes about Katheryn's "promiscuity without disapproval," calling her a "woman with a past" but without meaning to condemn her because "like many good-time girls, she was also warm, loving and good-natured" (Starkey, 2003:648 and 655). Lacey Baldwin Smith, in his lauded biography of Henry's fifth Queen, wrote that her life was "little more than a series of petty trivialities and wanton acts, punctuated by sordid politics", but lamented that her life was cut so tragically short by the backstairs politics that "transformed juvenile delinquency into high treason" (Smith, 2009:10). In his well-respected book about the King, *Henry VIII: The Mask of Royalty*, Smith was more blunt, saying that Henry had discovered his young wife had "been behaving like a common whore" (Smith, 1982:194). Both authors have a cordial attitude toward the fallen Queen, and they clearly view her as having been overly punished and victimized by forces beyond her control, but it is also clear they see her primarily as a sweet natured and simple-minded strumpet.

    Historians have rarely pointed out that her sexual history was far from extreme. Even her adulterous affair, which apparently never passed beyond flirtation, should be looked at in a mitigating light. This defence of Katheryn's actions is not a wholesale approval of adultery, but simply an acknowledgment that she was a young woman given very little choice about marrying her husband, who happened to be more than thirty years older than herself with leg wounds that stank and seeped pus. Her adulterous flirtation may not have been moral, but few would argue that it was not understandable. She was probably enthusiastically willing to marry the King, since she would finally have both the attention and material success she obviously craved, but when she said "I do" it is likely that she really meant "I do ... want to be the Queen". Her marriage was not a love match; it was her way out of obscurity and into importance, where both her family and her society would suddenly find her valuable and special. In all honesty, she was not renowned for being particularity intelligent, but that does not mean she was was necessarily a light-skirt.

    She was one of many children born to the obscure and scrounging younger brother of the Duke of Norfolk, Edmund

Howard, and his first wife, Jocasta Culpepper (Smith, 2009:39-42). Unfortunately, her mother died when Katheryn was still very young. Katheryn was then sent to live with Agnes Howard, the Dowager Duchess of Norfolk, who was the second wife of the Duke of Norfolk's father, and thus Katheryn's step-grandmother. Agnes Howard had a large household, and many major and minor noble families sent their younger daughters there to act as Ladies-in-Waiting to the Dowager Duchess, in order to fine tune their skills for court life. There were so many young women and girls in the household that there was actually a dormitory, called the Maidens' Chamber, where they all slept. Agnes had the door to this dormitory locked each night, in order to preserve the chastity, or at least the marriageability, of her wards (Starkey, 2003:644-646). However, several of the Dowager Duchess' Ladies-in-Waiting, like many young women throughout the centuries, were more interested in the opposite sex than they were anxious to preserve their virtue.

Katheryn, who was largely neglected during her childhood, found that she, like her cousin Anne Boleyn, possessed some magical characteristic that rendered her especially desirable. Men are, of course, drawn to women with this aura of sexual allure, but the women who are imbued with it are, with distressing frequency, blamed for attracting men. In patriarchal societies, women are considered the gatekeepers of morality, and thus it falls to the women to keep suitors at bay. Katheryn seemed to have little interest in safeguarding morality. Instead, she discovered that she could gain both affection and pleasure by being flirtatious and indulging in some physical romance with her beaux.

She must have been captivating, since her admirers always seemed to fall head over heels in love with her.

Katheryn's first suitor was her music teacher, Henry Manox, which did not work out well for the lovestruck Manox. He admitted that he was deeply infatuated with Katheryn and claimed she returned his interest, but it is unlikely that she felt any deep emotion toward him. For example, she told him emphatically that she would never marry him since she was a Howard by birth and could expect a much better match with a gentleman of rank (Lindsey, 1995:160). Although she apparently enjoyed his embraces, he clearly was not an object of her affection. Their semi-romance ended when Agnes Howard caught Manox and Katheryn canoodling. Agnes was vexed, and struck Katheryn, not so much for the licentiousness of her behavior, but rather for being foolish enough to risk her reputation with a commoner. She also forbade them to ever be alone together again (Starkey, 2003:646-647). The loss of Manox did not seem to have any lasting effect on Katheryn, because she quickly found another admirer to replace him.

Katheryn caught the eye of Francis Dereham. He was a more respectable beau, being a gentleman and, if not rich, at least financially comfortable (Starkey, 2003:647). Dereham seems to have fallen in love with the charming Mistress Howard, and repeatedly begged her to marry him, but although Katheryn liked him well enough, she did not consider him a serious marriage prospect (Lindsey, 1995:162). Nevertheless, she enjoyed his company enough to have sex with him, an act she appears to have found enjoyable. She didn't seem to worry that an unexpected pregnancy would force her to the altar: she believed that she knew how to "meddle with a man and yet conceive no child" (Loads, 2009:116). Several of the 'maidens' in the Maidens' Chamber appear to have been like-minded about the benefits of having a lover, so Katheryn was far from alone in her notions. The young women and girls who shared the dormitory bribed the dowager's maid to bring them the key to their door. At night, when they were supposed to be sleeping, they opened their door and allowed their suitors to come inside and woo them. The various boyfriends would bring alcoholic beverages, "strawberries, apples and other things to make good cheer" with, and would "commonly banquet and be merry there till two or three of the clock in the morning" (Starkey, 2003:647).

Manox was spitefully jealous. The musician bragged that Katheryn had promised him her virginity, and "from the liberties the young lady has allowed me, I doubt not of being able to effect my purpose" (Lindsey, 1995:161). However, he not only failed to convince her to have intercourse with him, Katheryn had actually chosen someone else to receive her maidenhead. Manox wanted to stop Dereham's visits so he slipped a note to Agnes Howard warning her of secret liaisons in the Maidens' Chamber. Manox was thwarted in his plans to separate Katheryn and Dereham, since the Dowager Duchess was more concerned with the effect that too much rich food might have on Katheryn's good looks than she was about the pre-marital sex (Starkey, 2003:648). Thus, the tomfoolery in the dormitory continued unabated. In such an atmosphere it is doubtful Katheryn ever learned to connect negative consequences with petting and/or copulation, and she was not wise enough to understand that the permissiveness allowed to a single woman of no importance in Agnes Howard's household would not be acceptable if that same young woman was married to a man of rank. She also did not seem to understand the strict standards to which she would need to adhere if she were a Queen, since it was unlikely she had even contemplated such a scenario.

Although she apparently relished her affair with Dereham

during its duration, Katheryn had no problems leaving him when she had a chance to attend court in the winter of 1539. When the lovesick Dereham tried to remind her they were engaged, she asserted that they most certainly were not. She was thrilled to leave the Dowager's household and become one of Anna of Cleves' Ladies-in-Waiting. When questioned later, Katheryn declared that she had never been pre-contracted to Dereham and that everyone "that knew me, and kept my company, know how glad and desirous I was to come to the court" (Starkey, 2003:648).

Most likely it is her ability to separate sex from love, and love from marriage, that has caused historians to revile her for centuries. The male courtiers of the Tudor era knew that having sex with a woman did not explicitly indicate they were in love with her and they also knew that there were women with whom one could have sex, or even love, but could never marry. Furthermore, gentlemen of this time knew that they must wed a woman of the correct social standing, preferably with a large dowry to sweeten the nuptials. There is a persistent myth that women, but not men, must be in an emotionally fulfilling relationship in order to enjoy sex. No matter how frequently it is scientifically disproved, this idea that women and men are *inherently* different in regards to sex and love, with its attendant belief that women are "naturally monogamous", continually rises from its grave, like a zombie, and staggers across the landscape of the popular media (Daniluk, 2003:213-215; Bay-Cheng, 2006:209). Since women are socially constructed as sexually disinterested and biologically driven to be chaste, any woman who does not conform to these ideologies is, by cultural definition, "abnormal". Even in modern times, these abnormal women are often punished for their deviant sexuality, usually with name calling and forms of social ostracization. In the sixteenth century penalties for female "deviant" sexual behavior could be much more severe. A woman in the Tudor era sometimes had to face more than being called a slut and getting the cold shoulder from her peers; in some circumstances she could lose her life if she exercised sexual autonomy, which is exactly what happened to Katheryn Howard. The past and current prohibitions about women's passions are therefore the reason that Henry's fifth wife, who usurped the male prerogative of enjoying sex *without love*, and considered marriage without starry-eyed idealism, has gained an enduring reputation as a wanton harlot.

  Court life was ideally suited to Katheryn. Her strongest accomplishments were her ability to flirt and gain popularity. These skills were perfect for the life of a Lady-in-Waiting. She soon attracted the eye of one of the court's most successful lotharios, Thomas Culpepper. He was a well known womanizer and one of Henry's special favorites. Culpepper was also a rapist and a murderer (Lindsey, 1995:168). He sexually assaulted the wife of a park-keeper and he was such a resounding coward that he had his attendants hold her down while he attacked her. When villagers tried to come to her aid, Culpepper killed one of her would-be rescuers. He was arrested for these heinous offences but as he was a good friend of the King he was granted a royal pardon (Ward, 2008:4). Either people in court were unaware of his crimes, or simply did not care what disgusting atrocities he had committed as long as the victims were members of the lower socio-economic classes, because his social success remained intact.

  Although the breach was probably unrelated to the fact he

was a rapist, the romance between Katheryn and Culpepper cooled off abruptly in early 1540. When a fellow courtier told Katheryn that he had heard she and Culpepper were engaged, she shrugged it off, telling him, "If you heard such a report you heard more than I do know" (Starkey, 2003:649). No one is precisely sure when or why Culpepper and Katheryn stopped keeping company, but it is possible that it was because she had attracted the notice of the King, and she wanted, or was ordered by her paternal uncle, to give all of her attention to Henry. The King had certainly become serious about her by April of 1540, and had probably been infatuated with her for some time before that, so the timing fits with her withdrawal from Culpepper. Someone informed Agnes Howard that Henry was besotted with Katheryn, "the first time that ever his Grace saw her" (Smith, 2009:95). Katheryn was not the type to have missed an opportunity to become a royal favorite, and a relationship with Culpepper would have hindered her ability to keep the King interested in her.

    For the Duke of Norfolk and his Catholic allies at court, Henry's interest in Katheryn was invaluable. Therefore, the formerly ignored young niece was spoken of to the King in glowing terms. Feasts were held in her honor. Agnes Howard sent stylish new clothes so Katheryn would look her best for His Majesty (Starkey, 2003:650). The young woman was also told "how to behave" and "in what sort to entertain the king's highness and how often" (Scarisbrick, 1970:429). She was probably coached on what to say about Cromwell in order to hasten his fall and execution, since the Duke was one of Cromwell's most bitter enemies. She had her full share of family pride, and was probably delighted to be of such importance and use to her crafty uncle. She also undoubtedly reveled in the attentions of a King.

Unlike Katheryn, the King was a romantic. He wanted attraction to be, at least for a time, a form of love. When he saw her acting as a Lady-in-Waiting to his wife, Anna of Cleves, he became infatuated by her looks. After he knew her better, Henry fell in love with her charming sweetness and flirtatious manner. Once he was in love, he was determined to make her the new Queen of England. The fact that this was an idiotic political move, one which would potentially alienate his Germanic allies and would certainly forward Norfolk's agenda, did not matter to the King. This decision, unlike so many of Henry's choices in the last years of his reign, was probably not the result of an unstable mental state resulting from the McLeod syndrome. It was most likely a remnant of the 'real' Henry, acting with the same determination to wed his true love as he did when he was a younger and healthier man. After all, he was once the dashing young King who rescued and married his destitute widowed sister-in-law, Katherina of Aragon. He was the same man who had been determined to honor his love for Anne Boleyn with a wedding, even at the expense of his first wife. This is precisely what he was trying to do again for Katheryn, at the expense of his marriage to Anna of Cleves. While it is likely that McLeod syndrome had profoundly altered the king's personality, at times the lover he used to be shone through, although this light was dimmed by his bone-deep narcissism and erratic temperament.

    The nuptials of Henry and Katheryn Howard were held quietly on July 28, 1540, the same day that Thomas Cromwell was beheaded. Henry's happiness with his new bride did not seem to alleviate his irrational need to eradicate his perceived "enemies", because just a few days later he executed six well-respected men for the feeblest of reasons. The oddest thing about these judicial murders was the fact that three of the men, Robert

Barnes, William Jerome, and Thomas Garret, were religious reformers, but the other three men, Edward Powell, Richard Fetherston, and Thomas Abel, were devout Catholics. There were no plausible explanations for any of their deaths and the French ambassador wrote that it was a "perversion of justice of which both parties complained .... they had never been called to judgment, nor knew why they were condemned" (Lindsey, 1995:156).

    Historians have struggled to explain why Henry would have killed so many prominent men for no given reason on the same day. Some historians have even argued that Henry is not to blame for these deaths; that the King was really a victim of conspiracies and skulduggery practiced by the bloodthirsty factions within his court. However, the King was the supreme authority and as such the decision to exterminate these men on a whim was ultimately his. These were distinguished men who were killed, not pickpockets apprehended at a market who could be punished with no public outcry. To give just one example, Thomas Abel had been Katherina of Aragon's personal chaplain for years and had written a book defending her marriage to Henry. The executions of these men were important enough for ambassadors to write home about. How on earth could the King not have know of and approved their executions? Those historians who theorize that Henry executed the men for a concrete purpose speculate that the King was possibly trying to show he was going to walk a line between Catholicism and the Reformation, and to demonstrate that those who strayed too far into either camp would die. While these arguments have merit, it may be that there was no *real* political or social motivation for the executions of the six men. It was possibly yet another sign that the King was slipping further into irrational paranoia and impulsive rage due to the effects of McLeod syndrome, and the men were all executed because of notions Henry formed while influenced by a delusional mental state.

When the King married Katheryn it had been less than eight months since he had married Anna of Cleves. Two weddings in one year was quite an accomplishment, even for someone who had grown as unpredictable as Henry. The King was now forty-nine years old and his bride was in her late teens or early twenties. For Henry, there was no question of impotence with Katheryn; her sexual allure was compelling and her youth titillated him. Within his kingdom peasants were starving because of a persistent drought that was killing crops and cattle, but Henry was too ecstatic in his nuptial bliss to care (Starkey, 2003:650). The cloudless skies that were causing such misery for the common populace were also ensuring that the King had sunny days for hunting and starry nights for feasting, dancing, and making love. Henry ignored governance to concentrate on his new Queen, and since there was no longer a figure like Cromwell to manage the kingdom for him, governance quickly deteriorated (Lindsey, 1995:156). Frankly, the King did not seem worried in the slightest about any of the larger problems surrounding him. At least for that short summer, Henry could fancy himself a young and virile man again, and that was all he cared to know.

To say that Henry was madly in love with his new bride is an understatement. He called Katheryn his "rose without a thorn" and boasted to his courtiers that she was a "jewel" (Lindsey, 1995:164). Naturally even-tempered and happy-go-lucky, Katheryn was content to submit to Henry in all things and to be showered with gifts in return for her docility. The King was enchanted, and gave her a motto that reflected her easy acquiescence: "no other wish save his" (Smith, 2009:138). Katheryn had a great deal of motivation to please her husband, which Henry saw as a delightfully feminine trait and a sign of her overwhelming love for him. The French ambassador wrote that Henry was so enamored of Katheryn that "he cannot treat her well enough" (Starkey, 2003:651). It was true. Henry bought her a warehouse-worth of beautiful and expensive gowns, gloves, shoes and headdresses. He practically buried her in gemstones and jewelry. Among the gifts he gave her was a necklace with 29 rubies, 116 pearls, and a gold pendant holding a large diamond, a large ruby and with a long baroque pearl hanging on the end. Another necklace he gave her had 33 diamonds, 60 rubies, and a border of pearls (Starkey, 2003:651). He also gave her earrings, bracelets, rings, and furs. The orphaned girl who had grown up as a neglected and poor dependent relation was now rolling in material wealth and adulation.

    Katheryn clearly loved to receive expensive presents from her enchanted husband, but she was as generous as she was acquisitive. She gave old friends and relations gifts, money and positions in her household, and asked Henry to give them jobs in the government or in his household as well. This behavior was considered to be an essential part of being a good person in the Tudor era (Starkey, 2003:661). Those who were given positions of authority were expected to do their very best to secure the fortunes of other members of their extended kin networks. Katheryn seemed more than willing to help those who came to her for a handout.

    She was also incredibly gracious to Anna of Cleves. The fact the two ladies were going to meet eventually at court must have caused the courtiers a fair amount of consternation. The Earl of Essex, who was the Lord Great Chamberlain and was therefore the man responsible for matters of etiquette pertaining to the royal household, must have been extremely anxious while he was arranging the meeting, since there was no precedent for such an occasion (Starkey, 2003:652). Katheryn had once waited on Anna of Cleves as a lowly member of her household. Now the young girl had usurped Anna's husband and the crown. How would Anna treat her successor? How would the present Queen treat the former Queen? If either woman behaved in a petty, jealous, or rude manner there would be a huge scandal. Happily, all worries were unnecessary. Just after New Year's Day in 1541, Anna of Cleves came to meet the new Queen, and Henry's former wife went down on her knees in respect before Katheryn, showing "as much reverence and punctilious ceremony as if she herself were the most insignificant damsel at court" (Starkey, 2003:653). Katheryn responded by pleading with Anna to stand and extended every courtesy imaginable to her. They had dinner together with Henry, which went well, and then stayed and danced with other courtiers after Henry went to bed (Lindsey, 2003:165).

The new Queen also used her influence over Henry to mitigate his blood-lust. She petitioned for Henry's mercy on behalf of both commoners and courtiers alike. Katheryn asked the King to stop the execution of a low-born spinning-woman named Helen Page, and also pleaded for the life of a courtier named John Wallop, both times with success (Lindsey, 1995:167). When Henry threw the famous English poet, Thomas Wyatt, into the Tower for the iniquitous crime of having formerly received Cromwell's patronage, Katheryn begged Henry to free him as well (Starkey, 2003:659). To oblige his pretty young wife, Henry released Wyatt. Nevertheless, the King made the odd stipulation that the poet had to reconcile with his estranged wife, even though he and his ex-wife hated each other. No one has ever been able to give a convincing argument as to why Henry made his unorthodox demand that Wyatt and his wife reunite. There may have been no reasonable explanation. McLeod syndrome might have caused the King to have such an erratic mental state by this point that Henry's ideas were no longer governed by any sort of logic.

  Katheryn, although not the hussy she is often depicted as, was not a saint either. She was a human being, and as such, had fights and disagreements in spite of her usually jolly temperament. Famously, she quarreled with Henry's eldest daughter, Mary. It is not surprising that Katheryn and Mary would have difficulties with one another. They were as different as chalk and cheese. Katheryn was somewhat flighty, flirtatious, fun, and apparently considered her religion (when she considered it at all) to be something that made her attend service on certain days but not anything she had to worry about (Starkey, 2003:654-655). Mary had suffered heinous emotional abuse at the hands of her father, had been torn away from the mother she loved dearly, had endured having her entire worldview blow up in her face, had been declared a bastard, was a serious thinker, and cared deeply about Catholicism. Considering their glaring dissimilarities, it is hard to imagine that the women would have an instant rapport. Additionally, the King had recently repudiated a woman that Mary loved in order to marry Anne Boleyn's sexually alluring cousin. This almost certainly reopened Mary's emotional wounds regarding her parents' acrimonious separation. It was probably Mary's loyalty to Anna of Cleves that caused her first battle with the new Queen.

  Historians are not sure exactly what happened between Mary and Katheryn, but it is known that the King's daughter did not treat the newest Queen with the "same respect" as she had treated Jane Seymour and Anna of Cleves (Lindsey, 1995:166). It was doubtlessly hard for Mary to treat a younger, lower-born, frivolous woman as her superior. This attitude, which Mary must not have hidden well, offended Katheryn, and she threatened to have some of Mary's personal Ladies-in-Waiting sent away. The threat of losing even more allies and people close to her must have terrified Mary, because she quickly "found means to conciliate" her stepmother (Whitelock, 2010:112). Katheryn, who was too good-natured to be truly vindictive, appears to have allowed the women to stay with Mary. The Queen displayed a further lack of maliciousness when she encouraged Henry to allow his daughter to come back to court full time.

    Katheryn also tried to knit Henry's fractured family unit back together. She made large gifts to Mary in an attempt to win her over, and she also gave small gifts to Elizabeth. Mary was a significant political figure and many at court, including the Duke of Norfolk, still looked to her with the hope of restoring Catholicism to England. Norfolk, as Katheryn's uncle, may have even pressured the Queen to try to win her oldest step-daughter's affections, in case Mary ever came into power after Henry's death. However, there was no reason for her to be nice to Elizabeth. It might even have been in her best interest to disassociate herself from Anne Boleyn's child. Instead, she went with her own inclinations to be kind to the little girl, and it was mostly because of Katheryn's efforts to unite the siblings as a family that Mary, Elizabeth, and Prince Edward all exchanged New Year's gifts with one another in 1543 (Starkey, 2003:660). Ironically, Henry had executed Katheryn several months earlier, so she was not alive to see her efforts to promote family unity bear fruit.

The Queen was often generous in a way that, to the modern eye, makes her seem foolish -- or at least painfully naive. For example, she appointed many of her friends from her days in the Dowager' service to her establishment at court, even though those friends were well aware that Katheryn had a former lover. Even more ill-advised is the fact that she appointed that same former lover, Dereham, to her household as well, in the capacity of her private secretary (Lindsey, 1995:167). It was especially problematic to have Dereham around, since he was such a colossal simpleton that he bragged about being an especial favorite of the Queen, and even claimed that if the King were to die "I am sure I might marry her" (Smith, 2009:148). Her seemingly imprudent patronage of the people from her less-than-chaste past was not, however, imbecilic: Tudor culture demanded that she give jobs to, or otherwise aid, her friends and relations. She was under tremendous pressure from the dowager Duchess and other noble relatives to give Dereham a place at court (Starkey, 2003:661). There was no reason for her to think that Dereham would risk his life by revealing he had once enjoyed a carnal relationship with the new Queen. If anyone, including Dereham, made her private secrets public then they would also have lost their advantageous place at court, and thus would have fallen almost as far and as fast as Katheryn.

The only truly asinine thing Katheryn did was risk her life by resuming her relationship with Thomas Culpepper. Moreover, it appears that she risked her life for the titillation of an illicit romance, rather than for actual sexual gratification, since both she and Culpepper swore that their flirtation had "not passed beyond words"(Smith, 1982:199). In fact, romance may not have been a significant inducement for Katheryn. She may have been more motivated by the thrill of *intrigue* than emotional impulse, since Culpepper would later testify that she loved him, but Katheryn herself refuted that claim (Lindsey, 1995:176). The Queen never loved Culpepper. In spite of her sweet words and promises to Culpepper, it is likely she indulged in the affair not as the result of a grand passion, but simply for personal amusement. Her beaux, Manox, Dereham, and Culpepper, even the King himself, were all convinced that Katheryn was as enamored of them as they were infatuated with her, but Katheryn seems to have given them all the style, but not the substance, of her affections. They touched her body, but not her heart.

If she wasn't in love, why did she want Culpepper? Why did Katheryn, who was silly but not stupid, risk her life to dally with him? Culpepper was a cold-blooded rapist and murderer, but he was also handsome, dashing, and charming, as many sociopaths are. She may have been willing to risk so much for their flirtations simply because she did not understand how much she had to lose. The Queen was amazingly uneducated about anything other than flirtation and fashion. She may have realized she would be in trouble if the King found out, but may not have understood that what she was doing was treason, especially since she was not actually physically intimate with Culpepper. She had also been getting away with breaking rules her entire life, thanks to her popularity, so she may not have realized it was impossible to continue her assignations with Culpepper without being discovered. Furthermore, since anyone complicit in her semi-affair would be in as much trouble as she was herself, she probably thought she was safe from anyone who would be able to tell tales. Finally, the court was full of intrigues, immorality, and infidelity so outrageous that they could be used as a basis for any modern television soap opera; if no one else died for their extramarital love lives, why should she? Finally, she might have thought that Henry, who was clearly unhealthy, would die relatively soon, which meant she only needed to be discreet for a little time.

Katheryn and Culpepper probably restarted their illicit relationship in the late winter or early spring of 1541. At first it was light coquetry, acceptable to the ears of others and possible to pass off as gallantry. As the affair intensified, they wanted more privacy to indulge in sexually charged flirtation. Their affair mainly consisted of these trysts. Doubtlessly it would have been consummated sooner or later, and Culpepper was frank when he said he had "intended and meant to do ill with the queen, and that in like wise the queen so minded to do with him" (Lindsey, 1995:176). Nevertheless, their romance was discovered before it reached that stage. Both Katheryn and Culpepper swore that it had remained unconsummated, even after they had been sentenced to death. Thus, they were executed for *lust,* rather than for physical adultery; yet mutual lust was enough for their relationship to be treason.

One of Katheryn's most serious mistakes was to trust one of her attendants, Lady Rochford. Lady Rochford was George Boleyn's widow, and her treachery had helped kill both her husband and her sister-in-law. Why would Katheryn place her faith in a woman who had been instrumental in the deaths of George and Anne Boleyn? It is possible that Katheryn just didn't think of Lady Rochford in that context, since the Queen was a young child when Anne and George were executed. All that seemed to matter to Katheryn was that Rochford was eager to help her meet with Culpepper. Unfortunately, the Queen didn't understand that Lady Rochford was inherently treacherous. If the Queen had been just a little more wise, or even just more mature, she would have realized she couldn't trust a woman like Lady

Rochford, who was known for her disloyalty and willingness to be an informer. The bigger mystery in the relationship between Katheryn and Lady Rochford is why George Boleyn's widow was willing to put her life in jeopardy to aid the Queen's illicit passion. Rochford would be executed for treason, just like Katheryn and Culpepper, should the dalliance be discovered. Did Rochford think that she could escape by turning informant, as she had with her late husband? Or was it that Lady Rochford just could not resist getting her malicious little claws into a juicy bit of subterfuge?

Whatever motivated the Queen, Lady Rochford, and Culpepper, it was a very foolish risk for them all to take. Henry was an extremely dangerous man to trifle with and at least two of the intriguers would have known that "the king's wrath is death" (Smith, 2009:64). Moreover, the King was feeling particularly touchy as his physical and mental health worsened, and not even his obsessive love for his new Queen was making him happy. His leg ulcers closed up in March of 1541; since the pus could not drain out of the newly closed sores the King became feverish and extremely ill, and his increased pain caused him to experience "a black gloom for weeks" (Scarisbrick, 1970:486). He would not even allow Katheryn to come to him during this time, probably because he did not want her to see him looking like such a sick old man. In addition to his episodes of depression, he was showing ever increasing signs of mental instability.

One example of his erratic thought processes is provided by his decision to order the beheading of his mother's first cousin, the elderly Countess of Salisbury, Margaret Pole, on May 27, 1541 (Fraser, 1992:342). Her execution was completely unnecessary, and politically injudicious. Although the King had killed her oldest son and her grandson already, one of her surviving sons, Cardinal Reginald Pole, was a serious political enemy and a continued thorn in Henry's side. Cardinal Pole lived in continental Europe, safely out of Henry's reach, where he continued to fight against England's political agendas and malign Henry's character. The only possible leverage Henry had over Pole was the fact that he had absolute control over the comfort, and fate, of the Cardinal's mother. By killing the Countess, he lost any power he might have had over the rebellious Pole. Yet in his paranoid state the King saw the venerable Countess as a source of danger, even though her threat to Henry was nonexistent. Henry's implacable and irrational paranoia had become so extreme that, even if it was not caused by worsening McLeod syndrome, it should at least be considered to be rooted in a mental illness of some kind.

    To make the matter of Margaret Pole's death even worse, there was an inexperienced young man filling in for the executioner that day and the beheading became a mutilation. Gruesomely, the innocent and well-respected Countess was struck several times around her head and shoulders before she finally, and mercifully, died (Fraser, 1992:342-343). A rumor, entirely unconfirmed, has grown up around the circumstances of Margaret Pole's legally sanctioned murder. The story recounts how the Countess, crying out that she was not a traitor and would not willingly be treated as one, fought with those trying to kill her, and boldly told the headsman that if he wanted to cut off her head "he must get it as he could" (Lindsey, 1995:172). This is probably more of a legend meant to acknowledge the strength of character Margaret Pole possessed than anything truthful, but it seems a fitting epitaph for the Countess of Salisbury, whom Henry's councilors called "rather a strong and constant man than a woman" (Lindsey, 1995:172).

Henry's new Queen may have been too busy enjoying her wardrobe and flirting with Culpepper to really give much thought to the King's behavior, but the other members of the Tudor court regarded the needless murder of the Countess of Salisbury with revulsion. His daughter Mary was one of the people who was most traumatized by the death of the Countess. Lady Salisbury had been Mary's governess and godmother, so Mary was yet again forced to experience the loss of a mother-figure at the whim of her beloved father. In spite of the horrors Henry was almost perpetually inflicting upon her, Mary, like most children, still loved her father. She must have been torn apart inside by her continued love for the father who kept destroying, in one way or another, women she loved. Moreover, she was a strict adherent to the religion her father was dismantling around her. She was probably plagued with fears for Henry's soul, just as her mother had been. Yet that same religion, and her entire culture, insisted that she obey her father in all things. The cognitive dissonance between the reality of what was happening to her and her socio-cultural upbringing must have been agonizing.

Mary was going to see Henry execute one more 'mother' in her life before a year had passed. Katheryn may not have felt much like a step-mother to Mary, but it must have been shocking to see her father kill another one of his wives.

The beginning of Katheryn's end came in November of 1541. Enemies of her powerful uncle, and those who were afraid of a potential return to Catholicism, discovered she had previously had sexual relations with Francis Dereham (Lindsey, 1995:174). Cranmer, as the Archbishop of Canterbury, wrote Henry a letter telling the King about these shocking accusations. Initially, Henry was incensed at the allegations, rather than at the

Queen. The King insisted she was maligned, that the rumors were "rather a forged matter than of truth" (Starkey, 2003:668), and that there should be an investigation only in order to clear his beloved Queen's good name. Everyone knew it was a small step from Henry's doubt, to his suspicion, and then to the Tower and a headsman's ax. What if he decided that those who had accused Katheryn were spreading calumny against the Queen? Would he see it as a plot against her and, thus, as a plot against the throne? Cranmer and the others were now strongly motivated to prove Katheryn's guilt since their lives would have been forfeit if the King turned against them.

Evidence, in the form of sworn statements from all parties, was not hard to obtain. Katheryn's former boyfriends, her current lover, and her 'friend' Lady Rochford all turned on her like jackals. The Queen was no better than her co-conspirators, blaming everyone but herself for her liaisons.

The King had appointed four men to scrutinize the Queen's past. The investigators first went after Katheryn's former music instructor, Manox. Revoltingly, Manox had bragged he had once had Katheryn, "by the cunt, and I know it among hundreds" (Starkey, 2003:669). He confessed that he had petitioned the Queen to be allowed to touch her genitals, and that she had agreed on the condition that he ask for nothing else. He maintained his assertion that he and Katheryn had never had sexual intercourse, even when he was questioned repeatedly, and possibly even tortured (Lindsey, 2003:175). At this point the revelations about Katheryn would be embarrassing, and might enrage Henry, but would not impugn her virginal state at marriage. If the search had stopped with Manox, she might have been safe.

Sadly for the Queen, Dereham was next to be

interrogated. Now the fox was truly set among the chickens, because Dereham, rather than defending his former love, confessed to having had sex with Katheryn. It might not have been a lack of chivalry that made him kiss and tell -- it may have been the rack or some other form of torture device that inspired him to give the details of their relationship (Starkey, 2003:674). Other women who had lived with Katheryn in the Maidens' Chamber testified they had heard Dereham and Katheryn "puffing and blowing", and they had all surmised that the couple were engaged in coitus (Starkey, 2003:670). Certainly Dereham could have argued that he and Katheryn had never gone beyond heavy petting, no matter what other people in the Maidens' Chamber might have heard, since it was so dark at night in Tudor bedrooms that no one was likely to have actually *seen* them having sex. The only person who claimed to have seen anything could only testify that she had witnessed Dereham lift Katheryn's dress and look at her body (Starkey, 2003:670). Why didn't Dereham simply maintain a lie? In all likelihood he was unable to prevaricate convincingly under the strain of unceasing and brutal questioning.

     When the news of Katheryn's prior relationships with Manox and Dereham was reported to Henry, he was devastated that his innocent young bride was not a maiden on their wedding night. He wept and raged so violently that his ministers feared for his sanity, which was already tenuous (Smith, 1982:198). Henry would vacillate between anger and sorrow, sometimes waving a sword and claiming the Queen would never have "such delight in her lechery as she should have pain and torture in her death", and at other times crying with such abandon it was considered "strange in [one of] his courage" (Smith, 1982:198). Feeling immeasurably sorry for himself, he lamented the fact he met with "such ill-conditioned wives" and tried to blame his council of advisors for his error in marrying Katheryn (Scarisbrick, 1970:432). Henry never saw his pretty young Queen again; he returned to Whitehall in London, leaving her at Hampton court without a farewell (Starkey, 2003:671). She was completely unaware of her impending doom.

There was worse news to come for Henry, much to Katheryn's detriment. Dereham's presence at court had made the investigators suspicious that he had continued the affair with Katheryn even after her marriage to the King. Dereham, who was desperate to prove that he had not resumed his romance with Katheryn, offered them the information that "Culpepper had succeeded him in the Queen's affections" (Starkey, 2003:674). This went beyond youthful indiscretions. Any dalliance Katheryn indulged in after she had married the King was high treason, and the death sentence for treason was particularly barbarous.

Culpepper and Lady Rochford were too well connected and of too high a rank to be tortured. Nevertheless, when questioned by the investigators they both revealed the reoccurring liaisons between Culpepper and Katheryn, but they were so clearly trying to save themselves at the expense of the Queen that there is every cause to doubt their veracity. Culpepper insisted that he was lured into the intrigue by Katheryn, who had pursued him so vigorously he had been given little choice but to begin the affair. He also maintained to the end that their amour had never been consummated. Lady Rochford, however, insisted that Culpepper and Katheryn must have been engaging in a physical, as well as an emotional, affair, "considering all the things that she hath heard and seen between them" (Lindsey, 1995:176). Lady Rochford also vowed that she was only a lowly servant of the Queen, forced against her will to abet Katheryn in her immoral acts, which was almost certainly a lie, since Rochford acted eagerly on the couple's behalf during the course of the intrigue (Lindsey, 1995:171, 176).

In all honesty, Katheryn showed no more scruples in blaming her romantic partners for her own folly than they had shown for her. When she was questioned, she accused Manox and Dereham of taking advantage of her before she met Henry, and also claimed that Culpepper and Rochford had coerced her into arranging trysts (Lindsey, 1995:175-176). This was very ignoble behavior, spurred by the Queen's desperation to save herself from a situation far more serious than she had ever supposed it might be. Katheryn probably had more brains than she has been given credit for, or was at least clever, but she was ignorant of the law and had no one to explain it to her, since her better educated relatives had completely abandoned her to preserve their own hides. Foolishly, she insisted she had not been pre-contracted to Dereham (Smith, 1982:199). Perhaps she initially thought it was her status as Queen, not her life, that was in danger and she wanted the King to be convinced their marriage was valid. Maybe she didn't understand that a pre-contract might save her, since it would nullify her marriage to Henry, leaving her an adulterer and a bigamist, but not a traitor to the crown.

Even without her acknowledgment of a pre-contract, there was no reason that Henry had to kill her. After all, her intimacies with Dereham occurred before she met the King, and thus could not be treason. Henry could have accepted Dereham's assertion that they were indeed pre-contracted, which would have made Katheryn Dereham's common-law wife, and in turn would have made their sex life socially permissible (Smith, 1982:196).

There were others who could testify that Dereham and Katheryn called each other 'husband' and 'wife' openly during their time in the Dowager Duchess' household (Strickland and Strickland, 1851:286). Moreover, a pre-contract would have voided her marriage to Henry, freeing the King to find another wife to please him. Katheryn could have been given to Dereham and sent from the court in penury and disgrace. Or she could have been consigned to one of the remaining nunneries, which would have been a serious punishment for such a sociable and fashionable young woman. Henry could have easily spared his frivolous but sweet natured young wife from the death penalty.

Yet the King was uninterested in mercy, or even justice. It is possible the blow to his ego, and his humiliation at being a dupe, would have given him enough cause to have Katheryn and her suitors exterminated, even if he had been mentally healthy. However, if the King suffered from McLeod syndrome, he was far from mentally healthy by this time in his life. He would have been deeply entrenched in illogical paranoia, and his rational thought processes would have been severely compromised. Thus, he would have acted with the willful and impulsive temper of an overwrought child, determined to see those who had hurt him scourged for their transgressions. Consistent with the theory that he suffered from McLeod syndrome, this is precisely what Henry did.

On December 10, 1541 he had Dereham executed as a traitor, with all the macabre tortures that entailed. Dereham was hauled off to Tyburn on a cart, hanged until he was semi-conscious, revived until he was aware of what was happening to him, then disemboweled, beheaded, and his corpse was cut into four pieces (Starkey, 2003:680-681). His only crime was the fact he had sex with Katheryn, his *de facto* common-law wife, when she was still living with her step-grandmother, long before she met the King. He was tortured to death simply because Henry had not married a virgin. Dereham had 'gotten' the Queen's maidenhead, 'depriving' her elderly and decrepit husband of that 'prize'. The idea rankled in the King's heart until he could only be comforted by Dereham's ghastly death. It was, like much of what Henry did in the last few years of his life, grossly unfair.

Culpepper was, irrationally, given an easier death. Thanks to his high status in society and Henry's strangely enduring favor, he was merely beheaded. It was a quick and easy death for the only man to have wooed Katheryn who had actually committed treason against the King. However, there is some satisfaction in the fact that, at last, Culpepper was being punished for one of his crimes. In light of the fact he was a rapist and murderer, his execution seems almost justified. Were the woman that he had raped, and the family of his murder victim, in the crowd gathered to watch his execution? If so, they may have received some small measure of comfort from the fact that Culpepper, who had committed his heinous acts without consequences simply because he was a favored courtier of the King's, was dying because he had tried to seduce Henry's wife.

Having executed Dereham and Culpepper, the King could concentrate his wrath on Katheryn and Lady Rochford. They were condemned by an Act of Attainder on February 11, 1542 (Starkey, 2003:682). The King had also determined to punish several members of his former Queen's family, including the Duke of Norfolk, for having allowed him to marry 'used goods'.

The Duke of Norfolk, in an attempt to save himself, wrote Henry one of the most wretched and groveling letters ever penned by a human hand. However, the Duke was too busy trying to prevent the loss of his own wealth, or even his own life, to spare a thought for any other of his family members that Henry was intent on punishing. Norfolk's letter begged Henry not to consider him as of the same caliber as his "ungracious mother-in-law", his "unhappy brother", or his "lewd sister", and took pains to decry the "abominable deeds" of his niece, whom he had not hesitated to procure for the King when Henry had show an interest in her (Starkey, 2003:681). Apparently the letter was sufficiently abject, since the King pardoned Norfolk and all other members of the Howard family, with the exception of the former Queen. Nothing could save her.

If only Katheryn had been more ruthless and conniving! If she had been of a Machiavellian mindset, she could have had her uncle use his ducal powers to have Manox arrested and executed on false charges as soon as Henry had indicated she would be his next Queen. She could have had the only person absolutely positive she was not a virgin, Dereham himself, quietly murdered or exiled. She could have preempted the rumors that could be spread about her past behavior by having Norfolk go to the King, before she married Henry, to complain she was being maligned in an attempt to injure *the family*, making any gossip about her seem to be a false attack by Howard enemies. Once Henry had imprisoned or executed anyone who 'slandered' the Queen, it would have been too dangerous for others to accuse her of impropriety. If she had been power-hungry and shrewd, she would never have risked a flirtation with Culpepper, or have been so foolish as to trust Lady Rochford. Sadly, nothing that Katheryn did was ever that well thought out. She lived in the moment, pursuing happiness and material goods, rather than accumulating power and guaranteeing her security.

Henry's fifth wife was beheaded February 13, 1542 and made a "most Godly and Christian end" (Starkey, 2003:684).

She was fortunate enough to have a competent executioner and her death was quick. Although she was executed for treason, her real crime was to believe her body was hers to do with as she chose. As a result of the fact that she had intercourse with one man, just *one*, other than the King, she has been denigrated for five hundred years as a "faithless slut" (Smith, 1982:198). The fact that she wanted to be happy, enjoying the attentions of a handsome and charming young man when her elderly husband was absent, has branded her forever as a scheming adulteress. Men sought romance outside of their loveless marriages with impunity, but for the Queen to do so was shocking, *because she was not a man*. It is the double-standard writ large on the historical page.

There is one way, however, in which Katheryn truly was the 'whore' she has been so frequently called. The second the King showed an interest in her, she and her family were willing to give Henry access to her body in exchange for financial gain, which is the very definition of prostitution. Once sold, the Queen's sexuality was supposed to stay in the service of her family and the man who bought her. It is the fact that Katheryn wanted to have sex where there was no profit for her family, and in violation of her husband's right to the exclusive use of her reproductive capabilities, that lead to her death. She didn't want to marry Dereham, and she wasn't interested in Culpepper for his money. She simply liked them and wanted to be with them because it was enjoyable to her. There was no great financial reward in it for her, or for her kin. It is very ironic that she, in short, died for those times in which she did not prostitute herself.

Chapter Nine
Kateryn Parr:
The Wise and Widowed Queen

    After the King beheaded Katheryn Howard, it would be almost 18 months before he remarried. Without a wife to claim most of his attention, he was able to turn more of his rapidly deteriorating thoughts to the governing of his realm. Since the lion's share of his decisions made no sense to anyone but himself, "the King's diplomatic and military labors during the 1540s ... [have been condemned as] wanton, extravagant, frivolous, stupid and even criminal" (Smith, 1982:164). There was no one like Wolsey or Cromwell to govern the kingdom by subtly governing the King. Even if some of his ministers had been as able to lead both King and country as Henry's former Chancellor and Chief Minister were, the King's mental state was so erratic it was unlikely that anyone could have controlled, or even influenced, him. His courtiers devoted their intellectual energies to self-preservation, since they needed all of their wits just to prevent the King from turning on them and having them beheaded on a passing fancy. Many of them were ultimately unsuccessful. Henry's irrationality and bad temper were also exacerbated by his dissatisfaction with his unmarried state. He was infatuated with no other woman when he killed his fifth wife, so there was no wedding to follow on the heels of the execution, which would have poured a psychological balm on his wounded ego. Henry was too melancholy, perhaps even too clinically depressed, to believe himself in love with any of the ladies at court, and few European royals were willing to offer their kinswomen as a match for a King who might repudiate her or kill her at his whim.

There was some thought that Henry could be persuaded to reunite with Anna of Cleves. She was still, whether she wanted to be or not, a political factor in his potential next marriage. Much of this speculation was due to the fact that the people of England adored her and were still holding out hope that Henry would come to love her as they did. There was even erroneous gossip that Anna had borne Henry's children (Lindsey, 1995:184). The French ambassador noted that the English were still unhappy that Henry had cast her aside, writing that they "all regret her [loss] more" than they missed the much-loved Katherine of Aragon (Starkey, 2003:687). The Duke of Cleves sent his ambassador to ascertain whether or not Henry was interested in reinstating Anna as his Queen. Fortunately for Anna, he was not. Some historians postulate that the Duke's overtures to Henry were a sign that Anna herself wanted to return to the King's side. They argue that she probably wanted to be Queen again because her status at court was "awkward and anomalous", and also because Henry had been "kind and generous" to her during their brief period as man and wife (Starkey, 2003:686). However, this assumes Anna wanted to be a wife and a Queen more than she wished to be untethered by male demands and safe from the King's displeasure. Henry's ire was no casual matter for a woman to consider, and the termination of Katheryn Howard's life was still fresh in the public mind. Anna of Cleves, as long as she remained the King's sister, was independently wealthy and could, for the most part, do as she pleased. If she became Henry's wife, she would not only be in jeopardy, she would have to constantly find ways to soothe her "repugnant and often inexplicably moody" husband (Scarisbrick, 2003:431). Anna would have been foolish to have desired to be Henry's wife, but since she was intelligent and lacked "neither prudence nor patience", it is more likely that she understood the advantages of remaining his sister (Starkey, 2003:687). However, no matter how lucky Henry's rejection of her was for Anna, it did nothing to alleviate the problem of his lack of marital partners.

    Henry had further reduced the pool of woman eligible to be his Queen by enacting a set of draconian laws regarding his potential wife. It was now legally required that any woman who married the King must tell him if she was "a pure and clean maid", and if she was less than honest about her condition it would be considered high treason (Lindsey, 1995:181). Moreover, if anyone else knew that her past was unsavory, they too would be committing high treason. Since proving that something is unknown, beyond a shadow of a doubt, is impossible, no one would be safe. It almost certainly made ambitious courtiers think twice about offering up their female relations as potential mates for Henry, because the offered girl's chastity had to be beyond doubt or her family would lose everything.

Fortunately for Henry, one of his daughter Mary's pretty attendants, Lady Latimer, became a widow. Lady Latimer (née Kateryn Parr), had caught Henry's eye in the past but was too virtuous to have been one of his former mistresses. Kateryn Parr's mother had served Katherina of Aragon as a Lady-in-Waiting and had probably named her daughter after the Queen. As fate would have it, Henry's last wife was probably his first wife's goddaughter and namesake (Starkey, 2003:691). She was only 31, more than 20 years younger than her new husband, but she was an emotionally mature and intellectual woman who had been widowed twice, so the age disparity was not as jarring. The new Queen was known to be a well-informed, wise, chaste, and respectable woman, as different from Katheryn Howard as an apple from an orange. Nonetheless, there was one significant drawback to marrying Lady Latimer: she was not a likely candidate to give the King more sons. It was assumed that she was infertile, since she had produced no offspring in either of her first two marriages. Why would Henry, who longed for sons more than anything else, choose a bride who was thought to be barren?

This also seemed to perplex Anna of Cleves. Chapuys, the Imperial ambassador who had seen and written so much about the King's tangled relationships for so many years, reported to Charles V that Henry's fourth wife and ersatz sister was "in despair" that Henry had picked a woman who was "inferior ... in beauty and gives no hope of posterity to the King" (Starkey, 2003:715). If the ambassador's information is correct, it would seem to lend credence to the theory that Anna wished to become Henry's wife once more. However, Chapuys was hostile to the alliance between Cleves and England, and thus may have exaggerated or simply preferred to report the most negative hearsay possible (Starkey, 2033:716). Even if it were true that Anna was upset because Henry had chosen Kateryn, this would not necessarily mean it was because she actually wanted to be Queen again. She may have merely been human enough to feel piqued when her vanity was affronted. Very few people enjoy rejection, regardless of whether or not it is in their best interests.

Interestingly, many historians think that Kateryn Parr's presumed infertility was actually one of the reasons *why* Henry chose her. The King was old, in ill health, and was now vastly obese. His excessive weight may have caused him to develop type II diabetes, which can be accompanied by erectile dysfunction. Even without type II diabetes, problems with obesity and blood pressure could have rendered Henry impotent. If the King could no longer consummate his marriage, the best way to protect himself from this fact becoming common knowledge would be to marry a woman whom the courtiers would not watch for signs of pregnancy. The lack of future children would be assumed to be a result of her sterile womb, not his impotence. In short, this discrete, faithful, and presumably infertile widow would be the perfect mask for Henry's own inadequacies.

For her part, Kateryn was more resigned than happy to become his Queen. She had developed an attachment to Thomas Seymour, the late Queen Jane Seymour's brother, and would later write that she would have preferred "to marry [him] before any man" (Lindsey, 1995:183). Henry's proposal posed a dilemma for his future bride. She did not love the King but she was secretly an ardent Reformer and a marriage might give her the opportunity to coax Henry further away from Catholicism. After much prayer and reflection, she felt that God had moved her to "renounce utterly mine own will and to follow His most willingly" (Starkey, 2003:711). Since the new Queen was sincerely devout, she did everything she could to fulfill her wedding vows to be obedient to her husband, yet she also did everything in her power to encourage him to favor the Reformation. Kateryn performed the delicate balancing act of satisfying both her husband and God to the best of her abilities, while simultaneously endeavoring to keep her head attached to her neck. It was not an easy task.

Henry's mental health was severely compromised by this point in his life and he was dangerously unpredictable. Courtiers, ministers, and ambassadors were all forced to cope with "the King's emotional instability … the sudden spasms of rage … [his] depression, moodiness and alternation between heavy lassitude and frenzied activity" (Smith, 1982:265-266). While it is possible that Henry's condition was caused entirely by the almost constant pain he suffered, or by a combination of discomfort, major depressive disorder and paranoia, it is also possible, even likely considering the fact he was almost undoubtedly Kell positive, that his psychological illness was induced by progressive McLeod syndrome. Regardless of the root cause of the King's psychological distress, it was an extremely perilous time to live at court or come to his attention. The life of any woman who married him was in danger.

Kateryn and Henry exchanged vows on July 12, 1543. A sixth marriage was somewhat astonishing, and one of his subjects wrote, "What a man the King is! How many wives *will* he have?" (Strickland and Strickland, 1851(v.3):85) Considering that his new wife sympathized with the aims of the Reformation, their union started inauspiciously since Henry had three

Protestants burned at the stake during the first two months following their wedding, which some people ascribed to the fact that "in July he married the widow of a noble named Latimer, and he is always wont to celebrate his nuptial by some wickedness of this kind" (Lindsey, 1995:186).

It was a very private ceremony, but both Mary and Elizabeth attended their father's last wedding. Henry's eldest daughter was now twenty-seven years of age, and the new Queen did everything she could to encourage Mary's presence at court, in spite of their radically differing religious beliefs. The Queen may have been a covert Reformist, and Mary a fierce defender of Catholicism, but there were still strong ties to connect them. Kateryn's mother had been close to Katherina of Aragon, so Henry's new wife had an inherited interest in the late Queen's daughter. Moreover, Kateryn and Mary were very close in age and had similar interests and educations (Starkey, 2003:718). Yet it may have just been Kateryn's natural kindness that endeared Mary to her. The Queen was always extremely kind to the ten-year-old Elizabeth as well, and fostered cordial relations between all the siblings. It is extremely likely that Kateryn cajoled Henry into softening his stance against his daughters' right to the throne (Starkey, 2003:720). He wouldn't budge an inch on their legitimacy, but he could and did restore his 'bastard' daughters to the succession. If he or his son did not produce lawful offspring, his unlawful daughter Mary would get the throne. If his daughter Mary died without issue, then the crown would come to Elizabeth. Without the new Queen's influence it would probably have been much harder for Mary to become the Queen of England after her brother Edward died in 1553.

Henry's new wife was influential in other ways also. She did her absolute best to keep the King and country from swinging away from the budding religious reforms and back to being Catholic in theology and practice, albeit without acknowledging the authority of the Pope. The naturally more traditionalist Henry was already becoming choleric about the spread of Bible-reading and the denial of transubstantiation, both linchpin theological doctrines of Protestants. Whichever way the King's religious inclinations were headed, the populace of England would be coaxed or bullied into following, so the battle for Henry's heart was literally a fight for the spiritual welfare and growth of the nation. His newest Queen was becoming more open about her Protestant leanings, and was seen "oftimes wishing, exhorting, and persuading the King, that as he had, to the glory of God, and his eternal fame, begun a good and godly work in banishing that monstrous idol of Rome, so he would thoroughly perfect and finish the same, cleansing and purging his church of England clean from the dregs thereof" (Mueller, 2011:22). Kateryn was soon known as a stalwart supporter of the Reformation, but this earned her bitter adversaries among the pro-Catholic faction, and Anne Boleyn's death stood as a warning of how dangerous it was for a Queen to have powerful enemies ranged against her.

There were two major religious forces at Henry's court: the first was Thomas Cranmer, the Archbishop of Canterbury, who represented Reformation sympathizers, and the second was Stephen Gardiner, the Bishop of Winchester, a traditional and reactionary Catholic. For most of 1543, Gardiner and his faction had Cranmer and his adherents at a disadvantage. Henry's religious leanings were profoundly conservative, and several prominent Reformers had been burned at the stake. Gardiner was clearly hoping that Cranmer would be executed as well. Cranmer was a close confidant of the King; if the Archbishop was out of the picture, it would be much easier to lure Henry back to the Mother Church, where he was most ideologically comfortable. Shortly before Christmas, Gardiner's faction asked Henry for permission to arrest Cranmer and imprison him in the Tower for heresy, and when the King agreed, it seemed to be the end for the Archbishop. However, the mercurial moods and erratic behavior of the King rendered nothing certain. Henry sent for Cranmer and warned him of the plot, telling him that "false knaves will soon be procured to witness against you and condemn you" (Scarisbrick, 1970:481). Henry then gave his royal ring to the Archbishop, an act which carried extreme significance since it indicated the possessor was in the King's favor. When Gardiner and his friends sprang their ambush on Cranmer, he dramatically whipped out the ring he had been given, causing his enemies immediate and pronounced consternation. When the conservative coalition retreated to confer with Henry, they were "savagely rebuked" by the irate King (Scarisbrick, 1970:481).

What changed Henry's mind, previously set upon imprisoning his Archbishop, and delivered Cranmer from almost certain death? If McLeod syndrome had eroded the King's mental faculties, then it may have just been another sudden mood swing that altered the paranoid monarch's perception of who his real 'enemies' were. It many have been a deliberate act on Henry's part, albeit influenced by McLeod-syndrome-induced paranoia, concocted to remind Bishop Gardiner that Cranmer was secure. However, historian David Starkey proposes that Kateryn herself may have been the significant factor in the survival of the Archbishop, since she was the only important new element in Henry's personal life (Starkey, 2003:728). This would certainly demonstrate the important role that a King's wife could play. Nevertheless, it is impossible to know just how big a part she might have had in Cranmer's survival, considering that the only way she could have influenced the King was to downplay her contribution to his decision-making process. She was, after all, merely a woman, and thus unfit to suggest policy. What is known, however, is that Henry was both unstable and suggestible by this time, possibly because of the psychological damage caused by McLeod syndrome, and therefore susceptible to supplications that contradicted his stated policy. This means that Henry may indeed have been cajoled by his wife and her pro-Cranmer suggestions but at the same time his illogical shifts in perspective made her just as vulnerable as his other courtiers to finding herself on the receiving end of his displeasure.

    Bishop Gardiner was certainly not the only courtier to be caught out by the King's emotional and political flip-flops. Although a "single example of perversity and mental sadism might be dismissed", Henry employed a double-bind subterfuge to ensnare his courtiers multiple times during the final years of his reign (Smith, 1982:31). Clearly, this game of cat and mouse appealed to Henry, and suited his ever-growing paranoia and need to test those around him. There was a second such incident in the spring of 1544 which involved the Reformist faction and the conservative cohort, but this time it was Gardiner himself who was saved from arrest by Henry's abrupt change of opinion. A nephew of the prelate, Germayne Gardiner, had just been executed for supporting Papal authority, and Henry was convinced that the Bishop was of the same mind as his kinsman (Scarisbrick, 1970:481). Members of Henry's council, including Archbishop Cranmer and the Duke of Suffolk, encouraged the King in his suspicions, and it was decided that Gardiner should be arrested in the morning. Forewarned, the Bishop hurried to Henry, where he threw himself upon the King's mercy and swore from "that day forward to reform his opinion" (Smith, 1982:32). Henry forgave Gardiner, but neglected to inform his council, leaving them to find out that the Bishop was pardoned on their own.

It was not only in court intrigues that Henry was displaying erratic notions, but also in the larger world of European politics. In the middle of 1544, Henry went off to fight yet another pointless war with France, and he left his Queen as regent to keep the country in good order. She also had to deal with the intermittent war between England and Scotland. The Scots, having no real desire to join their kingdom with England, had backed out of an agreement to have the infant Queen Mary wed Henry's young son, Prince Edward. The King was livid that the Scots preferred to be allied to France instead of England, incensed by the thought that they were rejecting his son, and enraged that they were thwarting his attempts to unite Scotland and England under one crown. Henry sent Edward Seymour to launch an attack on the impudent Scots, which resulted in five years of war termed the "Rough Wooing", and strengthened anti-English sentiment in that country so much that he lost any chance he may have had to achieve his political objectives (Magnússon, 2003:323). The crown was thus fighting a war on two fronts, and England's lack of resources meant that both campaigns were being strained. Poor planning and poor leadership also helped turn Henry's war in France into a disaster (Scarisbrick, 2003:448-451). Henry's one success came on September 14, 1544 when his forces captured Boulogne, a city in northern France less than one hundred miles from London that could potentially have been used as a stronghold for future English invasions (Pollard, 1919:412). However, further incursions into France had become impossible, since Henry had run out of money, which is needed to wage war. Having depleted his coffers on various domestic whims, the King couldn't afford to fund his own armies or hire more mercenaries to fight for him. On top of this, England's ally, Charles V, decided to start negotiating a peace with France without any English input, in spite of the fact that this infuriated Henry (Scarisbrick, 2003:450-451).

By the summer of 1545 England was dealing with myriad difficulties, largely because of the King's ineptitude and inability to plan for contingencies. France and Scotland were able to obtain mercenary troops with more success, primarily because the treasury of the French King was not so depleted, thus England was in real danger of being invaded simultaneously by two foreign powers from multiple fronts (Scarisbrick, 1970:454). This threat existed mainly because of Henry's ill-thought-out attacks on France and Scotland, which had only helped cement the Franco-Scots alliance against England and created an opportunity and reason for retaliation against England. Although such colossal mismanagement has been a dark stain on Henry's record, it could perhaps be viewed with more sympathy if it was known that he was operating under the burden of impaired brain function. Since his behavior would have been the result of a medical condition beyond his control, it hardly seems fair to judge the last years of his reign by the same standard used to judge the first years of his rule. After all, someone suffering from schizophrenia is not held accountable in a court of law in the same way as a person who is completely healthy. If the hypothesis that Henry was afflicted with McLeod syndrome is correct, then mental illness should be considered as a mitigating factor when assessing his kingship.

In spite of the potential disaster hanging over England, there was good news in store for the crown. The French didn't really want to commit themselves to the protracted land war that invading England would entail, so after landing their soldiers on English shores a few times that September, almost as if they were taunting Henry with what they *could* do if they chose, they withdrew their troops and sailed back to France (Scarisbrick, 1970:455). Henry returned home in October of 1545, where he was welcomed like a hero by his Queen and court, despite the fact he had gained very little, nearly caused the country to be invaded by hostile forces, and had driven England even deeper into a morass of debt.

With the King back at court, Kateryn had to watch herself carefully to make sure she never inadvertently eclipsed Henry's star. In spite of the Queen's nearly continuous efforts to keep the moody and irascible man she had married happy, she sometimes forgot herself in the heat of debate, and let her keen intelligence show through. Her sharp wits inadvertently provided an opening for her enemies to turn Henry against her. By late February of 1546 the court was hearing rumors that a new Queen might be forthcoming (Starkey, 2003:760). Then, in late March, after Kateryn had debated doctrine with the King and then been dismissed for the night, Henry began to complain to Gardiner how appalling it was "to come in mine old days to be taught by my wife" (Starkey, 2003:761). Gardiner disliked the whole Reformation movement intensely and, having been impeded in his attempt to have Cranmer brought low, he was doubtlessly eager to rid the court of the Reformist-sympathising Queen. Moreover, Gardiner was deeply misogynistic, and he freely admitted that one of the things he hated about Protestantism was that it gave "women courage and liberty to talk at their pleasure" about religious matters (Lindsey, 1995:193). The audacity of a mere female talking about the Gospels with the King must have infuriated him. Gardiner pounced on Henry's dissatisfaction with Kateryn and fanned the flames of Henry's ire with all his might. Gardiner convinced Henry that he should have the Queen and several of her like-minded Ladies-in-Waiting arrested and their illicit books on Biblical scholarship confiscated as evidence.

Gardiner quickly made plans with the Chancellor, Thomas Wriothesley, to arrest Kateryn and send her to the Tower. Wriothesley's most likely motives for abetting Kateryn's downfall appear to be simple ones; he was a sociopath who loved to persecute people, particularly women, and a sycophant devoted to pleasing powerful members of court. Like Gardiner, he seemed to harbor a special hatred for women involved in the Reformation. Wriothesley, who had once praised the Queen for her "virtue, wisdom, and gentleness" (Starkey, 2003:714-715), was eager to help Gardiner destroy the Queen if possible.

Gardiner, however, had not counted on the Queen's popularity -- or the loyalty of her supporters. Somehow, possibly through the efforts of one of Henry's physicians, Dr. Thomas Wendy, word of her impending arrest was leaked to Kateryn (Starkey, 2003:762). She had an absolute fit of hysterics. She was undoubtedly terrified since her life really was in danger, but her distress may have been exaggerated to soften Henry's heart (Lindsey, 1995:198). Kateryn's emotional affliction was such that Henry sent Dr. Wendy to check on her. Happily, the good doctor shared the Queen's Reformist tendencies. Therefore, he solemnly reported back to Henry that Kateryn was "dangerously ill from some mental distress" (Lindsey, 1995:198). Intrigued, the King came to her rooms and was suitably flattered when she told him her grief stemmed from her fears she had displeased him, which moved Henry to offer his wife a few words of comfort (Porter, 2010:257). Her dismay may have eased some of Henry's wrath, but the Queen knew she needed to act quickly if she were to avoid the Tower. Kateryn, accompanied by some of her Ladies-in-Waiting, went to Henry's chambers to seek an audience (Porter, 2010:258). After greeting his wife, the King, with little subtlety, asked her opinion on a religious topic. Kateryn, wisely, lost no time in begging him not to ask her to give him advice on religious matters since she was "a poor silly woman, so much inferior in all respects of nature to you" (Porter, 2010:258). Therefore she based her opinions on religion, "and all other cases, [on] your Majesty's wisdom, as my only anchor, Supreme Head and Governor here in earth, next under God" (Smith, 1982:260-261).

In spite of her impressive blandishments, the King was not so easily lulled out of his sulk. In response to her claims she could not presume to lecture him on theology, he declared, "Not so, by St. Mary, you are become a doctor, Kate, to instruct us, as we take it, and not to be instructed or directed by us" (Porter, 2010:258). Fortunately for her, Kateryn was a quick thinker, and immediately assured Henry that she only presented opposing views in order to draw his attention away from his painful legs, and as a way of hearing more of his wisdom, which she found so enlightening. Henry was finally placated, asking her, "And is it even so Sweetheart? And tended your argument to no worse end? Then perfect friends we are now again" (Porter, 2010:259). The King embraced her, and she was once again safe.

The Queen had been able to avoid imprisonment and possible beheading, probably because of the assistance of Dr. Wendy. In gratitude, Kateryn would later name Dr. Wendy her personal physician, and reward him with a manor and rectory that gave him a considerable financial benefit (Starkey, 2010:762).

Although the royal couple were once again in harmony, the King neglected to tell Wriothesley he had forgiven Kateryn. Thus it was that Henry and his wife were strolling in one of the palace gardens when the Chancellor showed up to arrest the Queen. Henry acted with what had become a typical display of mental aberration. Instead of stopping Wriothesley and simply sending him away, the King began shouting abuse at his Chancellor, calling him an "arrant beast" and a "knave" (Starkey, 2003:763). These aspersions may sound quaint to the modern ear, but they were ferocious insults during the Tudor era. Wriothesley was justifiably terrified. Kateryn, in either an act of Christian charity or an act of secret self-satisfaction, pleaded with Henry very cordially to forgive his Chancellor for her sake. This display of feminine compassion tugged on Henry's heartstrings, especially since he was unaware that Kateryn knew full well what Wriothesley had been doing. The King told his wife, "thou little knoweth how evil he deserveth this grace at thy hands" (Lindsey, 1995:199). In the game of courtly politics, the Queen had trumped the Knave.

The summer of 1546 was the last summer of Henry's life. As was typical of this fascinating monarch, he made it an interesting one. He attempted to punish Charles V for his betrayals during their last alliance by making treaties with the French and the Germans that would not be beneficial for the Holy Roman Empire (Scarisbrick, 1970:464). Henry also decided to put on a grand spectacle for the signing of a peace treaty between England and the Franco-Scots alliance, even though his kingdom was near bankruptcy. He made his eight-year-old son Edward the official statesman of this brouhaha, and sent 80 men to accompany and safeguard the Prince. The King created two new banquet houses at Hampton Court for his French guests, and sent them home with gifts that included horses, finely wrought silver goblets, and an entire set of solid gold plates (Smith, 1982:298). These ostentatious and unaffordable displays were probably Henry's defiant denial of the fact that his health was in serious decline, as well as an attempt to make his war in France seem as though it had been of great importance, rather than the lackluster affair it really was. He did manage to recoup some of his losses incurred during the strategically useless war and the grandiose showmanship of the parley by getting his Gallic rivals to agree to pay two million crowns over a period of eight years for the return of Boulogne to French control (Whitelock, 2010:121).

Once peace with the French was (at least temporarily) established, the Vatican made an attempt to woo Henry back to the Church. There were good reasons for the Catholic faction to be hopeful. Both major female figures in the schism, Katherina of Aragon and Anne Boleyn, were dead. Rome could finally offer Henry a nullification of his marriage to his first Queen; mainly because Katherina's nephew no longer held the Pope hostage, but also because there were no longer quite so many political ramifications from a divorce. Henry had a male heir now, after all, the English succession was no longer dependent on the validity of the King's first marriage. Moreover, his daughter Mary was no longer excluded from inheriting the throne, in spite of the fact that she was still officially 'illegitimate', which had been one of the most important goals for Catholic supporters in England. The King himself was clearly still more Catholic than Protestant in his theological leanings, and if the blame for the English break from the Holy See could be laid on the doorstep of the deceased Pope, Clement VII, then Henry might be prevailed upon to accept the authority of Clement's successor, Pope Paul III.

In August a papal envoy, Guron Bertano, arrived at Henry's court. Bertano was instructed to overlook everything Henry had done, including the unsanctioned divorce from Katherina and the dissolution of the monasteries, if the King would just agree that the Pope was the true Head of the Church (Scarisbrick, 1970:469-470). Bertano was quite hopeful at the outset of the talks; not only had he been allowed to come to court, which was more than Lutheran emissaries were allowed to do, he had had two meetings with William Paget, Henry's Secretary of State, and even had an audience with the King himself (Scarisbrick, 1970:469-470). In spite of these positive signs, after a stay of almost two months, Bertano was suddenly ordered to leave court immediately. Did Henry ever really consider rejoining the Holy Church? If so, what changed his mind? Was it another rapid mood swing activated by McLeod's syndrome, or were more prosaic forces in play? Although there were certainly inducements for the King to mend the breach between Rome and England, it is doubtful they were enough to overcome the enjoyment a man with Henry's robust ego would find in being the Supreme Head of the English Church. Furthermore, his wife, Kateryn, would have been whispering sweet compliments that reassured him that his schism from the Catholic faith was a manifestation of God's will. Even if Henry had been in perfect health, his self-importance and his supporters would have probably been enough to keep the King continuing down the path he had chosen more than a decade before. However, other instances of erratic behavior appear more likely to have been caused by the degenerative illness affecting his brain.

Although the summer's newly minted Anglo-French peace treaty had theoretically ended hostilities between the Scots and the English, only a few months after signing it Henry was sending such clear signals that he was planning another attack on his northern neighbors that Scotland had to send an appeal for aid to France (Scarisbrick, 1970:464). By the winter of 1546 the King had started amassing troops in preparation for a further invasion of Scottish territory, and the reason he gave for resuming his aggressive stance against Scotland was the accusation that the *Scots* had broken the peace treaty (Scarisbrick, 1970:464). Was this a legitimate complaint? Or a canny excuse to attack a country that had continually thwarted him? Or had McLeod syndrome given him paranoid fantasies of Scots treachery, so that he felt he was merely defending himself? Considering the dire financial situation England was in, and the repeated lack of success they had faced when dealing with the marriage of the infant Scots Queen, it does seem likely that McLeod syndrome played at least some part in Henry's "diplomacy" with Scotland.

Closer to home Henry continued to seem reasonably pleased with his wife, although it seems likely that Gardiner and his faction were still attempting to discredit her whenever they had an opportunity to bend the King's ear. Earlier in the summer Gardiner had tried to connect Kateryn to the "Fair Gospeler", Anne Askew, a well-known Protestant determined to share as much Biblical text as possible with lay people (Lindsey, 190-197). Askew was arrested in June, and Gardiner sent his bully-boys, Richard Rich and Chancellor Wriothesley, to interview her in the Tower of London, where they tried to ferret out any connection between the Gospeler and the Queen or the Queen's attendants. They were frustrated repeatedly by Askew's sharp wit. Outraged over being bested by a mere woman, they ordered her wracked. Since it was illegal for a woman of Askew's social class to be tortured, the lieutenant of the Tower, Anthony Knevet, was reluctant to participate. Once Knevet refused to continue, Wriothesley and Rich began to torture Askew themselves. Knevet rushed to the court and told the King what Gardiner's stooges were doing. Disgusted, Henry ordered the wracking stopped. It will never be known for sure if the Fair Gospeler had been the recipient of financial support from Queen Kateryn or any other noblewomen, since Askew died without ever betraying a connection (Lindsey, 1995:190-197). Askew was burned at the stake on July 16, 1546 (Askew and Beilin, 1996:xxxii).

Luckily for the Queen, after spending so much of his energy trying to precipitate Kateryn's downfall, Gardiner himself was undone by a small matter. The Bishop fell out of favor abruptly and spectacularly when, instead of exchanging some land on Henry's orders, he demanded to speak to the King about it first (Smith, 1982:301-302). Henry was livid he had not been obeyed posthaste. This may seem like a tempest in a teapot, but if Henry's brain was being affected by McLeod syndrome, his paranoia was likely beyond anything he could recognize or even attempt to control. Once the King associated Gardiner with "danger" or "disobedience", Gardiner could become fixed in Henry's mind as a dangerous person without the King having any recollection of the Bishop's past services. Gardiner, practiced supplicant though he may have been, never did talk his way back into Henry's good graces (Smith, 1982:303).

Other members of the court were also at risk of losing their sovereign's favor, since Henry seemed willing to believe any rumor "privately given him by any court-whisperer" (Smith, 1982:303). The whole court walked on eggshells around their unpredictable and mad King. Henry's mood was so unstable, and his wrath so violent and implacable, that no councilor would jeopardize himself by telling Henry what he really thought because of the risk that a "snare had been laid for him" (Smith, 1982:304). This is so unlike Henry's behavior as a younger man that it almost seems that he had become a completely different person. Rather than setting his courtiers against each other and picking quarrels with his councilors, prior to his fortieth birthday Henry had often shown a propensity for fostering peace and harmony in his court. In contrast, the old King manipulated his courtiers into fights, playing them against one another for his own amusement or advantage. It is likely that the mental deterioration that can accompany McLeod syndrome is the reason that Henry began his reign as a "much feted, glorious, and fun young monarch of the 1510s and 1520s" and ended it as an "overweight, suspicious, and ruthless tyrant" (Lipscomb, 2009:13). Fortunately for many of his courtiers, and his Queen, they didn't need to live in fear much longer. Unfortunately for others, his end would not come soon enough.

In December of 1546 the King turned suddenly on the Howard family. Henry had the Duke of Norfolk thrown into the Tower, stripped him of his titles and lands, and had the Duke's son, Henry Howard, the Earl of Surrey, who was a famous soldier and poet, charged with high treason based on less than credible evidence (Smith, 1982:289-296). There was little real reason for Henry to have turned on the Howards in that manner; Norfolk was hated by many people and was indisputably a wretched human being, but he had always been obsequiously devoted to the King's commands (Scarisbrick, 1970:484). Why did the King turn so suddenly, and so violently, against them? Or was it not really Henry's work at all?

The King was, obviously to anyone but himself, going to be leaving on a long journey with the Grim Reaper in the very near future. Two major political factions were vying for power, hoping that when Henry's young son became Edward VI they would be able to control English policy through the boy until he was old enough to rule for himself. Whoever held the reins when the King died would have regency over Edward, even if a will needed to be 'discovered' backing up their claims. For simplicity's sake, the warring factions can be thought of as the Seymours and the Howards.

By 1546, it was clear the Seymours had the upper hand. They were Edward's maternal uncles, and their late sister, Jane, retained a strong sentimental hold on Henry's affections. Henry seemed to trust them, as much as he was capable of trusting anyone, in part because they were a family of very humble origins who had been brought to distinction only by his notice. They were no threat to his throne and it was in their self interest to make sure Edward's ascent to the throne after Henry's death was unchallenged. The Howards, in spite of the Duke of Norfolk's never-ending toadying to the King, carried a threat to Henry's dynasty in their veins. They were one of the oldest and most powerful families in England, and Norfolk's eldest son, Henry Howard, the Earl of Surrey, was a particular problem for the King. Surrey's maternal grandfather, Edward Stafford (3rd Duke of Buckingham), was a direct male descendant of King Edward III, and that gave Surrey a more legitimate right to wear the English crown than that of any Tudor monarch (Childs,

2007:24). The King had executed Buckingham for treason more than twenty-five years before, on May 17, 1521, because the Duke was too outspoken about his better claim to England's throne. Like his grandfather, Surrey was well aware of his lineage, and made it clear he found the Seymours and their allies to be plebeian upstarts of inferior birth (Smith, 1982:290-291). This was extremely insulting to the Seymours, mainly because of its truth. Few people in the Tudor era admired a 'self-made man'. It was widely believed one's birth was determined by God's will, and those who were meant to be superior to their fellows were born to superior families. Those who tried to climb beyond their natal social class too quickly were regarded with suspicion. The Seymours, who were trying to establish themselves as one of the premier families in the court, wouldn't have liked any reminders that they had only become even modest country gentry just a few generations before, and would have doubtlessly preferred to emphasise their maternal connections, given that their mother was distantly related to the Plantagenets (Norton, 2009:7-9).

    The Duke of Norfolk, while a vile excuse for a man, was a canny political operator. He could see the writing on the wall, and faced with the reality of the Seymour ascension, he made plans to unite the Howards with their parvenu rivals. Since the upper nobility couldn't marry without royal permission, Norfolk petitioned the crown to allow a series of marriages to take place between the Howards and the Seymours (Smith, 1970:289). He had arranged that his daughter, Mary Howard, the widow of the King's illegitimate son, Henry Fitzroy, would marry one of Jane Seymour's younger brothers, Thomas. Thomas was the third eldest Seymour brother to survive to adulthood, and the focus of Queen Kateryn's passion before she was coerced into marriage to the King. Norfolk also proposed unions between some of his grandsons and the elder daughters of Edward Seymour, the late Queen Jane's eldest surviving brother, by his second wife, Anne (née Stanhope). Although this would have meant the Howards were marrying 'beneath them', it would have secured them powerful positions in any forthcoming regency controlled by the Seymours. Notwithstanding the political wisdom of the matches, none of them took place because Norfolk's son, the Earl of Surrey would not stand for it (Smith, 1970:289-290).

Surrey simply could not bear the humiliation of having his sons sink so low as to marry the granddaughters of a rural sheriff. Nor, despite his very strained relationship with his sister, did he want her to become the wife of a vulgar social climber. Instead, he suggested that she try to tickle the King's fancy, and rule over Henry the way successful mistresses had reigned in France. This did nothing to endear him to his sister, who, in spite of being no stranger to scandal, insisted that she would "cut her own throat [rather] than consent to such a villainy" as seducing the King, her own father-in-law (Smith, 1970:289-290). Surrey further alienated the Seymours by reportedly boasting that the Duke of Norfolk would be "meetest" to administer a regency government for Prince Edward upon the demise of the sovereign, rather than the men of "vile birth" who had only recently been "made" by the King's favors (Sessions, 2003:380-381).

Clearly, the Seymours had ample motive to arrange the judicial murder of Henry Howard. The Earl of Surrey's coat of arms was their method. Once again, Chancellor Wriothesley was happy to do the dirty work for men in power. Wriothesley was able to procure testimony from the Garter King of Arms, Herald Christopher Barker, stating that Surrey had knowingly and rebelliously used insignia on his coat of arms, and implying that the aforementioned insignia was that of the English King, Saint

Edward the Confessor (Sessions, 2003:396-398). Bearing the arms of Edward the Confessor without royal permission could easily be construed as treason, since it flaunted a connection to the throne equal to the King's (Smith, 170:290-291). However, there is good historical evidence that Surrey was never told he was forbidden to bear Edward the Confessor's designs in his arms (Sessions, 2003:398-397). Moreover, the chief witness to Surrey's crime, Christopher Barker, was suspiciously promoted to a Knight of the Bath as soon as the Seymours came to power, and he was just one of the many people who testified against Henry Howard that were similarly rewarded (Sessions, 2003:398).

Whatever the truth may be, the evidence the Seymours and their allies presented was enough to convince the King that Surrey was up to no good, and therefore Henry Howard, the Earl of Surrey, was beheaded on January 19, 1547. Unlike many of the King's other victims, Surrey did not follow the social conventions for those who were condemned; he did not go quietly or request that people pray for their sovereign. Instead, the Earl took the opportunity to chastise Henry and to reiterate his disgust of the Seymours by crying out, "Of what have you found me guilty? Surely you will find no law that justifies you; but I know that the King wants to get rid of the noble blood around him, and to employ none but low people" (Sessions, 2003:409).

Henry Howard was only 30 years old when he died, and in the prime of his creativity. The epitome of a Renaissance man, Surrey was renowned both as a warrior and one of the innovative forces behind the English sonnet form of poetry. Among modern literary scholars, he is remembered for his "extraordinary invention and influence" and his "position as the center of an

English poetic tradition" (Dimmock, 2006:117). For his contemporaries, Henry Howard was a luminary, gifted with both the pen and the sword. His execution was lamented and reviled throughout Europe, and seen as further evidence of the King's despotic nature. Edward Seymour was likewise criticized for his role in Surrey's death. John Foxe, in his *Book of Martyrs* (1563) declared that Seymour, who would have otherwise been lauded as a Protestant hero, brought "God's scourge and rod" upon himself because he had "distained his honour" and arranged the legal murder of the innocent Henry Howard (Sessions, 2003:5).

The 3rd Duke of Norfolk, proving yet again that there was nothing so important to him as his own hide, joined in condemning his own son, once it became clear Surrey was doomed. The wily old Duke wrote letters to the King in which he "bent; he ate humble pie; he pleaded for his life; and he confessed he had known and concealed the Earl's treason" (Smith, 1970:296). Norfolk's begging may have swayed Henry, since he delayed the Duke's execution by his inaction. The attainder against Norfolk was never signed by the King, but was instead validated by a cleric inking in Henry's embossed signature on a legal paper, a technique called a "dry stamp", the day before the King's death, when Henry lay too ill to be very aware of what was happening around him (Smith, 1970:296; Scarisbrick, 1968:491). Norfolk would escape the headsman's axe after all, and would continue to languish in the Tower for the totality of Edward VI's reign, before being restored to political life under the rule of Mary I (Head, 1995:228-229).

For some, Norfolk's survival during the Seymours' ascendancy as the powers behind the throne of the boy King Edward, is proof that it was Henry, not the Seymours, who provided the impetus for the tremendous carnage during the last years of his rule (Head, 1995:228). However, this may be too simple an explanation. While it is obvious that Henry, whether spurred by McLeod syndrome or not, had become determined to resolve any problems after 1536 with an execution or two, that does not mean the Seymours were innocent of plotting judicial murders. They had certainly aided and abetted Anne Boleyn's death, and were supremely unconcerned about the men who were also beheaded as a result. Since it was necessary for Anne to die before the Seymours could rise in rank and power, her destruction was a means to an end and those who perished with her were simply collateral damage. The fact it was the King who ordered his second Queen and her friends beheaded does not exempt the Seymours from the guilt of their collusion with Cromwell, the probable architect of Anne's downfall. There is every likelihood that the Seymours had learned from Cromwell's example and had manipulated Henry into commanding Surrey's annihilation. However, it was one thing to cajole an elderly King behind the scenes and let that monarch assume the responsibility for a peer's death; it was another to let the whole world know the sons of a jumped-up knight had executed the scion of one of the most noble lineages on English soil. The news of the Earl of Surrey's death was ill-received by foreign courts, and King Francis asked some very probing questions of Seymour's ambassador that made it clear he was skeptical about the reasons for Surrey's execution (Sessions, 2003:412-13). Imprisonment effectively neutralized Norfolk's threat to the Seymours' power, so there was very little reason for them to risk the disapproval of European powers by judicially murdering the Duke. What has been seen as evidence of mercy on the part of the Seymours may just have been political caution.

Henry died on January 28, 1547. He was in denial about his own mortality, even at the very end. He was asked if he wished for a priest to come to him, but he characteristically put it off because it was an unpleasant thought, saying he would "take a little sleep" first (Smith, 1982:313). It was as if he hoped he could ward off death by avoiding his last confession, or perhaps he felt he could avoid death by refusing to think about it. However, death came to the King, in spite of everything Henry did to avoid it. After a lifetime of bold action, the English lion simply slipped from sleep into a coma, and never awoke (Smith, 1982:313).

No one can say for sure which of the King's many ailments finally killed him. It is true that McLeod syndrome is associated with heart disease and congestive heart failure in patients around Henry's age, but there are too many other things that may have caused his death for us to be able to even speculate that his Kell positive blood group was a factor. He was massively and morbidly obese, which also wasn't doing his heart any good. He may have died from a stroke, an embolism, or a secondary infection from his ulcerated legs. It may have even been a combination of several health problems that killed him. Perhaps the oddest thing about Henry's death was the fact it was so quiet. It seems strange that such a dramatic life would end in such a calm manner.

There was a grand funeral for Henry, but his corpse was not present. The service centered around a massive wax effigy of Henry, crafted to give the appearance of a sleeping King, which was taken in slow procession to Windsor Chapel, followed by at least 1000 English soldiers and 250 paid mourners, among others

(Smith, 1982:314). The King's corpse was readied for burial, in the manner of his era, by being disemboweled, soaked in spices, wrapped in a shroud, and placed in a coffin (Smith, 1982:314). Henry's remains were interred on February 16, 1547, lowered into the grave of his "true and loving Wife Queen Jane", which was located under the floor of St. George's chapel (Fraser, 1992:394-395). There is also an unconfirmed report that the night before the burial his decomposing body burst the confines of his lead coffin and leaked onto the floor of the chapel, where dogs then licked it up, fulfilling Peto's prophesy that Henry would one day suffer the same fate as the Biblical monarch, Ahab (Skidmore, 2009:55).

Henry's tumultuous reign left a lasting legacy. His son became Edward VI, under the protection of a council of regents. The three most significant of these councilors were Edward Seymour, John Dudley, and William Paget. Henry had made Seymour the Earl of Hertford in 1537, since he was the male head of Queen Jane's family. John Dudley's military accomplishments had made him one of Henry's favorite courtiers, which inspired the King to grant him the title of Viscount Lisle and, later, name him Lord Admiral of England's navy. Sir William Paget, serving as Henry's secretary, was certainly less exalted, but he was a close friend and ally of Seymour and Dudley. As such, Paget was instrumental in assisting their rise, while simultaneously helping orchestrate the fall of the Howards. Hertford and Lisle, aided by Paget, lost no time in assuming power after Henry's death. They were, conveniently, in charge of his will, which was dry stamped and mysteriously contained a passage allowing them to grant themselves whatever lands or titles they wished (Skidmore,

2009:40-47). Hertford was declared the Lord Protector of the realm and became the *de facto* ruler of England. Eager to have a title that reflected his burgeoning power, Seymour authorised his own elevation to Duke of Somerset, which had formerly been one of the titles given to Henry Fitzroy (Sessions, 2003:362). Dudley was also promoted to great rank, becoming the Earl of Warwick and Lord Great Chamberlain (Starkey, 2001:66). However, karmic justice would come swiftly for them, and their ambitions would be their downfall. Popular sentiment turned against Somerset after he murdered his own brother during a power struggle, giving Dudley an opportunity to overthrow him and have him beheaded in January 1552, almost exactly four years after the Earl of Surrey's execution (Sessions, 2003:363). Dudley, just a few months prior to the judicial murder of his close friend, assumed the rank of Duke of Northumberland (Starkey, 2001:107). When young King Edward's health began to fail the next year, Northumberland married his son Guildford Dudley to Lady Jane Grey, Edward's designated heir to the throne. After Edward's death, Northumberland made an attempt to put the crown on Jane Grey's head and rule through her, but he was defeated by the forces of Edward's sister Mary, who executed him in the summer of 1553 (Starkey, 2001:109-119).

Mary herself would rule less than six years. She died childless, probably of ovarian cancer, in November 1558 (Watkins, 2009:79). Stability was finally restored by the ascension of Elizabeth I to the throne. Anne Boleyn's daughter would rule England, and rule it well, for more than 40 years, until her death in 1603. Elizabeth's passing was the passing of the Tudor dynasty, leaving the House of Stuart to rule after her. Only with his youngest daughter's demise did Henry VIII cease to have an effect on English history.

Chapter Ten
The Blood Burns:
How the Kell Antigen Changed the European History

Martin Luther once said that "Blood alone moves the wheels of history". Perhaps that overstates the case, but the blood of Henry VIII certainly affected history in a profound way. If the hypothesis that Henry VIII had a Kell positive blood type is correct, then a simple antigen caused a great many dramatic events. Think, if you will, of the things that would have changed if the King had not had a Kell positive blood type.

If the King had not been Kell positive, then there is every likelihood that more of the numerous offspring, and at least one of the several sons born to Henry and Katherina of Aragon, would have lived to reach adulthood. Therefore, the King would have never had a Great Matter because it is unlikely Henry would have ever have asked to nullify his marriage, no matter how much he yearned for Anne Boleyn; he would not have risked making any of his lawful male heirs illegitimate. Anne would be remembered, if she was remembered at all, as Henry's mistress. If she was able to successfully elude the King's interest, she would have lived in relative obscurity, the daughter of a minor court official and perhaps the wife of a noble and the mother of a large brood of children. Queen Elizabeth would never have existed. Even if Anne had borne the King's daughter, without a marriage between her mother and Henry, Elizabeth would have never come to the throne. Without a Great Matter to create a rift between the King and the Church, England would have doubtlessly remained officially Catholic, considering Henry's devotion to the old forms of worship.

  Had his first marriage never been annulled, Henry would not be notorious as a lecherous tyrant who married six women, but rather would be remembered, mostly by historians, as a rather average King with a loyal wife and a few mistresses. If Katherina had still died in 1536, leaving Henry free to remarry, it is doubtful he would have managed to wed another five women. Perhaps he would have wed Anne Boleyn, who would have possibly been his maitresse-en-titre, or official royal mistress. As an official royal mistress, Anne would have wielded enormous influence on the King, and perhaps have become as famous for her accomplishments and political machinations as Madame de Pompadour would become two hundred years later. Perhaps Anne Boleyn would have been unavailable or eclipsed by another mistress by the time Henry became widowed. He might still have chosen Jane Seymour, but it is perhaps more likely that he would have been persuaded to make a marriage for political reasons to a foreign princess or noblewoman. As a devoted Catholic, he would never have considered a Reformist bride, so Anna of Cleves would never have come to England or have been remembered by the grossly inaccurate soubriquet of "Great Flanders Mare." Whoever he took as a bride, she would have, if she survived childbirth and the other hazards of a woman's life in sixteenth century England, prevented him from being free to marry Katheryn Howard. The sweet but flighty Katheryn would have been happy to be the King's mistress, and would have been unlikely to have ever sought the position of Queen. She would have doubtlessly lived longer as Henry's mistress than she did as Henry's wife. Unless fate had made the King a widower once again, Kateryn Parr would have been free to marry Thomas Seymour, and would have lived quietly on the fringes of history. Thus, the lives of so many would have been altered drastically, if Henry's blood had not contained the Kell antigen!

With no Kell antigen to impede Henry's reproduction, the political climate would also have been very different. Not only would the lack of a Great Matter have kept England Catholic (the Reformation would certainly have had a harder time taking root), Cardinal Wolsey was unlikely to have been overthrown. Thomas Cromwell would have needed to find another route to power. Thomas More might have served as Henry's Chancellor much longer than two years, and it is extremely doubtful the King would ever have had his dear friend beheaded. Dozens of men who are now remembered as Catholic martyrs, like Edward Powell, Richard Fetherston, and Thomas Abel, would have survived unscathed. St. John Fisher might never have been canonized. However, it is likely that men devoted to the Reformation, such as Robert Barnes, William Jerome and Thomas Garret, would still have been executed. Under the influence of Thomas More, who believed that Reformists were vile heretics who not only deserved to be burned at the stake, but would also be sent to Hell "where the wretches [would] burn forever" (Marius, 1999:406), Henry would have probably consigned a great many more Protestants to the flames. With such staunch Catholic leadership, would England have experienced its own version of the St. Bartholomew's Day massacre, when thousands of Protestants would have been slaughtered by their Catholic neighbors at the instigation of the monarch?

If we assume that Henry not only had Kells but also developed McLeod syndrome, then the lack of a single Kx antigen also changed history because it altered the way Henry VIII governed his kingdom. As the McLeod syndrome increasingly affected him, his ability to make rational decisions deteriorated. He became paranoid, ruthless and vengeful. Nevertheless, he retained his cunning acumen, so that he was able to enforce his irrational decisions with articulate demands. This blend of insanity and intelligence has driven historians to despair for centuries, trying to explicate his motivations and policies based on historical documents and a logical analysis of the situation. Lacey Baldwin Smith noted that some of his fellow historians argue that the King's seemingly injudicious choices were the actions of a man determined to have "absolute power and independence", and were therefore part of a larger stratagem, while other historians posit that "instead of statesmanlike and calculated policies" Henry's resolutions were the result of a combination of "unreason and panic" (Smith, 1982:271). If an analysis of Henry's remains proved that he was Kell positive and almost certainly suffered from McLeod syndrome, knowing the effects of that illness on the King's mental faculties would give historians a better understanding of Henry's decisions, since McLeod syndrome would explain why the King was simultaneously clever and crazy.

Henry would probably have left a very different mark on history if his mind had remained intact. He was a talented and brilliant man who was deeply interested in humanism, including the studies of logic and moral philosophy; had he not lost his reason as a result of McLeod syndrome, he might be remembered today as one of the best and brightest of the Renaissance kings, as opposed to being conceptualized in popular culture as a tyrant and a murderer.

Without McLeod syndrome affecting his judgment, the King might not have pushed his entire kingdom into economic ruin. The dissolution of the monasteries in the 1530s had brought the crown a massive amount of wealth, but by 1545 Henry had squandered so much of it that England was on the verge of bankruptcy (Scarisbrick, 1970:456). It was not his extravagant clothes, or his love of jewels, or his love of pageantry and display, or even the generous gifts to his courtiers that had emptied the royal treasury. The most significant drain on the country's finances were the foolish wars the King insisted on fighting, which were hugely costly and made him look a buffoon. Every choice that Henry made to try to finance his wars, from debasing English coin to selling confiscated monastic lands at a fraction of their value, simply drove him further into penury (Scarisbrick, 1970:453-454). He did not seem to be able to keep his spending under control. It was almost as if he would forget, or simply be in denial about, the fiscal problems his kingdom was experiencing. Even while amassing a hideous amount of debt, he built or remodeled castles and manor houses in such numbers and with such opulence that it looks as if he thought he had the wealth of King Midas. One excellent example of this unwarranted building was Nonsuch Palace. In order to clear the land required for the construction of this huge new residence in Surrey, he destroyed the village of Cuddington and rerouted roads (Scarisbrick, 1970:504). It was called Nonsuch Palace because it was claimed there was no such palace like it in all the world. It was to be Henry's newest hunting lodge and was situated on over a thousand acres of parkland that was kept stocked with game for His Majesty's pleasure (Erickson, 1980:287). It was undoubtedly a beautiful building and a triumph of Renaissance architecture, but it was also an extravagance that England could not afford (Scarisbrick, 1970:506).

    Henry had been lauded as the "everlasting glory of his age" when he ascended the throne in the spring of 1509 (Robinson, 2008:37). His subjects had also entertained high hopes for their sovereign, and Lord Mountjoy bragged that the new king was "set not upon gold or jewels, or mines of ore, but upon virtue, reputation and eternal renown" (Crompton and Marty, 2004:4). It is a testament to Henry's nearly superhuman charisma that, in spite of the bloodthirsty tyranny of the last 15 years of his rule, he was "indisputably revered, indeed, in some strange way, loved. He had raised the monarchy to near-idolatry" (Scarisbrick, 1970:506). What more might not have been possible if this enthralling monarch had retained his mental perspicuity and psychological stability, as well as his charm? How very, very sad it is that because of a mutation in Henry's blood he became a monster, and is now known primarily as a savage tyrant who slaughtered wives and martyred scholars. Rather than achieving renown as the leader of the English Renaissance, he is thought of as a bloated despot whose best accomplishment was siring Good Queen Bess, Elizabeth I.

Martin Luther summed up the international popular opinion of Henry VIII when he said, "Junker Heintz will be God and does what he lusts" (Scarisbrick, 1970:526). What an ignoble epitaph for a King whose reign began with such promise!

BIBLIOGRAPHY

Adamson, Melitta Weiss. 2004. *Food in Medieval Times*. Greenwood Publishing Group.

Al-Andalusi, Said, Sema`an I. Salem, and Alok Kumar. 1996. *Science in the Medieval World*. University of Texas Press.

Albala, Ken. 2002. *Eating Right in the Renaissance*. University of California Press.

Anon. 1913. *The Catholic Encyclopedia: An International Work of Reference on the Constitution, Doctrine, Discipline and History of the Catholic Church*. The Encyclopedia press inc.

———. "The Evolution of Maternal Birthing Position" 43. http://journals.lww.com/obgynsurvey/Fulltext/1988/01000/The_ Evolution_of_Maternal_Birthing_Position.13.aspx.

Appleby, Andrew. 1979. "Diet in Sixteenth-century England: Sources, Problems, Possibilities." In *Health, Medicine, and Mortality in the Sixteenth Century*, 97–116. CUP Archive.

Arano, Luisa Cogliati, Oscar Ratti, and Adele Westbrook. 1976. *The Medieval Health Handbook Tacuinum Sanitatis: Luisa Cogliati Arano; [transl. and Adapted by Oscar Ratti and Adele Westbrook from the Original Italian Ed.]*. George Braziller.

Arsdall, Anne Van. 2002. *Medieval Herbal Remedies: The Old English Herbarium and Anglo-Saxon Medicine*. Psychology Press.

Askew, Anne, and Elaine V. Beilin. 1996. *The Examinations of Anne Askew*. Oxford University Press.

Balen, Adam H. 2005. *Polycystic Ovary Syndrome: a Guide to Clinical Management*. Taylor & Francis.

Ball, Philip. 2006. *The Devil's Doctor: Paracelsus and the World of Renaissance Magic and Science*. Macmillan.

Bates, David, Julia C. Crick, and Sarah Hamilton. 2006. *Writing Medieval Biography, 750-1250: Essays in Honour of Professor Frank Barlow*. Boydell Press.

Bay-Cheng, Laina Y. 2006. . In *Sex and Sexuality*, ed. Richard D. McAnulty and M. Michele Burnette, 203–228. Greenwood Publishing Group.

Beckmann, Charles R. B., American College of Obstetricians and Gynecologists, Barbara M. Barzansky, Frank W. Ling, and Douglas W. Laube. 2009. *Obstetrics and Gynecology*. Lippincott Williams & Wilkins.

Bernard, G. W. 2007. *The King's Reformation*. Yale University Press.

Bevan, Bryan. 1994. *Henry IV*. Palgrave Macmillan.

Block, Eric. 2010. *Garlic and Other Alliums: The Lore and the Science*. Royal Society of Chemistry.

Bober, Phyllis Pray. 2001. *Art, Culture, and Cuisine: Ancient and Medieval Gastronomy*. University of Chicago Press.

Bowman, J.M., J.M. Pollock, F.A. Manning, C.R. Harman, and S. Menticogou. 1992. "Maternal Kell Blood Group Alloimmunization." *Obstetricas and Gynecology* 79: 239–244.

Brewer, John S., Robert H. Brodie, and James Gairdner. 1862. *Letters and Papers, Foreign and Domestic, of the Reign of Henry VIII.: Preserved in the Public Record Office, the British Museum and Elsewhere*. His Majesty's Stationery Office.

Broomhall, Susan, and Stephanie Tarbin. 2008. *Women, Identities and Communities in Early Modern Europe*. Ashgate Publishing, Ltd.

Brundage, James A. 1990. *Law, Sex, and Christian Society in Medieval Europe*. University of Chicago Press.

Bullough, Vern L. 1996. *Handbook of Medieval Sexuality*. Taylor & Francis.

Burckhardt, Titus. 2001. *Mystical Astrology According to Ibn 'Arabi*. Fons Vitae.

Burke, S. Hubert. 1879. *Historical Portraits of the Tudor Dynasty and the Reformation Period*. J. Hodges.

Caine, M.E., and E. Mueller-Heubach. 1986. "Kell Sensitization in Pregnancy." *American Journal of Obstertics and Gynecology* January: 85–90.

Chamberlin, Frederick. 1931. *The Private Character of Henry the Eighth*. Washburn.

Chejne, Anwar G. 1983. *Islam and the West: The Moriscos, a Cultural and Social History*. SUNY Press.

Childs, Jessie. 2007. *Henry VIII's Last Victim: The Life and Times of Henry Howard, Earl of Surrey*. Macmillan.

Chrimes, Stanley Bertram. 1999. *Henry VII*. Yale University Press.

Cifu, David X., and Deborah Caruso. 2010. *Traumatic Brain Injury*. Demos Medical Publishing.

Comer, Ronald J. 2004a. *Fundamentals of Abnormal Psychology*. Macmillan.

———. 2004b. *Fundamentals of Abnormal Psychology*. Macmillan.

Committee, Knights of Columbus. Catholic Truth. 1913. *The Catholic Encyclopedia: An International Work of Reference on the Constitution, Doctrine, Discipline, and History of the Catholic Church*. Encyclopedia Press.

Constantine, Stephen M., and University of Massachusetts Amherst. 2006. *By a Gentle Force Compell'd: An Analysis of Rape in Eighteenth-century English Fact and Fiction*. ProQuest.

Conwell, Joseph F. 1997. *Impelling Spirit: Revisiting a Founding Experience, 1539, Ignatius of Loyola and His Companions : an Exploration into the Spirit and Aims of the Society of Jesus as Revealed in the Founders' Proposed Papal Letter Approving the Society*. Loyola Press.

Cressy, David. 1997. *Birth, Marriage, and Death: Ritual, Religion, and the Life-cycle in Tudor and Stuart England*. Oxford University Press US.

Crompton, Samuel Willard, and Martin E. Marty. 2004. *Desiderius Erasmus*. Infobase Publishing.

Cruz, Anne J., and Mihoko Suzuki. 2009. *The Rule of Women in Early Modern Europe*. University of Illinois Press.

Danek, A., J.P. Rubio, L. Rampoldi, M. Ho, C. Dobson-Stone, F. Tison, W.A. Stmmans, et al. 2001. "McLeod Neuroacanthocytosis: Genotype and Phenotype." *Annual Neurology* 50: 755–764.

Daniluk, Judith C. 2003. *Women's Sexuality Across the Life Span: Challenging Myths, Creating Meanings*. Guilford Press.

Dawson, Ian. 2005a. *Renaissance Medicine*. Enchanted Lion Books.

———. 2005b. *Medicine in the Middle Ages*. Enchanted Lion Books.

Deming, David. 2010. *Science and Technology in World History: The Ancient World and Classical Civilization*. McFarland.

Denny, Joanna. 2006. *Anne Boleyn: a New Life of England's Tragic Queen*. Da Capo Press.

Dewhurst, J. 1984. "The Alleged Miscarriages of Catherine of Aragon and Anne Boleyn." *Medical History* 28 (1) (January): 49–56.

Dimmock, Matthew. 2006. "Henry Howard, Earl of Surrey." In *The Oxford Encyclopedia of British Literature*, ed. David Scott Kastan, 5:117–120. Oxford University Press.

Dixon, Laurinda S. 2004. "Visual Prescriptions: In Sickness and in Health." In *In Sickness and in Health: Disease as Metaphor in Art and Popular Wisdom*, ed. Laurinda S. Dixon and Gabriel P. Weisberg. University of Delaware Press.

DUNDES, LAUREN. 1988. . *Obstetrical & Gynecological Survey*.

Dunn, P M. 1991. "Francois Mauriceau (1637-1709) and Maternal Posture for Parturition." *Archives of Disease in Childhood* 66 (1 Spec No) (January): 78–79.

Edwards, John. 2011. *Mary I: England's Catholic Queen*. Yale University Press.

Erickson, C. 1980. *Great Harry*. New York: St. Martin's Press.

Erickson, Carolly. 1998. *Mistress Anne*. Macmillan.

Eysenck, Michael W. 2000. *Psychology: a Student's Handbook*. Taylor & Francis US.

Feltoe, Richard. 1991. *Redpath: The History of a Sugar House*. Dundurn Press Ltd.

First, Michael B., and Allan Tasman. 2009. *Clinical Guide to the Diagnosis and Treatment of Mental Disorders*. John Wiley and Sons.

Fleming, Robin. . In .

Franklin, Robert R., Dorothy Brockman, and Dorothy Kay Brockman. 1995. *In Pursuit of Fertility: a Fertility Expert Tells You How to Get Pregnant*. Macmillan.

Freely, John. 2010. *Aladdin's Lamp: How Greek Science Came to Europe Through the Islamic World*. Random House Digital, Inc.

French, Roger. 1994. "Astrology in Medical Practice." In *Practical Medicine from Salerno to the Black Death*, ed. Luis García Ballester, 30–59. Cambridge University Press.

Frieda, Leonie. 2006. *Catherine De Medici: Renaissance Queen of France*. Harper Collins.

Friedmann, Paul, and Boleyn Anne (consort of Henry viii, king of England.). 1884. *Anne Boleyn: a Chapter of English History, 1527-1536*. Macmillan.

Froude, James Anthony. 1891. *The Divorce of Catherine of Aragon: The Story as Told by the Imperial Ambassadors Resident at the Court of Henry VIII ...* Longmans, Green & co.

Frye, Richard Nelson. 1975. *The Cambridge History of Iran: The Period from the Arab Invasion to the Saljuqs*. Cambridge University Press.

Furdell, Elizabeth Lane. 2001. *The Royal Doctors, 1485-1714: Medical Personnel at the Tudor and Stuart Courts*. University Rochester Press.

Gabbard, Glen O. 2005. *Psychodynamic Psychiatry in Clinical Practice*. American Psychiatric Pub.

Garland, Sarah. 2004. *The Complete Book of Herbs and Spices*. frances lincoln ltd.

Gelardi, Julia P. 2008. *In Triumph's Wake: Royal Mothers, Tragic Daughters, and the Price They Paid for Glory*. Macmillan.

Gifford, George. 2007. *A Dialogue Concerning Witches and Witchcrafts*. Puckrel Publishing.

Given-Wilson, Chris. 1996. *An Illustrated History of Late Medieval England*. Manchester University Press ND.

Glass, N. 2001. "Great Excavations." In *The Lancet*, 357:643.

Glick, Thomas F., Steven John Livesey, and Faith Wallis. 2005. *Medieval Science, Technology, and Medicine: An Encyclopedia*. Psychology Press.

Gostelow, Mary. 1998. *Blackwork*. Courier Dover Publications.

Grant, Alexander, and Keith John Stringer. 1995. *Uniting the Kingdom?: The Making of British History*. Psychology Press.

Gross, Gerd E. 2011. *Sexually Transmitted Infections and Sexually Transmitted Diseases*. Springer.

Gutas, Dimitri. 1998. *Greek Thought, Arabic Culture: The Graeco-Arabic Translation Movement in Baghdad and Early 'Abbāsid Society (2nd-4th/8th-10th Centuries)*. Psychology Press.

Haile, Martin. 1910. *Life of Reginald Pole*. Longmans, Green, and co.

Hall, Manly Palmer. 2005. *The Story of Astrology: The Belief in the Stars as a Factor in Human Progress*. Cosimo, Inc.

Hartel, Joseph Francis, and Pontificia Università gregoriana. 1993. *Femina Ut Imago Dei in the Integral Feminism of St. Thomas Aquinas*. Gregorian&Biblical BookShop.

Head, David M. 1995. *The Ebbs and Flows of Fortune: The Life of Thomas Howard, Third Duke of Norfolk*. University of Georgia Press.

Herbst, Judith. 2006. *Germ Theory*. Twenty-First Century Books.

Holmes, David Lynn. 1993. *A Brief History of the Episcopal Church: With a Chapter on the Anglican Reformation and an Appendix on the Annulment of Henry VIII*. Continuum International Publishing Group.

Hull, Suzanne W. 1996. *Women According to Men: The World of Tudor-Stuart Women*. Rowman Altamira.

Hunt, Alice. 2009. "The Monarchial Republic of Mary." *The Historical Journal* 52 (3): 557–572.

Hutchinson, R. 2005. *The Last Days of Henry VIII: Conspiracy, Treason and Heresy at the Court of the Dying Tyrant*. London Phoneix: Weidenfeld &Nicolson 2005 Orion Books Ltd. 2006.

Ives, Eric. 2009. *Lady Jane Grey: a Tudor Mystery*. John Wiley and Sons.

Ives, Eric William. 2004. *The Life and Death of Anne Boleyn: "The Most Happy"*. Wiley-Blackwell.

Jansen, Sharon L. 2002. *The Monstrous Regiment of Women: Female Rulers in Early Modern Europe*. Palgrave Macmillan.

Jung, H.H., and H. Haker. 2004. "Schizophrenia as a Manifestation of X-Linked McLeod-Nuerocanthocytosis Syndrome." *Journal of Clinical Psychology* 65: 722–723.

Kamen, Henry. 1998. *Philip of Spain*. Yale University Press.

Kandeel, Fouad R. 2007. *Male Reproductive Dysfunction: Pathophysiology and Treatment*. CRC Press.

Kaser, Karl. 2010. *The Balkans and the Near East: Introduction to a Shared History*. LIT Verlag Münster.

Kendall, Paul Murray. 1956. *Richard the Third*. W. W. Norton & Company.

Khanbaghi, Aptin. 2006. *The Fire, the Star and the Cross: Minority Religions in Medieval and Early Modern Iran*. I.B.Tauris.

Klepp, Susan E. 2009. *Revolutionary Conceptions: Women, Fertility, and Family Limitation in America, 1760-1820*. UNC Press Books.

Kybett, S.M. 1989. "Henry VIII -- A Malnourished King?" *History Today* September: 19–25.

Lancaster, Henry Oliver. 1990. *Expectations of Life: A Study in the Demography, Statistics, and History of World Mortality*. Springer.

Lilly, William. 1835. *An Introduction to Astrology, Rules for the Practice of Horary Astrology [an Abstract of Christian Astrology]: To Which Are Added, Numerous Emendations, by Zadkiel*.

Lindemann, Mary. 1999. *Medicine and Society in Early Modern Europe*. Cambridge University Press.

Lindsey, K. 1995. *Divorced, Beheaded, Survived: A Feminist Reinterpretation of the Wives of Henry VIII*. Reading, Massachusetts: Addison-Wesley Publishing Company.

Loades, D. M. 1999. *Politics and Nation: England, 1450-1660*. Wiley-Blackwell.

———. 2009. *Tudor Queens of England*. Continuum International Publishing Group.

Loades, David. 2009. *The Six Wives of Henry VIII*. Amberley Publishing.

Loades, David M. 2006. *Elizabeth I: A Life*. Continuum International Publishing Group.

Lovejoy, Arthur O. 1976. *The Great Chain of Being: a Study of the History of an Idea : the William James Lectures Delivered at Harvard University, 1933*. Harvard University Press.

Lutz, Peter L. 2002. *The Rise of Experimental Biology: An Illustrated History*. Humana Press.

Lyons, Clare A. 2006. *Sex Among the Rabble: An Intimate History of Gender & Power in the Age of Revolution, Philadelphia, 1730-1830*. UNC Press Books.

Magnússon, Magnús. 2003. *Scotland: The Story of a Nation*. Grove Press.

Marius, Richard. 1999. *Thomas More: a Biography*. Harvard University Press.

Marsh, W.L. 1990. "Biological Roles of Blood Group Antigens." *The Yale Journal of Biology and Medicine* 63: 455–460.

Marsh, W.L., E.F. Schnipper, C.L. Johnson, K.A. Mueller, and S.A. Schwartz. 1983. "An Individual with McLeod Syndrome and the Kell Bollod Group Antigen K(K1)." *Transfusion* 23: 336–338.

Marshall, Peter. 2006. *Religious Identities In Henry VIII's England*. Ashgate Publishing, Ltd.

Mayne, K., P. Bowell, and G. Pratt. 1990. "The Significance of Anti-Kell Sensitization in Pregnancy." *Clinical and Labratory Haematology* 12: 379–385.

Merriam-Webster, and Inc. 2005. *Merriam-Webster's Medical Desk Dictionary*. Merriam-Webster Inc.

Murphy, C. 2001. "Second Opinions: History Winds Up in the Waiting Room." In *The Atlantic*, 287:16–18.

North, John David. 2008. *Cosmos: An Illustrated History of Astronomy and Cosmology*. University of Chicago Press.

Norton, Elizabeth. 2009. *Jane Seymour: Henry VIII's True Love*. Amberley Publishing.

Okerlund, Arlene Naylor. 2009. *Elizabeth of York*. Macmillan.

Orme, Nicholas. 2003. *Medieval Children*. Yale University Press.
Parr, Katherine, and Janel Mueller. 2011. *Katherine Parr: Complete Works and Correspondence*. University of Chicago Press.
Petere Murray Jones. 2008. "Herbs and the Medieval Surgeon." In *Health and Healing from the Medieval Garden*, ed. Peter Dendle and Alain Touwaide, 162–179. Boydell Press.
Pinto-Correia, Clara. 1998. *The Ovary of Eve: Egg and Sperm and Preformation*. University of Chicago Press.
Pollard, Albert Frederick. 1904. *Thomas Cranmer and the English Reformation, 1489-1556*. G.P. Putnam's Sons.
——. 1919. *Henry VIII*. Longmans.
Porter, Linda. 2007. *The First Queen of England: The Myth of "Bloody Mary"*. Macmillan.
——. 2010. *Katherine the Queen: The Remarkable Life of Katherine Parr, the Last Wife of Henry VIII*. Macmillan.
Porter, Roy. 1999. *The Greatest Benefit to Mankind: a Medical History of Humanity*. W. W. Norton & Company.
Rabin, Sheila. 2002. "Unholy Astrology: Did Pico Always View It That Way?" In *Paracelsian Moments: Science, Medicine, & Astrology in Early Modern Europe*, 151–162. Ed. Williams, G.S. Truman State Univ Press.
Rao. 2008. *Textbook of Gynaecology*. Elsevier India.
Raubenhemier, Otto. 1918. "The History of Mercury." *The National Druggist* 48: 317–318.
Richardson, Tim. 2003. *Sweets: A History of Candy*. Bloomsbury Publishing USA.
Rickman, Johanna. 2008. *Love, Lust, and License in Early Modern England: Illicit Sex and the Nobility*. Ashgate Publishing, Ltd.
Ridley, Jasper Godwin. 1988. *The Tudor Age*. Constable.
Robinson, Jon. 2008. *Court Politics, Culture and Literature in Scotland and England, 1500-1540*. Ashgate Publishing, Ltd.

Roden, Timothy, Craig Wright, and Bryan R. Simms. 2009. *Anthology for Music in Western Civilization*. Cengage Learning.

Roger French. 1994. "Astrology in Medical Practice." In *Practical Medicine from Salerno to the Black Death*, ed. Luis Garcia Ballester, 30–59. Cambridge University Press.

Scarisbrick, J. J. 1968. *Henry VIII*. University of California Press.

Schaus, Margaret. 2006a. *Women and Gender in Medieval Europe: An Encyclopedia*. CRC Press.

———. 2006b. *Women and Gender in Medieval Europe: An Encyclopedia*. CRC Press.

Schultz, James Alfred. 2006. *Courtly Love, the Love of Courtliness, and the History of Sexuality*. University of Chicago Press.

Sessions, William A. 2003. *Henry Howard, the Poet Earl of Surrey: A Life*. Oxford University Press.

Shepard, Alexandra. 2006. *Meanings of Manhood in Early Modern England*. Oxford University Press.

Shora, Nawar. 2008. *The Arab-American Handbook: a Guide to the Arab, Arab-American & Muslim Worlds*. Cune Press.

Shore, M.F. 1972. "Henry VIII and the Crisis of Generativity." *Journal of Interdisiplinary History* 2: 359–390.

Sim, Alison. 2001. *The Tudor Housewife*. McGill-Queen's Press - MQUP.

———. 2005. *Food & Feast in Tudor England*. Sutton.

Simon, Bennett. 2008. "Mind and Madness in Classical Antiquity." In *History of Psychiatry and Medical Psychology: With an Epilogue on Psychiatry and the Mind-body Relation*, ed. Edwin R. Wallace and John Gach, 175–197. Springer.

Simon, Rita James. 1998. *Abortion: Statutes, Policies, and Public Attitudes the World Over*. Greenwood Publishing Group.

Siraisi, Nancy G. 1990. *Medieval & Early Renaissance Medicine: An Introduction to Knowledge and Practice*. University of Chicago Press.

Skidmore, Chris. 2009. *Edward VI: The Lost King of England*. Macmillan.

Smith, David Eugene. 1958. *History of Mathematics*. Courier Dover Publications.

Smith, Lacey Baldwin. 1973. *Henry VIII: The Mask of Royalty*. Panther.

———. 2009. *Catherine Howard: The Queen Whose Adulteries Made a Fool of Henry VIII*. Amberley Publishing.

Starkey, David. 2001. *Elizabeth: The Struggle for the Throne*. HarperCollins.

———. 2003. *Six Wives : the Queens of Henry VIII*. Chatto & Windus.

———. 2006. *Monarchy: From the Middle Ages to Modernity*. HarperCollins.

Stiehm, E. Richard, Hans D. Ochs, and Jerry A. Winkelstein. 2004. *Immunologic Disorders in Infants and Children*. Elsevier Health Sciences.

Stone, Jean Mary. 1904. *Reformation and Renaissance (circa 1377-1610)*. Duckworth.

Strausz, Ivan K. 1996. *Women's Symptoms: a Comprehensive Guide to Common Symptoms and Diseases : Their Causes and Treatments*. Random House, Inc.

Strickland, Agnes. 1853. *Memoirs of the Queens of Henry VIII., and His Mother, Elizabeth of York*. Blanchard and Lea.

Strickland, Agnes, and Elisabeth Strickland. 1851. *Lives of the Queens of England: From the Norman Conquest*. H. Colburn.

Sullivan, William. 1838. *Historical Causes and Effects: From the Fall of the Roman Empire, 476, to the Reformation, 1517* ... J.B. Dow.

Symmans, W.A., C.S. Shepherd, W.L. Marsh, R. Oyen, S.B. Shohet, and B.J. Linehan. 1979. "Hereditary Acanthocytosis Associated with the McLeod Phenotype of the Kell Blood Group System." *Bristish Journal of Haematology* 42: 575–583.

Temkin, Owsei. 2006. *The Double Face of Janus and Other Essays in the History of Medicine*. JHU Press.

Tillotson, Alan Keith, ROBERT /TILLOTSON/TILLO ABEL, Nai-Shing Hu Tillotson, and Robert Abel (Jr.). 2001. *The One Earth Herbal Sourcebook: Everything You Need to Know About Chinese, Western, and Ayurvedic Herbal Treatments*. Kensington Books.

Travis, Frederick, Harald S. Harung, and Yvonne Lagrosen. 2011. "Moral Development, Executive Functioning, Peak Experiences and Brain Patterns in Professional and Amateur Classical Musicians: Interpreted in Light of a Unified Theory of Performance." *Consciousness and Cognition* (April). doi:10.1016/j.concog.2011.03.020. http://www.sciencedaily.com/releases/2011/05/110505083421.htm?utm_source=feedburner&utm_medium=feed&utm_campaign=Feed%3A+sciencedaily+%28ScienceDaily%3A+Latest+Science+News%29&utm_content=Google+Reader.

Turkington, Carol, and Mitchell Edelson. 2005. *The Encyclopedia of Women's Reproductive Cancer*. Infobase Publishing.

Vogel, Friedrich, and Arno G. Motulsky. 1997. *Human Genetics: Problems and Approaches*. Springer.

Voigts, Linda Ehrsam. 2008. "Plants and Planets: Linking the Vegetable with the Celestial in Late Medieval Texts." In *Health* and Healing from the Medieval Garden, ed. Peter Dendle and Alain Touwaide, 29–46. Boydell Press.

Vries, Manfred F. R. Kets de. 2009. *Reflections on Character and Leadership: On the Couch with Manfred Kets De Vries*. John Wiley & Sons.

Wada, M., M. Kimura, M. Daimon, K. Kurita, T. Kato, Y. Johmura, K. Johkura, Y. Kuroiwa, and G. Sobue. 2003. "An Unusal Phenotype of McLeod Syndrome with Late Onset Axonal Neuropathy." *Journal of Neurology and Nuerosurgical Psychiatry* 74: 1697–1698.

Walker, Greg. 2003. *The Private Life of Henry VIII*. I.B.Tauris.

Waller, Maureen. 2006. *Sovereign Ladies: The Six Reigning Queens of England*. Macmillan.

Ward, Joseph P. 2008. *Violence, Politics, and Gender in Early Modern England*. Macmillan.

Warnicke, Retha M. 1991. *The Rise and Fall of Anne Boleyn: Family Politics at the Court of Henry VIII*. Cambridge University Press.

———. 2000. *The Marrying of Anne of Cleves: Royal Protocol in Early Modern England*. Cambridge University Press.

Watkins, John. 2009. . In *Queens and Power in Medieval and Early Modern England*, ed. Carole Levin and R. O. Bucholz, 76–97. U of Nebraska Press.

Watson, Katherine Denise. 2009. *Forensic Medicine in Western Society: A History*. Taylor & Francis US.

Wear, Andrew. 2000. *Knowledge and Practice in English Medicine, 1550-1680*. Cambridge University Press.

Weir, A. 2001. *Henry VIII: The King and His Court*. New York and Toronto: Ballantine Books.

Weir, Alison. 2000. *The Six Wives of Henry VIII*. Grove Press.

Whetstone, George, and Diana Shklanka. 1987. *A Critical Edition of George Whetstone's 1582 An Heptameron of Civill Discourses*. Garland.

Whitelock, Anna. 2010. *Mary Tudor: Princess, Bastard, Queen*. Random House, Inc.

Whitley, Catrina Banks, and Kyra Kramer. 2010. "A New Explanation for the Reproductive Woes and Midlife Decline of Henry VIII." *The Historical Journal* 53 (4) (December): 827–848.

Whitney, Elspeth. 2004. *Medieval Science and Technology*. Greenwood Publishing Group.

Wilson, C. Anne. 1991a. *Food & Drink in Britain: From the Stone Age to the 19th Century*. Academy Chicago Publishers.

———. 1991b. *Food & Drink in Britain: From the Stone Age to the 19th Century*. Academy Chicago Publishers.

Wilson, Derek. 2003. *In the Lion's Court: Power, Ambition, and Sudden Death in the Reign of Henry VIII*. Macmillan.

Wimer, B.M., W.L. Marsh, H.F. Taswell, and W.R. Galey. 1977. "Haenmatological Changes Associated with with the McLeod Phenotype of the Kell Blood Group System." *British Journal of Haematology* 36: 219–224.

Woodford, Donna. 2004. *Understanding King Lear: a Student Casebook to Issues, Sources, and Historical Documents*. Greenwood Publishing Group.

Woolgar, C. M. 2006. *The Senses in Late Medieval England*. Yale University Press.

Wright, J. Edward. 2002. *The Early History of Heaven*. Oxford University Press US.